A FIELD GUIDE
TO THE
BIRDS OF KOREA

LG Evergreen Foundation

A FIELD GUIDE TO THE
BIRDS OF
KOREA

Text by Woo-Shin Lee, Tae-Hoe Koo, Jin-Young Park

Illustrations by Takashi Taniguchi

Distributions maps by Satori Hamaya

Supervising maps by Woo-Shin Lee, Tae-Hoe Koo, Jin-Young Park

Translation & English adaptation by Desmond Allen

Editor in Chief Noritaka Ichida(Wild Bird Society of Japan)

Published by Bon-Moo Koo

LG Evergreen Foundation

LG Evergreen Foundation

LG Twin Towers, 20, Yeoeuido-dong,
Yeongdeungpo-gu, Seoul, 150-721, Korea
Phone:+82-2-3773-2269,+82-2-3773-2038
Fax:+82-2-3773-2077
Website:http://www.lg.co.kr, http://foundation.lg.or.kr
Registration number No. 13-1058(April 14, 2000)
First Edition December1, 2000

ISBN 89-951415-0-6 06490

Printing:Toyokan Publishing, Co.,Ltd. Tokyo Japan

Contents

Foreword

Birds stand at the apex of the ecosystem, which itself is a barometer for measuring the health of the natural environment. It is said that over 100 species of plants and animals will disappear from the face of the earth with the extinction of one bird species. Regrettably, however, the rate of bird extinction is gaining speed with the passage of time. This can only serve as a grim warning of how serious environmental pollution is to us all.

Birds freely migrate across national boundaries to nest and reproduce, so all nations must be committed to preserving the natural environment if we are to protect the birds. Saving the birds is not only linked with protecting nature; it is a way to foster international cooperation. This also coincides with the idea of respecting one's fellow human beings. We who are alive today as well as our descendents must work hard to protect nature or the future of humankind will be dark, indeed.

Korea, surrounded on three sides by water, occupies a very important geographical location with respect to protecting many bird species. The Korean Peninsula lies along the migration route that runs from Australia, New Zealand and Southern Asia to Siberia. Moreover, Korea is richly endowed with estuaries, which are ecological treasure troves. However, indiscriminate land reclamation and development are diminishing Korea's estuaries and other wetlands. As a very sad result, migrating birds are losing places to rest and the ecological balance is being disturbed.

I love birds, and bird-watching has long been an interest of mine. I would often take foreign bird-watching guides along on my outings, prompting me to wish that a handy guidebook on birds could be made available in Korean. At last, the LG Evergreen Foundation has come out with such a book, with descriptions in both Korean and English, as part of our nature preservation activities. This is a source of great pleasure for me personally.

I believe this volume will serve as an excellent companion for people who love to watch birds. Hopefully, it will help to encourage more people-especially our youth-to come to love birds, enjoy bird-watching, and develop a greater interest in preserving nature.

Birds symbolize freedom, peace and hope, and we all hope that our sons and daughters will be able to enjoy a rich and happy future. By referring to this book, you can learn the names of many birds and expand your understanding of ecology. Over the long run, I hope this volume will provide valuable knowledge that can help people better connect with nature and live more in harmony with the environment.

In closing, let me thank everyone who contributed their knowledge and talents to create an illustrated book on birds that is on a par with any other found in the world today.

Bon-Moo Koo
Chairman
LG Evergreen Foundation
September 2000

Preface

In the coming new millennium, many believe the environment and information will be the factors that decide the quality of human life. In my childhood, the cuckoo's call informed me of the coming of spring and the song of the Black-naped Oriole in deep green glades made me feel the summer. I saw off autumn and welcomed winter with a lonely heart when the flying skeins of ducks and wild geese arrived here from thousands of miles away. There used to be so many birds, those restless, natural beauties, that they enriched our spirit and comforted us. Nowadays, however, the habitats of many wild birds have been destroyed because of modernization, most obviously with the construction of cities and roads. Less obviously but perhaps of even greater concern, reclamation and pollution of wetlands increasingly endangers the habitats of waterbirds, such as wild ducks and geese, and the large flocks of visiting shorebirds, for which Korea is such an important international destination.

In my high school days, I used to watch so many ducks and wild geese at estuary of the River Nakdonggang, one of the most important wintering sites for wildfowl in Asia. In graduate school days I began a serious study of wildlife in the Gwangneung forest in Gyeonggi-do, a paradise for birds in Korea. I watched many birds there, and I really wanted to know the names of a large, black one and a blue one with a long tail and a lustrous eye-ring. I was disappointed because I did not have a good field guide at that time.

I believe that knowing the names of animals or plants is an important first step to feeling close to them. Unlike insects or plants, birds cannot be observed thoroughly on the palm of the hand with a pictorial guide. Until recently, Korean bird lovers have had to use foreign field guides because we did not have a good guide of our own with which to identify birds in the field. Recently, the number of bird watchers in Korea has increased and many bird books have been published, and they are a great help. But birdwatching in the field has been hampered by the lack of a pocket-sized guide with accurate and attractive illustrations. Mr. Bon-Moo Koo, LG chairman, and himself a great bird lover, has been eager to publish this field guide in order to satisfy bird watchers, and to help Korean people to enjoy watching birds, and come to love nature.

After we began to write this book in the summer of 1997, thanks to the many people concerned with bird observation, Citrine Wagtail, Long-billed Dowitcher, and Black-winged Cuckoo-Shrike were added to the list of Korean birds. Furthermore, some birds breeding in or recorded from North Korea have been included, giving as complete a coverage of the Korean peninsula as is presently possible, and preparing for the reunification of Korea. In total, there are 450 species illustrated in this book.

We have made efforts, both for ordinary people and for experts, to provide a variety of pictures to help easy identification. Birds are shown in characteristic postures and, where appropriate, both males and females are depicted showing breeding and non-breeding plumages; some juveniles or immatures are also shown, as are the eclipse plumages of ducks, and flight views of selected species. Also given are English names, Scientific names, body length and migratory status, as well as distribution maps for each species. In addition, we have made a special map of Korea showing information about breeding areas, wintering places and habitats of birds.

Finally, I truly hope that this book will be a valuable educational resource in an age when the value of the natural environment is again recognised, that it will enable many more people both to love birds, and to love and protect nature, and that it will be of help in conserving the beauty and richness of nature in Korea, improving the quality of life for us all now and for posterity.

June. 2000

Woo-Shin Lee, Ph.D.
Representative of Authors,
Professor of Wildlife Ecology and Management,
Department of Forest Resources, Seoul National University

Acknowledgements

For the publication of this picture book, Mr. Wee-Haeng Hur and Mr. Chang-Yong Choi, graduate students of Seoul National University, assisted the document research, arrangement and proofreading of the texts; Mr. Jeong-Yeon Lee, a graduate student of Kyunghee University, collaborated in the checking and correction of the pictures of snipes and waders. Ms. Satori Hamaya drew the distribution maps and Mr. Noritaka Ichida, Mr. Makoto Kawanabe and Ms. Cho-Ryon Shim, staff members of the Wild Bird Society of Japan, helped us to edit the book. I think this illustrated guide could not have been published, were it not for the efforts and support of many scholars, including Prof. Pyong-Oh Won and Dr. Han-Jeong Woo, who have devoted themselves to research on birds. The authors would like to express our sincere gratitude to Mr. Bon-Moo Koo, LG chairman and all others who worked heartily to publish this book. And this book was 'translated' by Mr. Desmond Allen. I appreciate for his endeavours for English edition.

The staff at the Natural History Museum at Tring, U.K., are also thanked for access to specimens in the Walter Rothschild collections.

Introduction

● **Identification**

This book is a guide to the field identification of every bird species that has been recorded in the Korean Peninsula up to August 2000. There are color illustrations and descriptions of the 18 orders, 72 families and 450 species including descriptions and illustrations of all subspecies that can be easily identified in the field. Names are given for each species in English, in Latin (the scientific name) and in Korean using the Roman alphabet rather than Hangeul (Korean characters). There are many English names but this book chooses the most common name. However, for birds with two kinds of common English name, both are described to allow an easy comparison with other publications.

The classification and the scientific and English names were based on the check-lists of the birds in the world published by Howard & Moore (1998) and by Clements (1991), but some species differ where these have been reclassified as a result of recent detailed studies. Moreover, advances in taxonomy are being made continually, so further changes may be necessary in the future.

● **Text**

This guide has departed from the standard taxonomic order in which families of birds are usually presented. Each family description includes the total number of species in the world and Korea, and their general characteristics (shape, colour and ecology). The characteristics of distinct subfamilies is also described; for example, ducks are subdivided into marsh ducks, diving ducks, geese, swans etc., which roughly correspond with ecological types. The order of description for each species is as follows:

Species Name (English, Scientific and Korean name)
Migration and status in Korea(symbols)
Size of birds (L:total length W: wingspan)
Identification points

Voice
Similar Species
Habitat in Korea
Status

●The Illustrations

To help birdwatchers, we have tried to include as many illustrations as we could. Each species has illustrations of some or all of the following: adult male, adult female, immature, juvenile, summer plumage, winter plumage, in flight, typical standing posture, etc. The arrows on the illustrations indicate the field marks.

● The Range map

The area covered is Northeast Asia, centered on the Korean Peninsula. The maps show the breeding range in pink, and the wintering range in yellow-green. The area where the bird may be found in either season is indicated in brown.

● Subspecies

We have described the subspecies of some species, when these are clearly distinguishable in the field by the colour or pattern of their plumage, for example Dusky Thrush.

● Symbols of migration and status in Korea

Res	Resident
SV	Summer Visitor
WV	Winter Visitor
PM	Passage Migrant
Vag	Vagrant
Probably extinct	
(s)	South part of Korea
(n)	North part of Korea
(I)	Offshore islands of Korea
ab	abundant
c	common
uc	uncommon
sc	scarce
r	rare

[]   alternative English name

● **Technical terminology**

Adult: a mature bird in definitive plumage. Some species have the same appearance in both summer and winter; others have distinct of adult summer and adult winter plumages. Some small birds reach adult plumage within a year, but large species, such as some birds of prey or albatrosses, take several years to attain adult plumage.

Altricial: chicks born with eyes closed and little or no down, which are unable to leave the nest and are fed by the parents for more than for 2 weeks, e.g. most small birds, Rufous Turtle Dove.

Brood Parasitism: the exploitation by one species of the parental behaviour of another species. The cuckoo family (Cuculidae) is well-known for this, although only about 50 species of the 139 in the family are actually brood parasites.

Cere: bare skin at the base of the upper mandible and around the nostrils of raptors.

Chick: a newly-hatched bird unable to fly. In the case of small birds it becomes juvenile after fledging.

Colony: a number of birds breeding gregariously, the term vaguely including the location and the nests, e.g. egrets,gulls etc.

Crest: a tuft of feathers on the crown of the head, which in many species can be raised or lowered.

Eclipse: cryptic, female-like plumage attained by male ducks in summer after breeding, during which the flight-feathers are moulted and the duck becomes flightless, thus needing camouflage. (c.f. breeding plumage.)

Frontal Shield: the unfeathered forehead/forecrown of certain rail species, e.g. Coot, Moorhen, which often has a distinctive colour and shape.

Hovering: holding a stationary position in the air by rapid wing beats.

Immature: a bird wearing any plumage other than adult after the first moult. Some species have no obvious moult.

Incubation: the process whereby the heat necessary for embryonic development is applied to an egg after it has been laid.

Juvenile: a young, fledged bird wearing its first set of true feathers (the juvenile plumage), but which has not yet moulted any of these feathers.

Lobate: having the toes separately fringed by lobes of skin, as distinct from webs connecting the toes, e.g. Little Grebe, Coot, Red-necked Phalarope.

Moult: a natural process of renewal of the plumage, whereby the old feathers are shed and new ones grown. Most species moult in autumn, but some species moult in spring, or moult different feather groups at different times of year. Plumage colour is often changed as a result of moulting, but it can also be caused by feather wear.

Nuptial feather : special feathers attained for courtship.

Parental Care: the protection, feeding, and general care of the young by one or both parents from the time of hatching to independence.

Passage Migrant: a bird which regulary passes through an area on its migration without remaining there for either the summer or the winter. Transient, e.g. sandpipers, shorebirds.

Plumes: long, showy feathers only worn during the breeding season, e,g, Egrets.

Precocial: active immediately after hatching, with open eyes and a covering of down; a precocial chick leaves the nest within the first day or two, is independent of the parents, but follows them to find its own food or to be fed by them; e.g. shorebirds, Ring-necked Pheasant. (see altricial)

Resident: a bird which lives in the same location all year.

Soaring: a bird's own muscles are not necessarily the only source of energy for flight. Energy can often be extracted from the upward movement of the air in which the bird flies, e.g. seabirds or birds of prey, enabling the bird to counteract the downward force of gravity.

Speculum: a distinctive, glossy patch on the upper surface of the secondaries of many species of ducks.

Summer Plumage (Breeding Plumage): usually a more colorful set of feathers gained by many birds, primarily males, either through feather abrasion or by a spring moult. However, some species, such as ducks or the Little Egret,acquire summer plumage in January or February.

Summer Visitor: a bird which comes to an area for breeding. In Korea, summer visitors mainly arrive in spring (from the end of April to early May) from South-east Asia, returning in the same direction in autumn (early-middle September), e.g. Black-naped Oriole, Common Cuckoo, Barn Swallow, egrets, etc.

Total Length(L) : the length of a moderately stretched museum specimen of a bird from the tip of the bill to the tip of tail.

Upperparts, Underparts: these are usually separated by a line along the body connecting the eyes and the wings.

Vagrant : a bird which has wandered far off its normal range, often joining flocks of other species, sometimes because of typhoons, or disorientation during migration, e.g. Short-tailed Albatross, Emperor Goose, Demoiselle Crane, etc.

Wing-span: distance from wing-tip to wing-tip.

Winter Plumage: the plumage worn by birds when they are not breeding, also known as non-breeding plumage. Many species show little or no difference between summer and winter plumages.

Winter Visitor: a bird which breeds mainly in more northern areas, particularly Siberia, in spring and summer and comes Korea to spend the winter, e.g. many geese, ducks, swans, and cranes.

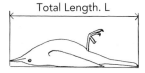
Total Length. L

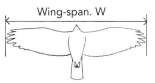
Wing-span. W

● Topography

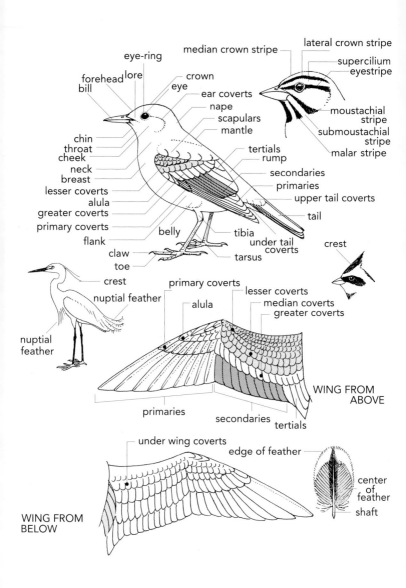

eye-ring
median crown stripe
lateral crown stripe
forehead · lore
supercilium
eyestripe
bill
crown
eye
ear coverts
nape
scapulars
mantle
moustachial stripe
submoustachial stripe
malar stripe
chin
throat
cheek
neck
breast
lesser coverts
alula
greater coverts
primary coverts
flank
belly
tertials
rump
secondaries
primaries
upper tail coverts
tail
tibia
under tail coverts
claw
toe
tarsus
crest
crest
nuptial feather
primary coverts
alula
lesser coverts
median coverts
greater coverts
nuptial feather
WING FROM ABOVE
primaries
secondaries
tertials
under wing coverts
edge of feather
center of feather
shaft
WING FROM BELOW

Checklist of Korean Birds

- **ORDER GAVIIFORMES**
  Family Gaviidae
  Red-throated Diver [Red-throated Loon] *Gavia stellata*
  Arctic Diver [Arctic Loon] *Gavia arctica*
  Pacific Diver [Pacific Loon] *Gavia pacifica*
  Yellow-billed Diver [Yellow-billed Loon] *Gavia adamsii*

- **ORDER PODICIPEDIFORMES**
  Family Podicipedidae
  Little Grebe *Tachybaptus ruficollis*
  Red-necked Grebe *Podiceps grisegena*
  Great Crested Grebe *Podiceps cristatus*
  Horned Grebe [Slavonian Grebe] *Podiceps auritus*
  Black-necked Grebe *Podiceps nigricollis*

- **ORDER PROCELLARIIFORMES**
  Family Diomedeidae
  Short-tailed Albatross *Diomedea albatrus*

  Family Procellariidae
  Bonin Petrel *Pterodroma hypoleuca*
  Streaked Shearwater *Calonectris leucomelas*
  Flesh-footed Shearwater [Pale-footed Shearwater] *Puffinus carneipes*
  Short-tailed Shearwater [Slender-billed Shearwater] *Puffinus tenuirostris*

  Family Hydrobatidae
  Oceanodroma monorhis Swinhoe's Storm Petrel

●ORDER PELECANIFORMES

Family Pelecanidae
Dalmatian Pelican *Pelecanus crispus*

Family Sulidae
Masked Booby *Sula dactylatra*
Brown Booby *Sula leucogaster*

Family Phalacrocoracidae
Great Cormorant *Phalacrocorax carbo*
Temminck's Cormorant *Phalacrocorax capillatus*
Pelagic Cormorant *Phalacrocorax pelagicus*
Red-faced Cormorant *Phalacrocorax urile*

Family Fregatidae
Lesser Frigatebird *Fregata ariel*

●ORDER CICONIIFORMES

Family Ardeidae
Grey Heron *Ardea cinerea*
Purple Heron *Ardea purpurea*
Great Egret [Large Egret] *Egretta alba*
Intermediate Egret *Egretta intermedia*
Little Egret *Egretta garzetta*
Swinhoe's Egret [Chinese Egret] *Egretta eulophotes*
Pacific Reef Heron *Egretta sacra*
Cattle Egret *Bubulcus ibis*
Chinese Pond Heron *Ardeola bacchus*
Striated Heron *Butorides striatus*

Black-crowned Night Heron   *Nycticorax nycticorax*

Japanese Night Heron   *Gorsachius goisagi*

Chinese Little Bittern [Yellow Bittern]   *Ixobrychus sinensis*

Schrenck's Bittern   *Ixobrychus eurhythmus*

Cinnamon Bittern   *Ixobrychus cinnamomeus*

Black Bittern   *Ixobrychus flavicollis*

Eurasian Bittern   *Botaurus stellaris*

Family Ciconiidae

Black Stork   *Ciconia nigra*

Oriental White Stork   *Ciconia boyciana*

Family Threskiornithidae

Oriental Ibis   *Threskiornis melanocephalus*

Crested Ibis [Japanese Crested Ibis]   *Nipponia nippon*

Eurasian Spoonbill   *Platalea leucorodia*

Black-faced Spoonbill   *Platalea minor*

ORDER ANSERIFORMES

Family Anatidae

Mute Swan   *Cygnus olor*

Whooper Swan   *Cygnus cygnus*

Tundra Swan   *Cygnus columbianus*

Swan Goose   *Anser cygnoides*

Bean Goose   *Anser fabalis*

White-fronted Goose   *Anser albifrons*

Lesser White-fronted Goose   *Anser erythropus*

Greylag Goose   *Anser anser*

Snow Goose   *Anser caerulescens*

Emperor Goose *Anser canagicus*

Canada Goose *Branta canadensis*

Brent Goose *Branta bernicla*

Ruddy Shelduck *Tadorna ferruginea*

Common Shelduck *Tadorna tadorna*

Crested Shelduck *Tadorna cristata*

Mandarin Duck *Aix galericulata*

Eurasian Wigeon *Anas penelope*

American Wigeon *Anas americana*

Falcated Teal *Anas falcata*

Gadwall *Anas strepera*

Baikal Teal *Anas formosa*

Common Teal [Green-winged Teal] *Anas crecca*

Mallard *Anas platyrhynchos*

American Black Duck *Anas rubripes*

Spot-billed Duck *Anas poecilorhyncha*

Pintail *Anas acuta*

Garganey *Anas querquedula*

Northern Shoveler *Anas clypeata*

Red-crested Pochard *Netta rufina*

Canvasback *Aythya valisineria*

Pochard *Aythya ferina*

Redhead *Aythya americana*

Baer's Pochard *Aythya baeri*

Tufted Duck *Aythya fuligula*

Greater Scaup *Aythya marila*

Harlequin Duck *Histrionicus histrionicus*

Oldsquaw [Long-tailed Duck] *Clangula hyemalis*

Black Scoter [Common Scoter] *Melanitta nigra*

Velvet Scoter [White-winged Scoter]   *Melanitta fusca*

Barrow's Goldeneye   *Bucephala islandica*

Common Goldeneye   *Bucephala clangula*

Smew   *Mergus albellus*

Red-breasted Merganser   *Mergus serrator*

Chinese Merganser [Scaly-sided Merganser]   *Mergus squamatus*

Common Merganser [Goosander]   *Mergus merganser*

●ORDER FALCONIFORMES

Family Accipitridae

Osprey   *Pandion haliaetus*

Oriental Honey Buzzard   *Pernis ptilorhynchus*

Black Kite   *Milvus migrans*

White-tailed Sea Eagle   *Haliaeetus albicilla*

Steller's Sea Eagle   *Haliaeetus pelagicus*

Cinereous Vulture [Black Vulture]   *Aegypius monachus*

Lammergeier [Bearded Vulture]   *Gypaetus barbatus*

Crested Serpent Eagle   *Spilornis cheela*

Grey-faced Buzzard   *Butastur indicus*

Hen Harrier   *Circus cyaneus*

Pied Harrier   *Circus melanoleucus*

Eastern Marsh Harrier   *Circus spilonotus*

Chinese Sparrowhawk   *Accipiter soloensis*

Japanese Lesser Sparrowhawk   *Accipiter gularis*

Eurasian Sparrowhawk   *Accipiter nisus*

Goshawk [Northern Goshawk]   *Accipiter gentilis*

Common Buzzard   *Buteo buteo*

Rough-legged Buzzard   *Buteo lagopus*

Upland Buzzard   *Buteo hemilasius*

Greater Spotted Eagle   *Aquila clanga*
Steppe Eagle   *Aquila nipalensis*
Imperial Eagle   *Aquila heliaca*
Golden Eagle   *Aquila chrysaetos*
Mountain Hawk Eagle   *Spizaetus nipalensis*

Family Falconidae
Common Kestrel   *Falco tinnunculus*
Amur Falcon   *Falco amurensis*
Merlin   *Falco columbarius*
Eurasian Hobby   *Falco subbuteo*
Saker Falcon   *Falco cherrug*
Peregrine Falcon   *Falco peregrinus*

ORDER GALLIFORMES
Family Tetraonidae
Black Grouse   *Tetrao tetrix*
Hazel Grouse   *Bonasa bonasia*

Family Phasianidae
Japanese Quail   *Coturnix japonica*
Ring-necked Pheasant   *Phasianus colchicus*

ORDER GRUIFORMES
Family Turnicidae
Yellow-legged Buttonquail   *Turnix tanki*

Family Gruidae
Common Crane   *Grus grus*

Hooded Crane   *Grus monacha*

Sandhill Crane   *Grus canadensis*

Red-crowned Crane   *Grus japonensis*

White-naped Crane   *Grus vipio*

Siberian White Crane   *Grus leucogeranus*

Demoiselle Crane   *Anthropoides virgo*

Family Rallidae

Water Rail   *Rallus aquaticus*

Swinhoe's Rail   *Coturnicops exquisitus*

Baillon's Crake   *Porzana pusilla*

Ruddy Crake [Ruddy-breasted Crake]   *Porzana fusca*

Band-bellied Crake   *Rallina paykullii*

White-breasted Waterhen   *Amaurornis phoenicurus*

Watercock   *Gallicrex cinerea*

Moorhen [Common Gallinule]   *Gallinula chloropus*

Coot   *Fulica atra*

Family Otididae

Great Bustard   *Otis tarda*

●ORDER CHARADRIIFORMES

Family Jacanidae

Pheasant-tailed Jacana   *Hydrophasianus chirurgus*

Family Rostratulidae

Painted Snipe   *Rostratula benghalensis*

Family Haematopodidae
Eurasian Oystercatcher   *Haematopus ostralegus*

Family Recurvirostridae
Black-winged Stilt   *Himantopus himantopus*
Avocet   *Recurvirostra avosetta*

Family Glareolidae
Oriental Pratincole   *Glareola maldivarum*

Family Charadriidae
Northern Lapwing   *Vanellus vanellus*
Grey-headed Lapwing   *Vanellus cinereus*
Pacific Golden Plover   *Pluvialis fulva*
Grey Plover   *Pluvialis squatarola*
Common Ringed Plover   *Charadrius hiaticula*
Long-billed Plover   *Charadrius placidus*
Little Ringed Plover   *Charadrius dubius*
Kentish Plover   *Charadrius alexandrinus*
Mongolian Plover [Lesser Sand Plover]   *Charadrius mongolus*
Greater Sand Plover   *Charadrius leschenaultii*
Oriental Plover   *Charadrius veredus*

Family Scolopacidae
Black-tailed Godwit   *Limosa limosa*
Bar-tailed Godwit   *Limosa lapponica*
Little Curlew   *Numenius minutus*
Whimbrel   *Numenius phaeopus*
Eurasian Curlew   *Numenius arquata*

Far Eastern Curlew [Eastern Curlew]   *Numenius madagascariensis*

Spotted Redshank   *Tringa erythropus*

Redshank   *Tringa totanus*

Marsh Sandpiper   *Tringa stagnatilis*

Greenshank   *Tringa nebularia*

Spotted Greenshank [Nordmann's Greenshank]   *Tringa guttifer*

Greater Yellowlegs   *Tringa melanoleuca*

Green Sandpiper   *Tringa ochropus*

Wood Sandpiper   *Tringa glareola*

Terek Sandpiper   *Xenus cinereus*

Common Sandpiper   *Actitis hypoleucos*

Grey-tailed Tattler   *Heteroscelus brevipes*

Ruddy Turnstone   *Arenaria interpres*

Wilson's Phalarope   *Phalaropus tricolor*

Red-necked Phalarope   *Phalaropus lobatus*

Grey Phalarope [Red Phalarope]   *Phalaropus fulicarius*

Eurasian Woodcock   *Scolopax rusticola*

Solitary Snipe   *Gallinago solitaria*

Latham's Snipe   *Gallinago hardwickii*

Pintail Snipe   *Gallinago stenura*

Swinhoe's Snipe   *Gallinago megala*

Common Snipe   *Gallinago gallinago*

Jack Snipe   *Lymnocryptes minimus*

Long-billed Dowitcher   *Limnodromus scolopaceus*

Asiatic Dowitcher [Asian Dowitcher]   *Limnodromus semipalmatus*

Red Knot   *Calidris canutus*

Great Knot   *Calidris tenuirostris*

Sanderling   *Calidris alba*

Red-necked Stint   *Calidris ruficollis*

Little Stint   *Calidris minuta*

Temminck's Stint   *Calidris temminckii*

Long-toed Stint   *Calidris subminuta*

Pectoral Sandpiper   *Calidris melanotos*

Sharp-tailed Sandpiper   *Calidris acuminata*

Dunlin   *Calidris alpina*

Curlew Sandpiper   *Calidris ferruginea*

Spoon-billed Sandpiper   *Eurynorhynchus pygmeus*

Broad-billed Sandpiper   *Limicola falcinellus*

Buff-breasted Sandpiper   *Tryngites subruficollis*

Ruff   *Philomachus pugnax*

Family Stercorariidae

Arctic Skua [Parasitic Jaeger]   *Stercorarius parasiticus*

Family Laridae

Ivory Gull   *Pagophila eburnea*

Black-tailed Gull   *Larus crassirostris*

Mew Gull [Common Gull]   *Larus canus*

Herring Gull   *Larus argentatus*

Heuglin's Gull   *Larus heuglini*

Yellow-legged Gull   *Larus cachinnans*

Slaty-backed Gull   *Larus schistisagus*

Glaucous-winged Gull   *Larus glaucescens*

Glaucous Gull   *Larus hyperboreus*

Iceland Gull   *Larus glaucoides*

Relict Gull   *Larus relictus*

Black-headed Gull   *Larus ridibundus*

Saunders' Gull   *Larus saundersi*
Ross's Gull   *Rhodostethia rosea*
Black-legged Kittiwake   *Rissa tridactyla*
Sabine's Gull   *Xema sabini*
Gull-billed Tern   *Gelochelidon nilotica*
Whiskered Tern   *Chlidonias hybridus*
White-winged Black Tern   *Chlidonias leucopterus*
Common Tern   *Sterna hirundo*
Sooty Tern   *Sterna fuscata*
Little Tern   *Sterna albifrons*
Great Crested Tern [Crested Tern]   *Thalasseus bergii*

Family Alcidae
Guillemot [Thin-billed Murre]   *Uria aalge*
Spectacled Guillemot   *Cepphus carbo*
Marbled Murrelet   *Brachyramphus marmoratus*
Ancient Murrelet   *Synthliboramphus antiquus*
Crested Murrelet [Japanese Murrelet]   *Synthliboramphus wumizusume*
Least Auklet   *Aethia pusilla*
Whiskered Auklet   *Aethia pygmaea*
Rhinoceros Auklet[Horn-billed Puffin]   *Cerorhinca monocerata*

●ORDER COLUMBIFORMES
Family Pteroclididae
Pallas' Sandgrouse   *Syrrhaptes paradoxus*

Family Columbidae
Hill Pigeon   *Columba rupestris*
Stock Dove   *Columba oenas*

Black Wood Pigeon   *Columba janthina*

Rufous Turtle Dove   *Streptopelia orientalis*

Collared Dove   *Streptopelia decaocto*

Red-collared Dove   *Streptopelia tranquebarica*

White-bellied Green Pigeon   *Treron sieboldii*

●ORDER CUCULIFORMES
Family Cuculidae

Red-winged Crested Cuckoo [Chestnut-winged Cuckoo]

Clamator coromandus

Hodgson's Hawk Cuckoo   *Cuculus fugax*

Indian Cuckoo   *Cuculus micropterus*

Common Cuckoo   *Cuculus canorus*

Oriental Cuckoo   *Cuculus saturatus*

Little Cuckoo   *Cuculus poliocephalus*

●ORDER STRIGIFORMES
Family Strigidae

Eurasian Scops Owl   *Otus scops*

Collared Scops Owl   *Otus lempiji*

Eurasian Eagle Owl   *Bubo bubo*

Snowy Owl   *Nyctea scandiaca*

Tawny Owl   *Strix aluco*

Ural Owl   *Strix uralensis*

Northern Hawk Owl   *Surnia ulula*

Little Owl   *Athene noctua*

Brown Hawk Owl   *Ninox scutulata*

Long-eared Owl   *Asio otus*

Short-eared Owl   *Asio flammeus*

●ORDER CAPRIMULGIFORMES
Family Caprimulgidae
Jungle Nightjar [Grey Nightjar]   *Caprimulgus indicus*

●ORDER APODIFORMES
Family Apodidae
White-throated Needle-tailed Swift   *Hirundapus caudacutus*

White-rumped Swift   *Apus pacificus*

House Swift   *Apus affinis*

●ORDER CORACIIFORMES
Family Alcedinidae
Greater Pied Kingfisher   *Megaceryle lugubris*

Common Kingfisher   *Alcedo atthis*

Ruddy Kingfisher   *Halcyon coromanda*

Black-capped Kingfisher   *Halcyon pileata*

Family Coraciidae
Broad-billed Roller [Dollarbird]   *Eurystomus orientalis*

Family Upupidae
Hoopoe   *Upupa epops*

●ORDER PICIFORMES
Family Picidae
Wryneck   *Jynx torquilla*

Japanese Pygmy Woodpecker   *Dendrocopos kizuki*

Grey-capped Woodpecker   *Dendrocopos canicapillus*

Lesser Spotted Woodpecker   *Dendrocopos minor*

Rufous-bellied Woodpecker   *Dendrocopos hyperythrus*

White-backed Woodpecker   *Dendrocopos leucotos*

Great Spotted Woodpecker   *Dendrocopos major*

Three-toed Woodpecker   *Picoides tridactylus*

White-bellied Woodpecker   *Dryocopus javensis*

Black Woodpecker   *Dryocopus martius*

Grey-headed Woodpecker   *Picus canus*

ORDER PASSERIFORMES
Family Pittidae

Fairy Pitta   *Pitta brachyura*

Family Alaudidae

Greater Short-toed Lark   *Calandrella brachydactyla*

Asian Short-toed Lark   *Calandrella cheleensis*

Crested Lark   *Galerida cristata*

Eurasian Skylark   *Alauda arvensis*

Family Hirundinidae

Sand Martin   *Riparia riparia*

Barn Swallow [House Swallow]   *Hirundo rustica*

Red-rumped Swallow   *Hirundo daurica*

Asian House Martin   *Delichon urbica*

Family Motacillidae

Forest Wagtail   *Dendronanthus indicus*

Yellow Wagtail   *Motacilla flava*

Citrine Wagtail   *Motacilla citreola*

Grey Wagtail   *Motacilla cinerea*

White Wagtail   *Motacilla alba*
Black-backed Wagtail   *Motacilla lugens*
Japanese Wagtail   *Motacilla grandis*
Richard's Pipit   *Anthus richardi*
Blyth's Pipit   *Anthus godlewskii*
Olive-backed Pipit   *Anthus hodgsoni*
Rosy Pipit   *Anthus roseatus*
Red-throated Pipit   *Anthus cervinus*
Pechora Pipit   *Anthus gustavi*
Buff-bellied Pipit   *Anthus rubescens*

Family Campephagidae
Black-winged Cuckoo Shrike   *Coracina melaschistos*
Ashy Minivet   *Pericrocotus divaricatus*

Family Pycnonotidae
Brown-eared Bulbul   *Hypsipetes amaurotis*

Family Laniidae
Thick-billed Shrike [Tiger Shrike]   *Lanius tigrinus*
Bull-headed Shrike   *Lanius bucephalus*
Brown Shrike   *Lanius cristatus*
Long-tailed Shrike   *Lanius schach*
Great Grey Shrike [Northern Shrike]   *Lanius excubitor*
Chinese Great Grey Shrike   *Lanius sphenocercus*

Family Bombycillidae
Waxwing [Bohemian Waxwing]   *Bombycilla garrulus*
Japanese Waxwing   *Bombycilla japonica*

Family Cinclidae
Brown Dipper   *Cinclus pallasii*

Family Troglodytidae
Winter Wren   *Troglodytes troglodytes*

Family Prunellidae
Alpine Accentor   *Prunella collaris*
Siberian Accentor   *Prunella montanella*

Family Turdidae
Japanese Robin   *Erithacus akahige*
Rufous-tailed Robin [Swinhoe's Robin]   *Luscinia sibilans*
Siberian Rubythroat   *Luscinia calliope*
Siberian Blue Robin   *Luscinia cyane*
Bluethroat   *Luscinia svecicus*
Red-flanked Bluetail [Orange-flanked Blue Robin]   *Tarsiger cyanurus*
Black Redstart   *Phoenicurus ochruros*
Daurian Redstart   *Phoenicurus auroreus*
Common Stonechat   *Saxicola torquata*
Grey Bushchat   *Saxicola ferrea*
Pied Wheatear   *Oenanthe pleschanka*
Black-eared Wheatear   *Oenanthe hispanica*
White-throated Rock Thrush   *Monticola gularis*
Blue Rock Thrush   *Monticola solitarius*
Siberian Thrush   *Zoothera sibirica*
White's Thrush [Scaly Thrush]   *Zoothera dauma*
Grey-backed Thrush   *Turdus hortulorum*
Grey Thrush   *Turdus cardis*

Blackbird   *Turdus merula*

Brown Thrush   *Turdus chrysolaus*

Pale Thrush   *Turdus pallidus*

Eye-browed Thrush   *Turdus obscurus*

Black-throated Thrush   *Turdus ruficollis*

Dusky Thrush   *Turdus naumanni*

Family Timaliidae

Chinese Babbler   *Rhopophilus pekinensis*

Family Panuridae

Bearded Tit   *Panurus biarmicus*

Vinous-throated Parrotbill   *Paradoxornis webbianus*

Family Sylviidae

Japanese Bush Warbler   *Cettia diphone*

Short-tailed Bush Warbler [Asian Stubtail]   *Urosphena squameiceps*

Spotted Bush Warbler   *Bradypterus thoracicus*

Japanese Marsh Warbler   *Locustella pryeri*

Lanceolated Grasshopper Warbler   *Locustella lanceolata*

Pallas' Grasshopper Warbler   *Locustella certhiola*

Middendorff's Grasshopper Warbler   *Locustella ochotensis*

Styan's Grasshopper Warbler   *Locustella pleskei*

Gray's Grasshopper Warbler   *Locustella fasciolata*

Black-browed Reed Warbler   *Acrocephalus bistrigiceps*

Oriental Great Reed Warbler   *Acrocephalus orientalis*

Thick-billed Warbler   *Acrocephalus aedon*

Fan-tailed Warbler [Zitting Cisticola]   *Cisticola juncidis*

Dusky Warbler   *Phylloscopus fuscatus*

Radde's Warbler   *Phylloscopus schwarzi*
Pallas' Leaf Warbler   *Phylloscopus proregulus*
Yellow-browed Warbler [Inornate Warbler]   *Phylloscopus inornatus*
Arctic Warbler   *Phylloscopus borealis*
Greenish Warbler   *Phylloscopus trochiloides*
Pale-legged Willow Warbler   *Phylloscopus tenellipes*
Eastern Crowned Willow Warbler   *Phylloscopus coronatus*
Lesser Whitethroat   *Sylvia curruca*
Goldcrest   *Regulus regulus*

Family Muscicapidae
Grey-spotted Flycatcher [Grey-streaked Flycatcher]   *Muscicapa griseisticta*
Sooty Flycatcher [Dark-sided Flycatcher]   *Muscicapa sibirica*
Asian Brown Flycatcher   *Muscicapa dauurica*
Tricolor Flycatcher [Yellow-rumped Flycatcher]   *Ficedula zanthopygia*
Narcissus Flycatcher   *Ficedula narcissina*
Mugimaki Flycatcher   *Ficedula mugimaki*
Red-throated Flycatcher   *Ficedula parva*
Blue-and-white Flycatcher   *Cyanoptila cyanomelana*

Family Monarchidae
Asian Paradise Flycatcher   *Terpsiphone paradisi*
Black Paradise Flycatcher   *Terpsiphone atrocaudata*

Family Aegithalidae
Long-tailed Tit   *Aegithalos caudatus*

Family Remizidae
Chinese Penduline Tit   *Remiz consobrinus*

Family Paridae

Marsh Tit   *Parus palustris*

Willow Tit   *Parus montanus*

Coal Tit   *Parus ater*

Great Tit   *Parus major*

Varied Tit   *Parus varius*

Family Sittidae

Eurasian Nuthatch   *Sitta europaea*

Chinese Nuthatch   *Sitta villosa*

Family Certhiidae

Common Treecreeper [Eurasian Treecreeper]   *Certhia familiaris*

Family Zosteropidae

Chestnut-flanked White-eye   *Zosterops erythropleurus*

Japanese White-eye   *Zosterops japonicus*

Family Emberizidae

Pine Bunting   *Emberiza leucocephala*

Meadow Bunting   *Emberiza cioides*

Jankowski's Bunting [Rufous-backed Bunting]   *Emberiza jankowskii*

Japanese Reed Bunting   *Emberiza yessoensis*

Tristram's Bunting   *Emberiza tristrami*

Grey-headed Bunting [Chestnut-eared Bunting]   *Emberiza fucata*

Little Bunting   *Emberiza pusilla*

Yellow-browed Bunting   *Emberiza chrysophrys*

Rustic Bunting   *Emberiza rustica*

Yellow-throated Bunting   *Emberiza elegans*

Yellow-breasted Bunting *Emberiza aureola*

Chestnut Bunting *Emberiza rutila*

Red-headed Bunting *Emberiza bruniceps*

Yellow Bunting *Emberiza sulphurata*

Black-faced Bunting *Emberiza spodocephala*

Grey Bunting *Emberiza variabilis*

Pallas' Reed Bunting *Emberiza pallasi*

Reed Bunting *Emberiza schoeniclus*

Lapland Longspur *Calcarius lapponicus*

Snow Bunting *Plectrophenax nivalis*

Family Fringillidae

Brambling *Fringilla montifringilla*

Oriental Greenfinch *Carduelis sinica*

Siskin *Carduelis spinus*

Common Redpoll *Carduelis flammea*

Hoary Redpoll *Carduelis hornemanni*

Rosy Finch *Leucosticte arctoa*

Long-tailed Rosefinch *Uragus sibiricus*

Common Rosefinch [Scarlet Rosefinch] *Carpodacus erythrinus*

Pallas's Rosefinch *Carpodacus roseus*

Pine Grosbeak *Pinicola enucleator*

Common Crossbill [Red Crossbill] *Loxia curvirostra*

White-winged Crossbill *Loxia leucoptera*

Bullfinch *Pyrrhula pyrrhula*

Hawfinch *Coccothraustes coccothraustes*

Chinese Grosbeak *Eophona migratoria*

Japanese Grosbeak *Eophona personata*

Family Ploceidae
Russet Sparrow   *Passer rutilans*

Tree Sparrow   *Passer montanus*

Family Sturnidae
Violet-backed Starling [Chestnut-cheeked Starling]   *Sturnus philippensis*

Daurian Starling   *Sturnus sturninus*

Common Starling   *Sturnus vulgaris*

Grey Starling [White-cheeked Starling]   *Sturnus cineraceus*

Grey-backed Starling [White-shouldered Starling]   *Sturnus sinensis*

Family Oriolidae
Black-naped Oriole   *Oriolus chinensis*

Family Dicruridae
Black Drongo   *Dicrurus macrocercus*

Ashy Drongo   *Dicrurus leucophaeus*

Hair-crested Drongo [Spangled Drongo]   *Dicrurus hottentottus*

Family Artamidae
White-breasted Wood Swallow   *Artamus leucorhynchus*

Family Corvidae
Jay   *Garrulus glandarius*

Azure-winged Magpie   *Cyanopica cyana*

Black-billed Magpie   *Pica pica*

Spotted Nutcracker   *Nucifraga caryocatactes*

Red-billed Chough   *Pyrrhocorax pyrrhocorax*

Daurian Jackdaw   *Corvus dauuricus*
Rook   *Corvus frugilegus*
Carrion Crow   *Corvus corone*
Jungle Crow   *Corvus macrorhynchos*

How to identify birds

Most of us do not know the names of very many birds so you might be surprised to know that 450 species of bird have been recorded in the Korean Peninsula. Though there are many birds around us, it is impossible to see all these kinds of birds in a short period because they do not occur in one place or at the same time of a year, and their habitats are different from each other. As with many other skills, learning to correctly identify birds requires time and effort. The most important factor in learning to identify birds is, above all, observing them in the field. Furthermore, you need to become familiar with birds' features through the illustrations and texts in this pictorial guide. This is because the ability to identify birds depends upon how much information you have on their characteristics.

One of the most usual ways in deciding a bird's name is by eliminating those birds that it clearly is not. In order to do so, you should judge which group the bird in question, such as flycatchers, woodpeckers or egrets, belongs to. The size, form, posture, behaviour, and habitat should be carefully observed. You will find pictures of the shape of various different kinds of birds in the inside cover of the book. You can refere to these to find out which groups they are in. Then, you should look at the body shape, the length of the bird's bill, head, foot, leg, wing, and tail.

After your observation, you will look for matching pictures in the book. If you are a beginner, however, it will be better for your work to browse through it several times first. When you have time before going to bed or after a meal, you should look through it from cover to cover and then you will become familiar with the birds in it. You will soon get to know their appearance and characteristics. You should pay attention to the parts of the birds indicated by arrows for when you go birdwatching outdoors. The arrows indicate the most prominent points or 'field marks' which help you to identify birds in the field. You will soon find them a great help when you are birdwatching. They are distinctive points such as the yellow bill-tip of the Spot-billed Duck, the white wing-patch of the Black-capped Kingfisher and the ribbon-like crest of the Northern Lapwing. Of course, there are some bird species which are very similar in colour and shape and so are hard to identify, but you will be able to distinguish them when you get to know more details of their characteristics and you have built up your experience in the field.

When you watch birds in flight, you should pay special attention to their shape and way of flying, the pattern and distribution of colours, and any calls they may make. Birds move in characteristic ways which often make identification fairly certain even if the colours cannot be clearly seen; for example, the head-jerking of a swimming Moorhen, or the bobbing of the Common Sandpiper; or they may cock their tails like the Wren, or wag them like the Wagtails. Looking out for these behaviour patterns always makes birdwatching interesting. Experienced birdwatchers usually locate birds first by their songs or calls, especially in forest. Even the most shy birds have distinctive calls, and indeed they may the only way to correctly identify some species in the field. Recording and listening to birds' songs and calls is an excellent way to expand your knowledge of birds, and is a much easier way of providing a record of a bird's presence than a photograph.

Remember that most species of birds prefer a particular habitat in each species, or occur during a particular season. For example, Cranes do not sit on trees, they like fields and marshes. So a bird which looks like a crane in a tree might well be a egret, a bird which does like trees. So you should check the habitat section of the description before deciding on your identification.

You are very unlikely to find a rarity but of course it is not impossible. Your chances are much higher in bad weather in spring and autumn when migrating birds are blown off course; in autumn in particular, immature birds are likely to become disorientated and lost and reach Korea from a distant place. It is really interesting when we find birds at unexpected places or in an unusual season. However, especially if you are a beginner, you should consider carefully whether or not your observation is correct.

There are various situations of bird watching in the field, and you can never know the name of every bird you see. But if you have some experience of bird watching, you can, at least, identify them as to which family or group they belong to. After much practice, you will be able to identify most of birds. When you find a bird you should remember that not every bird is always identifiable, and you should not jump to conclusions, but rather check the various field characters as caerfully as possible and be cautious about your identification.

You also need to get accustomed to recording the bird's appearance, behaviour, song, habitat, and so on. Such practice will be the best way to build up your bird watching skills and experience. You should make simple sketches as well as writing down details of colour, behaviour and calls. So you should be sure to take a small notebook and pencil along with this field guide.

VISIBLE FIELD MARKS

Size and Shape: Compare the overall size of the bird to that of familiar species:

Body Shape: Is the bird plump like a Hawfinch or slender like a wagtail?

Bill Size and Shape: Is the bill short or long? Thick or thin? Straight or curved?

The Length and Shape: Is the tail long or short? Is it forked, square, notched, rounded, or wedge-shaped?

Wingspan and Shape: Are the wings long or short? Pointed or rounded?

Face and Head: Does it have a stripe throught the eye or crown? A ring around the eye?

Underparts: Is its belly light or dark, barred, plain, or patterned

Upper Surfaces of Wings and Body: Are there distinctive marks, spots, or stripes?

Rump and Tail: Is the rump light or dark? What about the tail? Does the tail have a dark or light band at the tip?

Wings: Are there prominent bars or stripes on the wings? Do the wings contrast with the back?

Posture at Rest: How does the bird sit or perch?

Tail-wagging: Does it wag its tail? If so, is it up and down or in a circle?

Tree Climbing: Does it climb straight up like a woodpecker, in spirals like a creeper, or go down head first like a nuthatch?

Flying: A. Does the bird dip up and down in flight like a woodpecker or fly straight like a Grey Staring?

B. Does it soar?

C. Does it hover?

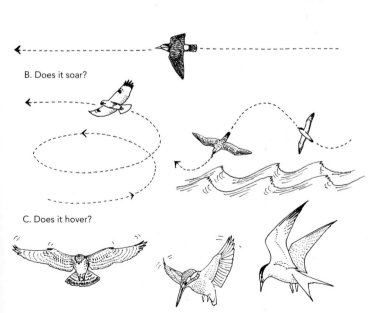

Divers Family Gaviidae (World : 5 species, Korea : 4 species) Medium large waterbirds. Streamlined body, with legs set far back, is well adapted to dive and catch fish underwater. Swim low in water. Sexes similar.

RED-THROATED DIVER [Red-throated Loon] *Gavia stellata* <Abi> WV/uc L 63cm. Slender bill often held pointed upwards; lower mandible uptilted; rather uniform grey-brown upperparts. **Br:** face and sides of neck pale-grey; finely striped on hindneck; large, dark reddish-brown patch on foreneck. **Non-Br:** extensive white on sides of neck and face, so eye is conspicuous; upperparts speckled with white. **Juv:** crown and nape darker than non-Br. White spots on upperparts less bold. **Habitat:** coasts, estuaries.

PACIFIC DIVER [Pacific Loon] *Gavia pacifica* <Hoesaengmeoriabi> WV/uc L 65cm. Shorter, straighter bill and more rounded head shape than Arctic Diver. **Br:** black foreneck has metallic-purple sheen; pale hindneck visible from a distance and contrasts with blackish face. **Non-Br:** dusky mottling on ear coverts makes face dark; many show dark chinstrap. **Juv:** pale fringes to feathers on mantle/scapulars. **Similar species:** Arctic Diver. **Habitat:** coasts, estuaries.

ARCTIC DIVER [Arctic Loon] *Gavia arctica* <Keunhoesaengmeoriabi> WV/uc L 72cm. White on rear flanks usually above water-line and conspicuous; stout bill often held straight. **Br:** black foreneck has metallic-green sheen; stripes on chin and sides of neck are wider than Pacific Diver; grey hindneck shows little contrast with face. **Non-Br:** blackish body shows clear contrast with clear white neck line and white oval on rear flanks just above water-line. **Juv:** pale fringes on mantle/scapulars. **Habitat:** cosats.

YELLOW-BILLED DIVER [Yellow-billed Loon] *Gavia adamsii* <Huinburiabi> WV/r L 89cm. Thick neck and 'lumpy' forehead; pale bill has curved lower mandible and is held pointing upwards. **Br:** head and hindneck black; bill ivory. **Non-Br:** pale around eye contrasts with dark patch behind ear coverts. Crown and hindneck greyish-brown, merging into white of foreneck. **Juv:** pale fringes to upperparts give neat scaly pattern. **Habitat:** coasts, estuaries.

Divers

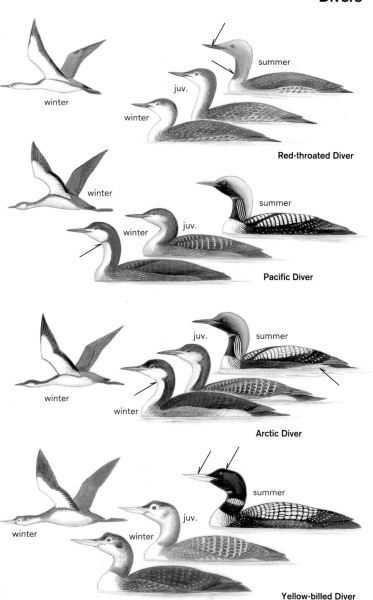

winter

juv.

winter

summer

Red-throated Diver

winter

winter

juv.

summer

Pacific Diver

winter

juv.

summer

winter

Arctic Diver

winter

juv.

winter

summer

Yellow-billed Diver

49

Grebes
Family Podicipedidae (World : 21 species, Korea : 5 species)
Diving birds. Fly with rapid wingbeats, the neck extended and held lower than the back. Diagnostic upperwing patterns. Tail very short.

LITTLE GREBE *Tachybaptus ruficollis* <Nonbyeong-ari> WV/c·Res/c L 26cm. Smallest grebe. Iris yellow. **Br:** dark-looking with cheeks and sides of neck chestnut; yellow gape patch. **Non-Br:** underparts and face sandy-buff, throat and rearend paler; upperparts darker; bill pale. **Juv:** paler body, black head with white stripes becomes like non-br. In flight, lacks obvious white on wings. **Habitat:** rivers, lakes, reservoirs.

BLACK-NECKED GREBE *Podiceps nigricollis* <Geomeunmongnonbyeong-ari> WV/c L 31cm. Peaked crown and steep forehead; short, dark, upturned bill. **Br:** black neck and yellow ear-tufts. **Non-Br:** blackish crown with sooty grey through eye and down across ear coverts; grey mottling forms band across neck, contrasting with whitish throat and breast. In flight, white confined to rear of inner wing. **Habitat:** lakes, estuaries, coasts.

HORNED GREBE [Slavonian Grebe] *Podiceps auritus* <Guippullonbyeong-ari> WV/uc L 33cm. Straight black bill. **Br:** black head with yellowish-orange head plumes, chestnut neck and flanks. **Non-Br:** sloping, black crown is peaked at rear; crown and dark hind neck show clear contrast with white lower face and throat. In flight, small white triangle on forewing, and white across rear of inner wing. **Habitat:** lakes, estuaries, coasts.

RED-NECKED GREBE *Podiceps grisegena* <Keunnonbyeong-ari> WV/uc L 45cm. Longish dark bill has yellow base. **Br:** grey face with whitish upper edge contrasts with black crown and chestnut neck. **Non-Br:** duller grey-brown, white throat extending to grey-white patch behind dusky ear coverts; lacks chestnut on neck and black on crown. **Habitat:** coasts, estuaries.

GREAT CRESTED GREBE *Podiceps cristatus* <Ppullonbyeong-ari> WV/c · Res/r L 49cm. Long, slender neck. with clear white foreneck and black crown. In flight, white on leading and rear edge of wings and across scapulars. **Br:** chestnut and black plumes on ear coverts and black crests. **Non-Br:** white foreneck and white face with black loral line, with conspicuous eye and cap. **Habitat:** lakes, rivers, estuaries, coasts.

Grebes

Little Grebe

Black-necked Grebe

Horned Grebe

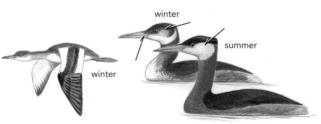

Red-necked Grebe

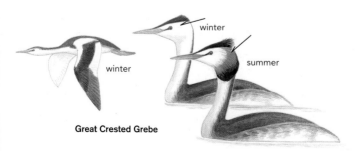

Great Crested Grebe

Shearwaters

Family Procellariidae (World : 72 species, Korea : 4 species) Typical seabird spend their life on the open sea except breeding season. Lay 1 eggs in digged tunnel.

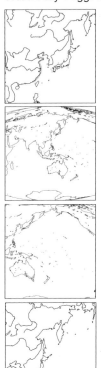

STREAKED SHEARWATER *Calonectris leucomelas* <Seumsae> SV/c(l) L 49cm·W 120cm. Dark-brown upperparts, white underparts. White forehead and lores, pale bill. Variable amount of dark-brown streaking or scaling on head, from almost pure white, to dark capped. **Habitat:** sea.

FLESH-FOOTED SHEARWATER [Pale-footed Shearwater] *Puffinus carneipes* <Bulgeunbalseumsae> PM/r L 43cm·W 103cm. Dark-brown body looks darker/browner than Short-tailed Shearwater, with longer, noticeably pink bill with dark tip, and pinkish legs. In flight, rather sluggish. **Habitat:** sea.

SHORT-TAILED SHEARWATER [Slender-billed Shearwater] *Puffinus tenuirostris* <Soeburiseumsae> PM/r L 42cm·W 98cm. Dark-brown on upperparts, looks brighter on under wing-coverts, but individuals vary. Short, slender, dark bill and dark-brown legs. In flight, rapid beats followed by gliding. **Similar species:** Flesh-footed Shearwater looks pink on bill and legs, dark-brown underwing-coverts. **Habitat:** sea.

BONIN PETREL *Pterodroma hypoleuca* <Huinbaeseumsae> Vag L 31cm·W 69cm. Grey upperparts, appearing scaly on mantle; lower back and rump blackish-brown, with wings showing M-pattern; tail dark-grey. Underparts white, narrow blackish trailing edge to wing widens at primaries, with a blackish patch at the primary coverts, and a diagonal bar across the secondary coverts. Pinkish legs. **Habitat:** sea.

Storm Petrels

Family Hydrobatidae (World : 20 species, Korea : 1 species) Typical seabirds. Tube-shaped nostril and webfoot. Eat the invertebrate; shrimps and cuttlefishes. Lay 1 eggs at digged tunnel in islands.

SWINHOE'S STORM PETREL *Oceanodroma monorhis* <Badajebi> SV/c(l) L 20cm·W 45cm.The only petrel recorded so far in Korea. Small, all dark-brown, with paler wing-coverts; blackish primaries have very pale bases; pale bar across rump may also be present; long wing; medium-forked tail; black bill and legs. **Habitat:** sea.

Shearwaters, Storm Petrels

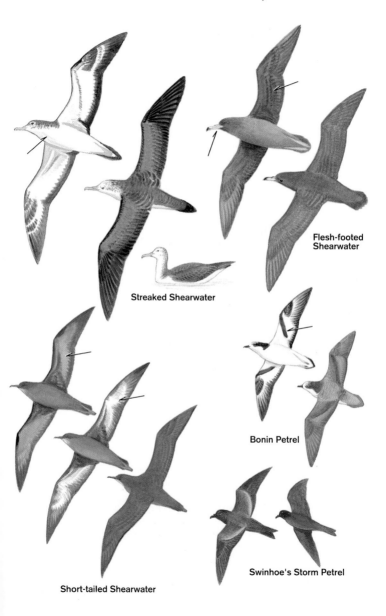

Flesh-footed Shearwater

Streaked Shearwater

Bonin Petrel

Swinhoe's Storm Petrel

Short-tailed Shearwater

Albatrosses
Family Diomedeidae (World : 14 species, Korea : 1 species) Long and narrow wings, and thick billed large seabirds. Colonial breeder in island far from the land. Sexes similar, but male larger than female.

SHORT-TAILED ALBATROSS *Diomedea albatrus* <Albatross> Vag L 91cm・W 210cm. Huge. **Ad:** Huge, pale pink bill; white body; pale yellow crown and nape; flight feathers, primary coverts black, and tip of short tail black. **Juv:** Blackish-brown body with pink bill and legs; white bar on wing gets broader to adult. (Juv. Black-footed Albatross could occur, which has very similar plumage but is smaller and has narrow white line around base of relatively smaller bill, and blackish feet). **Habitat:** sea. **Status:** One captured, Busan, June 1885.

Pelicans
Family Pelecanidae (World : 8 species, Korea : 1 species) Pelicans are very large, white or whitish waterbirds with long, broad wings and short tails. The huge bill has a pouch for storing caught fish.

DALMATIAN PELICAN *Pelecanus crispus* <Sada-sae> Vag L 170cm・W 327cm. **Br:** Greyish white with short crest; small area of pink skin around eye; orange gular pouch. Flight feathers blackish above but underwing appears all-white except for dark tips (not as illustrated). **Imm:** Grey-brown back and wing-covert; pale brown bill. Similar Great White Pelican has whiter plumage and black flight feathers on underwing; yellow gular pouch, and extensive pink skin around eye; imm. also has dark line across underwing-coverts; this species could also occur as a vagrant. **Habitat:** lakes, rivers, seashore. **Status:** each single records at Incheon in 1914, and Marado, Jeju-do in 1978.

Short-tailed Albatross

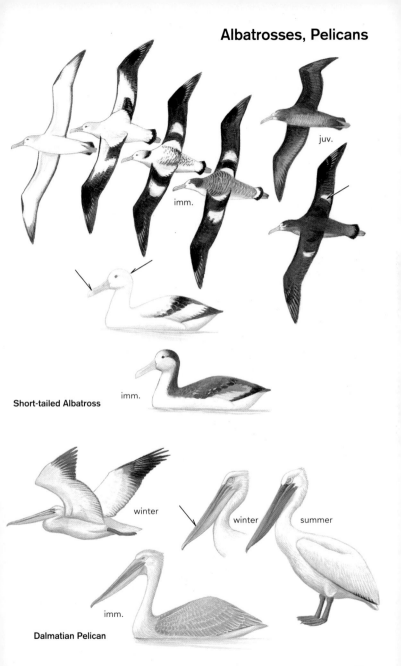

juv.

imm.

Short-tailed Albatross

imm.

winter

winter

summer

imm.

Dalmatian Pelican

Boobies

Family Sulidae (World : 9 species, Korea : 2 species) Large seabirds with long wings, wedge-shaped tail and long graduated bill making them look pointed at both ends. Often fly higher than most other seabirds, plunge-diving into sea for food.

BROWN BOOBY *Sula leucogaster* <Galsaegeolganisae> Vag L 69cm•W 140cm. Legs and bill yellowish. **Ad:** dark brown upperparts; white belly and centre of underwing. **Male:** blue facial skin. **Female:** yellow facial skin. **Juv:** underparts and underwings greyish brown, becoming white with age. **Similar species:** Juv. Masked Booby is larger with darker bill, white upper breast and neck collar. **Habitat:** sea, coasts.

MASKED BOOBY *Sula dactylatra* <Pureuneolgureolganisae> Vag L 86cm•W 152cm. Very large. **Ad:** white with black flight feathers and tail; large, yellowish bill; blue-grey facial skin and gular pouch appear dark at sea. **Juv:** brown head, back and wings with whitish neck collar; greyish bill darker at base. **Similar species:** see Brown Booby. **Habitat:** sea, coasts.

Frigatebirds

Family Fregatidae (World : 5 species, Korea : 1 species) Large soaring seabirds with deeply forked tails and long wings. They almost never land on water. Colonial breeder in tropical oceanic islands. Sexes differ; male have inflatable red pouches.

LESSER FRIGATEBIRD *Fregata ariel* <Gunhamjo> Vag L 76cm. Characteristic black shape, with long pointed wings, deeply forked tail, white 'spurs' across axillaries and long, hooked, pink bill. **Male:** glossy black above; underparts mostly black, except for white bar from side to underwing, and red throat (can be difficult to see). **Female:** blackish above; white on breast and sides extends on to underwing; buffy wingbar across inner wing. **Imm:** similar to female, but head pale, often yellowish or rusty; dark breastband, white lower belly becoming scaly, then black, with age; bill greyish-pink; inner wing bar paler. Robs food from other birds. **Habitat:** open ocean, occasionally blown inshore or inland. **Status:** each records at Hangang, Nakdonggang, and Dongjingang.

Boobies, Frigatebirds

juv.

♂
♀

Brown Booby

juv.

Masked Booby

♂
juv.
♀
imm.
juv.

Lesser Frigatebird

Cormorants

Family Phalacrocoracidae (World : 33 species, Korea : 4 species) Medium to large, fish-eating diving birds; most species coastal. Plumages usually dark with metallic sheen; hooked bills; long necks.

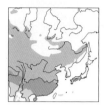

GREAT CORMORANT *Phalacrocorax carbo* <Minmulgamauji> WV/c L 82cm・W 130cm. Upperparts blackish with green or bronze-brown gloss. **Br:** white patch on thigh. Varying amount of whitish hair-like plumes on rear of head and neck. **Non-Br:** lacks filoplumes on head and neck, and white patch on thigh; greyish bill. **Juv:** blackish brown. Underparts paler. **Habitat:** coasts, estuaries, rivers, lakes.

TEMMINCK'S CORMORANT *Phalacrocorax capillatus* <Gamauji> Res/c L 84cm・W 133cm. Very similar to Great Cormorant, but typically coastal. Glossed green rather than bronze, specially on upperparts. Bare, yellow area at base of bill is smaller than Great, and cuts into the white feather area forming a point; white area behind eye larger, extending higher than the eye level; white on throat; bill dark-grey. **Non-Br:** extensive white on face and throat; bill largely yellowish. **Juv:** bill shows much yellow. **Habitat:** coasts, estuaries, lakes.

PELAGIC CORMORANT *Phalacrocorax pelagicus* <Soegamauji> Res/c L 73cm・W 98cm. Head and bill slender. **Br:** black with variable greenish or violet gloss, distinct purple gloss on thin neck; two ragged, short crests; bill thin, brownish, with yellowish base, lacking any blue; large white flank patch. **Non-Br:** lacks red facial skin and crests on head and white patch on thigh. **Juv:** dark brown. Underparts paler **Habitat:** coasts.

RED-FACED CORMORANT *Phalacrocorax urile* <Bulgeunppyamgamauji> Res/sc(n) L 84cm・W 116cm. Black body; bill looks yellowish, with dark tip; gape bluish. Black with variable greenish or violet gloss. **Br:** two distinct crests on crown and nape. Bare red facial skin extends from behind eye through lores and across forehead, on to chin; brighter when aroused. **Non-Br:** lacks crests and thigh patches. **Juv:** Dark-brown body, yellowish or greyish bill. Larger size, with slightly thicker neck and bill than Pelagic Cormorant. **Habitat:** coasts.

Cormorants

Great Cormorant
winter · summer · juv.

Temminck's Cormorant
winter · winter · summer · juv.

Pelagic Cormorant
summer · winter · summer · winter · juv.

Red-faced Cormorant
summer · summer · winter · juv.

Herons, Bitterns and Egrets

Family Ardeidae (World : 61 species, Korea : 17 species) Middle to large wading birds. Flight direct with slow wingbeats, necks pulled back in S-shape, though occasionally will fly briefly with neck extended. Sexes usually similar. Bitterns tend to be shy, inhabiting well-vegetated wetlands; most herons and egret species tend to feed in more open situations and nest colonially.

CHINESE LITTLE BITTERN [Yellow Bittern] *Ixobrychus sinensis* <Deombulhae-oragi> SV/c L 37cm. In flight, strong contrast visible between yellow-brown wing-coverts, dark-brown back and black flight-feathers. **Male:** grey or blackish crown; yellow-brown body. **Female:** crown reddish-brown; brown streaks on underparts. **Juv:** rich brown, heavily streaked above and below; underparts pale. **Habitat:** reservoirs, lakes, rivers, rice-fields.

SCHRENCK'S BITTERN *Ixobrychus eurhythmus* <Keundeombulhae-oragi> SV/uc L 39cm. Very skulking. Tibia unfeathered; rear edge of pupil appears split, so pupil is not circular. **Male:** crown to back deep chestnut, darker on crown; creamy-white underparts, and pale grey wingpatch on secondary coverts; dark stripe down centre of foreneck. **Female:** back and wings densely spotted white; underparts yellowish streaked with brown. **Juv:** as female, but browner and more heavily streaked. **Habitat:** reservoirs, lakes, rivers, rice-fields. .

CINNAMON BITTERN *Ixobrychus cinnamomeus* <Yeoldaebulgeunhae-oragi> Vag L 41cm. Rufous-brown wings in flight. **Male:** rufous-brown upperparts, underparts much paler; whitish chin. **Female:** rich brown upperparts spotted with white; streaked below. **Juv:** as female, but densely marked with buff. **Habitat:** reservoirs, lakes, rivers, rice-fields.

BLACK BITTERN *Ixobrychus flavicollis* <Geomeunhae-oragi> Vag L 58cm. In flight, upperparts appear black, with contrasting neck patch. Legs and feet usually dark but may be greenish. Shy. **Male:** crown and upperparts black; yellowish-buff neckpatch; white throat and streaked white breast. **Female:** as male, but blackish-brown. **Juv:** as female, but upperparts fringed paler. **Habitat:** reservoirs, lakes, rivers, rice-fields.

Bitterns

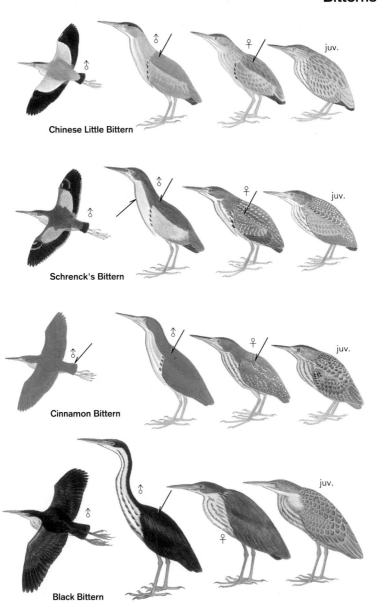

Chinese Little Bittern

Schrenck's Bittern

Cinnamon Bittern

Black Bittern

JAPANESE NIGHT HERON *Gorsachius goisagi*
<Bulgeunhae-oragi> Vag L 49cm. **Ad:** short,
thick, dark bill and blue facial skin and eye-ring.
Upperparts including crown chestnut, rufous on
sides of head; underparts creamy streaked
irregularly with chestnut and buff. In flight, black
primaries and secondaries have conspicuous tawny
trailing edge. **Juv:** fine pale vermiculations over all
upperparts. Facial skin creamy. **Similar species:**
Imm. Black-crowned Night Heron is overall
brownish but more streaky, with white spots on
wing coverts, larger bill and red iris. **Habitat:**
feeds in marshes, streams in dense forests. **Status:**
caught several times at Busan and Jeju-do.

BLACK-CROWNED NIGHT HERON *Nycticorax
nycticorax* <Hae-oragi> Res/c·SV/c L 57cm. A
widespread species near rivers, often heard calling
at night, and seen flying from roost at dusk. Bulky,
but compact and short-necked. **Ad:** crown to
mantle black, forehead white, wings grey; two or
three long white plumes on hindneck; black back
and uniform grey wings are conspicuous in flight;
underparts white, sometimes grey. **Juv:** body
brown with whitish spots along wing coverts, buffy
streaks on upperparts, denser on underparts. Juv.
has dark moustache. **Similar species:** Juv. Striated
Heron is dark brown from mantle to wings, has
less thick bill, yellow iris, white submoustachial.
Habitat: all kinds of wetlands, especially rivers.

STRIATED HERON *Butorides striatus* <Geom-
eundaenggihae-oragi> SV/c L 52cm. A small, dark
heron with rapid wing beats. **Ad:** Forehead, crown
and moustache black; back and wing coverts slaty-
grey with green gloss; wing coverts edged whitish;
underparts grey with white streaks; bill long; facial
skin, legs and feet yellow. **Juv:** body dark brown
with whitish streaks on wing coverts, head and
neck; white submoustachial; buff streaks on
underparts; legs greenish yellow. **Similar species:**
see Black-crowned Night Heron; imm. Black
Bittern scaly, has yellowish neckpatch. **Habitat:**
wetlands, especially rivers and rice-fields.

Night Herons

Japanese Night Heron

juv.

Black-crowned Night Heron

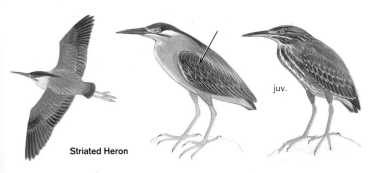

Striated Heron

juv.

CHINESE POND HERON *Ardeola bacchus* <Huinnalgaehae-oragi> SV/r L 45cm. Conspicuous contrast in flight between white wings and black back. **Br:** head and neck chestnut becoming purplish on breast; back black; white wings and tail not always visible at rest. **Non-Br:** head to breast white streaked grey-brown; back darker; wings white. Seems to disappear on landing when white wings are folded under long back feathers. **Habitat:** rice-fields, marshes, grasslands.

CATTLE EGRET *Bubulcus ibis* <Hwangno> SV/c L 50cm. Shorter legs and neck and heavier-jowled than other white egrets; bill shorter with upper mandible curving down to meet tip of straight lower mandible; feathering on lower mandible gives heavy-jowled look; legs blackish. **Br:** conspicuous orange plumes on head, breast and back; red base to bill; facial skin becomes bright pink or bluish, and legs reddish. **Non-Br:** pale yellowish facial skin; lacks plumes; body all-white though some have orange tinge remaining on head or back. **Habitat:** marshes, rice-fields, grasslands. Often follows cattle and feeds on insects they disturb.

PACIFIC REEF EGRET *Egretta sacra* <Heungno> Res/uc L 58cm. Plumes on nape, foreneck and lower back in Br. plumage. Legs and feet greenish or yellow; legs rather thick with short thigh; chin and neck rather thick, notably upper neck; crown appears rounded from bill base to nape. **Dark morph:** dark slaty-grey overall; most have narrow white mark on throat; bill yellow to blackish, upper mandible slightly curved along its length. **White morph:** usually all-white. **Habitat:** rocky coasts. **Status:** white morph not yet recorded in Korea.

EURASIAN BITTERN *Botaurus stellaris* <Allakhae-oragi> WV/r L 76cm. Highly skulking. When alarmed, points bill upward to align plumage stripes with reeds and remains motionless for a while. Thick bill and neck make eye appear small. **Ad:** sides of head pale brown; crown and moustachial stripe black; body buffy with blackish stripes and fine V-shaped bars; legs/feet greenish. **Habitat:** reedbeds, marshes.

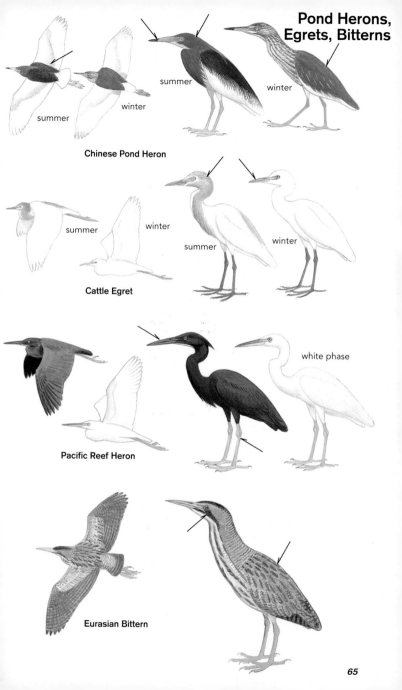

Pond Herons, Egrets, Bitterns

Chinese Pond Heron
summer
winter
summer
winter

Cattle Egret
summer
winter
summer
winter

Pacific Reef Heron
white phase

Eurasian Bittern

GREAT EGRET [Large Egret] *Egretta alba* <Jungdaebaengno> SV/c•WV/uc L 90cm. All-white body with long bill, neck and legs. Gape extends well behind eye; forehead usually slopes gently to bill. Flies with slow wingbeats. Northern subspecies *E. a.* usually has yellowish tibia in winter, black feet with yellow soles; smaller southern subspecies *E. a. modesta* (widespread in summer) has all-black feet. **Br:** bill black; facial skin blue-green; plumes on lower back; legs reddish. **Non-Br:** bill, facial skin yellow; no plumes. **Habitat:** wetlands, tidal flats.

INTERMEDIATE EGRET *Egretta intermedia* <Jungbaengno> SV/c L 68cm. Typically in rice-fields. Bill shorter than Little and Great Egrets; gape extends to rear edge of eye but not beyond; forehead often rounded; legs/feet black. **Br:** bill black; facial skin yellow, at times becoming greenish; plumes on upper breast and lower back. **Non-Br:** dull yellow bill has dusky tip. **Habitat:** marshes, rice-fields.

LITTLE EGRET *Egretta garzetta* <Soebaengno> SV/c•Res/c L 61cm. All-white with conspicuous yellow feet and long black bill; facial skin yellow or grey or white. **Br:** two long plumes from rear crown; also plumes on breast and lower back. Facial skin at times becomes dark pink and feet red. **Non-Br:** lacks plumes. **Juv:** lower mandible yellowish; legs greenish-grey with yellower feet. **Habitat:** all kinds of wetlands.

SWINHOE'S EGRET [Chinese Egret] *Egretta eulophotes* <Norangburibaengno> SV/uc L 68cm. All-white plumage; neck and legs appear shorter and thicker than Little Egret; tibia and tarsus longer than Pacific Reef Egret; bill becomes steadily narrower from base to tip. **Br:** bill orange-yellow; blue skin on lores; plumes on nape and lower back. Legs black; feet bright yellow. **Non-Br/Juv:** no plumes; lores greenish or greyish, legs greenish with black shins and yellowish feet; bill black usually with clearly defined orange base to lower mandible. **Similar species:** non-Br white morph of Reef Heron. **Habitat:** tidal flats, estuaries, lakes, rice-fields. **Status:** in summer confined to Yellow Sea.

Egrets

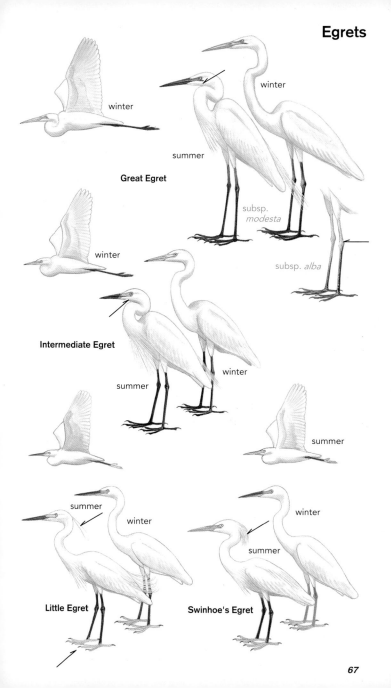

winter

Great Egret

winter

summer

winter

subsp. *modesta*

subsp. *alba*

summer

winter

Intermediate Egret

summer

summer

summer

winter

summer

winter

summer

winter

Little Egret

Swinhoe's Egret

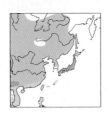

GREY HERON *Ardea cinerea* <Waegari> SV/c·
Res/c L 93cm. **Ad:** white head and neck with black
lateral crown stripes which become plumes in Br.
season; underparts white with black stripes down
throat and on sides of belly black. In flight, grey
upperwing wing-coverts contrast with black flight
feathers; white patch at base of primaries;
underwings greyish; black shoulder-patch visible
at rest. **Br:** at times shows red bill with yellow tip,
red legs; white crown. **Non-Br:** streaked crown,
grey bill. **Juv:** head, neck greyer; mantle and wing-
coverts browny-grey. **Habitat:** wetlands.

PURPLE HERON *Ardea purpurea* <Bulgeun-
waegari> PM/sc L 79cm. **Ad:** black crown and
moustache meet at nape; black stripes run down
neck at sides and back; long, grey scapulars. In
flight, shows large feet, less contrast between grey
wing-coverts and black flight feathers than Grey
Heron; patch at base of primaries is chestnut;
underwing-coverts mostly chestnut. **Juv:**
upperparts scaled with brown. **Habitat:** wetlands,
especially reedbeds.

Storks Family Ciconiidae (World : 19 species, Korea : 2 species)

Large wading birds with long and thick bills. Unlike herons and egrets, fly
with the neck extended. Feeding fishes, amphibians in wetlands. Sexes
similar, but males are usually larger than female.

ORIENTAL WHITE STORK *Ciconia boyciana*
<Hwangsae> WV/r L 112cm·W 195cm. Blackish
bill; legs and skin around eye red; whitish iris;
white body with black flight feathers which cover
tail when at rest. In flight, neck outstretched, like
cranes, wings showing white edgings to black
flight feathers above, and to outer secondaries
below. **Habitat:** estuaries, lakes, riversides,
reservoirs.

BLACK STORK *Ciconia nigra* <Meokhwangsae>
WV/r L 95cm. **Ad:** black glossed with purple and
green; underparts from breast to tail, including
inner underwing-coverts, white; red bill, legs, eye-
ring. **Juv:** brownish upperparts bill, and head;
white underparts flecked with brown; greenish
legs; small white patch on neck. **Habitat:**
ricefields, estuaries, reservoirs, rivers.

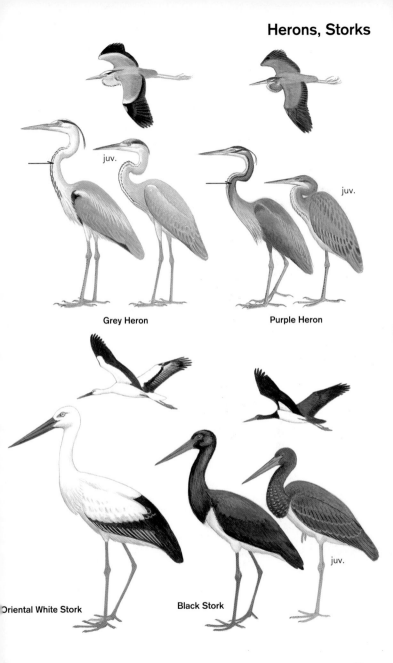

Grey Heron

Purple Heron

Oriental White Stork

Black Stork

juv.

Ibises and Spoonbills

Family Threskiornithidae (World : 31 species, Korea : 4 species) Spoonbills have long legs and necks and all-white plumage, and so can be confused with egrets at a distance. However, unlike herons and egrets, they fly with the neck extended. They sleep with bill tucked into wings, often on one leg.

EURASIAN SPOONBILL *Platalea leucorodia* <Norangburijeo-eosae> WV/r L 86cm. White body, black legs and bill with yellowish tip; narrow, black line from eye to bill base. **Br:** pale yellow crest on back of head, wide yellow bar on neck and upper breast, orange-red patch on throat. **Juv:** wing tips black; pinkish-yellow bill. **Similar species:** Black-faced Spoonbill is smaller and has black face. **Habitat:** estuaries, tidal flats, reservoirs.

BLACK-FACED SPOONBILL *Platalea minor* <Jeo-eosae> SV/r • Res/r L 74cm. **Ad:** entirely white wings and body, black facial skin across forehead through lores to eyes; small yellowish skin patches below eyes; creased black bill, black legs. Female smaller than male. **Br:** pale yellow crest on back of head, pale yellow upper breast. **Juv:** paler, unwrinkled bill. **Imm:** dark tips to primaries, reducing year by year; bill creases form from third year. **Habitat:** estuaries, tidal flats, reservoirs. **Status:** breeds on uninhabited islands in the sea on the west of Korea.

CRESTED IBIS [Japanese Crested Ibis] *Nipponia nippon* <Ttaogi> WV/r L 76.5cm. White body and head with long crest; pinkish-orange flight feathers are largely covered at rest; long, decurved black bill with red tip: naked red face; red legs that do not project beyond tail in flight. **Br:** dark grey plumage on head and back caused by tar-like secretion. **Non-Br:** slightly shorter crest. **Similar Species:** Oriental Ibis has black head and legs. **Habitat:** grassy wetlands, rice-fields. **Status:** no records since 1980.

ORIENTAL IBIS *Theskiornis melanocephalus* <Geomeunmeorihuinttaogi> Vag L 68cm. White body; decurved bill, bare black head and black legs. Flight purposeful with neck extended, showing thin line of pink bare skin on underwing, and with feet extending beyond tail. **Imm:** primary tips black, nape and hind neck with blackish feathers. **Similar Species:** Japanese Crested Ibis. **Habitat:** grassy wetlands, rice-fields.

Spoonbills, Ibises

winter

summer

juv.

Eurasian Spoonbill

winter

summer

juv.

Black-faced Spoonbill

winter

summer

Crested Ibis

juv.

summer

juv.

Oriental Ibis

71

Geese, Swans, and Ducks
Family Anatidae (World : 149 species, Korea : 45 species) Excellent swimmers, typically with broad bills, long neck, short tail, short legs, and webbed feet.

Geese
(World : 14 species, Korea : 9 species) Heavy-set waterfowl. Feeding on grasses, seeds and aquatic plants. Sexes similar.

CANADA GOOSE *Branta canadensis* <Kaenada-gireogi> Vag L 67cm. Brownish goose with black head and neck, with white chinstrap. Rump and tail black with contrasting white band of uppertail coverts; vent, undertail coverts white.Bill, legs black. **Habitat:** rivers, reservoirs, cultivated fields, grasslands, rice-fields.

BRENT GOOSE *Branta bernicla* <Heukgireogi> WV/r L 61cm. Head, neck, breast and upper belly black; wings, back and rump blackish-brown; upper throat and neck sides have streaky white patch from first winter onwards; flanks barred with white; rear of body white, contrasting in flight with black rump. **Similar species:** Canada Goose. **Habitat:** intertidal-flats, bays.

SNOW GOOSE *Anser caerulescens* <Huingireogi> WV/r L 67cm. **Ad:** all-white with black primaries; bill short and thick, pink; legs pink. **Imm:** blackish bill and legs; plumage greyish-brown above, including crown, dark pattern persisting above and behind eye. **Similar species:** swans; other species of leucistic or albino geese lack black primaries, bill different. **Habitat:** coastal marshy areas.

EMPEROR GOOSE *Anser canagicus* <Huinmeori-gireogi> Vag L 67.5cm. Dark, bluish-grey body has fine, black and white scaling, black throat and foreneck; white head and hindneck often stained orange; small pink bill with bluish base; bright orange legs; white tail. **Habitat:** rocky seashore, rice fields. **Status:** one record in Cheolwon in December 1995.

SWAN GOOSE *Anser cygnoides* <Gaeri> WV/sc・PM/sc L 87cm. Long, sloping, black bill and long neck; dark-brown crown and hindneck contrast with much paler sides of head and very pale foreneck. Breast and upper mantle washed orange; back, sides and wings pale grey-brown; legs orange. **Habitat:** often feeds by digging in muds; rivers, marshes or estuaries.

Geese

Canada Goose

Brent Goose

imm.

Snow Goose

imm.

Emperor Goose

imm.

Swan Goose

imm.

GREYLAG GOOSE *Anser anser* <Hoesaekgireogi> Vag L 84cm. Uniform brownish-grey with paler head than other geese, and showing contrasting pale grey forewing in flight. **Ad:** bright-pink bill has white line at base and white nail; legs pinkish; may have black marks on belly. **Imm:** bill and legs paler than Ad. **Habitat:** rivers, rice-fields and reservoirs.

WHITE-FRONTED GOOSE *Anser albifrons* <Soegireogi> WV/c L 72cm. Compact body with shortish neck. **Ad:** bold black patches on belly; white around base of pinky-orange bill with whitish nail; legs orange. **Imm:** lacks white on face. **Similar species:** Ad. Bean lacks belly patches, has longer neck. Juv. Bean lacks contrasting cheek. Lesser White-fronted Goose. **Habitat:** rice-fields, reservoirs, rivers, reclamation fields.

LESSER WHITE-FRONTED GOOSE *Anser erythropus* <Huinimagireogi> Vag L 58cm. The smallest grey goose with short, bright-pink bill, with white nail; white patch at bill base extends to rounded crown of smaller head; few black patches on belly; bright-yellow eye ring; legs orange. **Imm:** no white at base of bill, nail usually pale. **Similar species:** White-fronted Goose. **Habitat:** rice-fields, reservoirs, reclamation fields, estuaries.

BEAN GOOSE *Anser fabalis* <Keungireogi> WV/c L 85cm. Two distinct forms occur. Both have dark brown back and head contrasting with paler breast; black bars on flanks only; narrow white wing bars, dark underwing and terminal tail band; bill black with orange near tip; legs orange. Subspecies A.f. *middendorffi* (Taiga Goose) is larger, with long neck and larger bill. Subspecies A.f. *serrirostris* (Tundra Goose) has shorter neck and bill. **Imm:** legs duller. **Voice:** 'gahang-gahang', deeper in A.f. *middendorffi*. **Similar species:** White-fronted Goose, Swan Goose, Greyleg Goose. **Habitat:** A.f. *middendorffi* favors feeding in shallow lakes, A.f. *serrirostris* rice-fields.

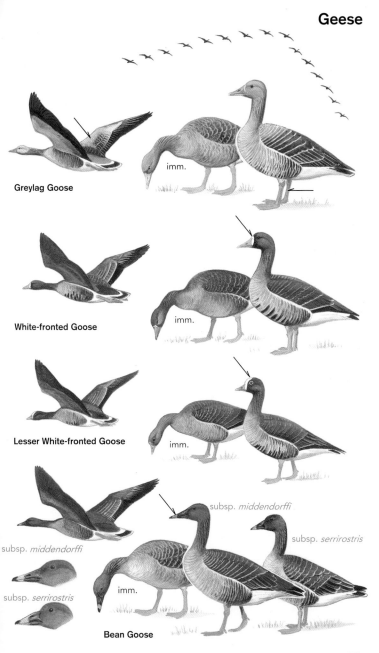

Geese

Greylag Goose

imm.

White-fronted Goose

imm.

Lesser White-fronted Goose

imm.

subsp. *middendorffi*

subsp. *serrirostris*

subsp. *middendorffi*

subsp. *serrirostris*

imm.

Bean Goose

Swans

(World: 6 species, Korea: 3 species) Large waterbirds with long and slender necks. Form flocks based on family units in non-Br period. Sexes are similar, adults being all-white, while immatures are greyish-brown. Flight is attained by running for take-off, Feed on aquatic plants.

MUTE SWAN *Cygnus olor* <Hokgoni> WV/r L 152cm. Orange-red bill with black knob at base; legs black. **Imm:** greyish-brown, darker above; bill dark grey, becoming pinkish by 1stW. Swims with neck slightly curved in S-shape, sometimes with wings arched upward. **Habitat:** lakes, estuaries, grassy wetlands. **Status:** most rare visiting species among swans to lagoons in west coast.

WHOOPER SWAN *Cygnus cygnus* <Keungoni> WV/uc L 140cm. Bill black with extensive yellow base extending as wedge down upper mandible reaching nostrils; head and bill wedge-shaped. Swims with neck vertical. **Imm:** grey-brown, darker on head; bill pattern is similar to adult but is dirty-pink at base with black tip. **Voice:** loud 'whoop, whoop'. **Similar Species:** Tundra Swan. **Habitat:** reservoirs, lakes, rivers, estuaries, and marshes.

TUNDRA SWAN *Cygnus columbianus* <Goni> WV/uc L 120cm. Resembles Whooper Swan in plumage and in holding neck vertical, but is smaller and has different bill pattern. **Ad:** rounded head profile; bill black with rounded yellow patch of variable size. **Imm:** bill as adult but yellow area is pale pink, black areas are dark pink, with black tip. Wintering numbers are smaller than Whooper Swan's. The American subspecies *C. c. columbianus* has a largely black bill. **Voice:** like Whooper Swan's but lower and softer. **Habitat:** reservoirs, lakes, rivers, estuaries and marshes.

Feeding

Ducks   Geese   Swans

Swans

Mute Swan

Whooper Swan

Tundra Swan

Shelducks (World: 7 species, Korea: 3 species) Tadorna are large, goose-like ducks with longish necks and legs. Habits similar to Geese.

RUDDY SHELDUCK *Tadorna ferruginea* <Hwang-ori> WV/uc L 64cm. Distinctive orange body with paler head; tail and uppertail-coverts black; wings above and below show black tips, green-glossed secondaries and contrasting white coverts; bill, legs black. **Male Br:** narrow black collar. **Non-Br:** collar indistinct. **Female:** lacks collar; face whiter. **Habitat:** rivers, estuaries, reservoirs, rice-fields.

COMMON SHELDUCK *Tadorna tadorna* <Hok-buriori> WV/c L 63cm. Mostly white with dark greenish head and neck, black scapulars, orange band round breast and upper mantle, and black stripe down belly; black flight feathers and tail tip; wing-coverts and tail white; tertials chestnut; red bill, orange legs. **Male Br:** red knob at base of bill. **Non-Br:** duller, loses bill knob; white marks on face. **Female:** generally duller. **Imm:** body colours paler than female. **Habitat:** mudflats, saline brackish lakes.

CRESTED SHELDUCK *Tadorna cristata* <Won-angsachon> Probably extinct L 64cm. **Male:** black crown, crest and breast contrast with pale grey face and neck, and slaty-grey flanks and belly; wings above and below show black tips, green-glossed secondaries, and contrasting white coverts; tertials show chestnut above; tail black; bill and legs orange. **Female:** body finely barred brownish-grey; black crown with white spectacles, neck and throat. **Status:** only two specimens from Nakdonggang and Geumgang.

Dabbling Ducks (Korea: 13 species) Generally found in shallow water where they feed either by dabbling on the surface or by immersing heads and necks and up-ending. Take off directly from surface.

MANDARIN DUCK *Aix galericulata* <Wonang> Res/uc • WV/uc L 45cm. Often perches in trees. **Male:** very distinctive with mane-like crest on rear crown and broad buffy white supercilium; inner webs of tertials form orange 'sails'; bill bright pinkish-red with white tip; legs orange. **Female:** grey-brown with white spectacles, throat and white at base of brownish or pinkish bill; sides spotted whitish. **Male eclipse:** as female but bill usually pink. **Habitat:** streams, lakes, rivers, reservoirs.

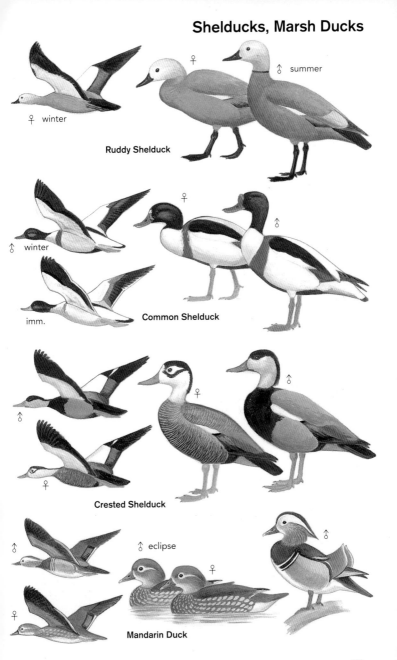

Shelducks, Marsh Ducks

♀ winter

♀

♂ summer

Ruddy Shelduck

♂ winter

♀

♂

imm.

Common Shelduck

♂

♀

♀

♂

Crested Shelduck

♂

♀

♂ eclipse

♀

♂

Mandarin Duck

MALLARD *Anas platyrhynchos* <Cheongdung-ori> WV/ab•Res/uc L 59cm. Most abundant and major species among ducks, and some breed in Korea; original species of domestic ducks; hybrid and grouping with domestic ducks. **Male:** green-glossed head with white collar; dark chestnut breast; pale greyish body; white tail has contrasting black centre with up-curled feathers and black coverts; bill yellow to olive. **Female:** brown marked darker; tail edged whitish; black bill has orange tip and edges. **Male eclipse:** like female, but more uniform above, less streaked; bill yellow to olive. **Similar species:** Spot-billed Duck. **Habitat:** rivers, estuaries, reservoirs, lakes, rice-fields, coasts.

SPOT-BILLED DUCK *Anas poecilorhyncha* <Huinppyamgeomdung-ori> WV/ab•Res/c L 61cm. Commonly breed grassland around waters; many flocks, come from northern area overwinter as groups. Dark body with pale face noticeable at a distance. Brown body marked darker; creamy-brown face shows black eye-stripe and lower stripe from bill base; bill black with yellow tip; folded wing shows white tertials; legs and feet orange. In flight, white underwing-coverts: and bulky body distinctive. **Similar species:** female Gadwall. **Habitat:** widespread in rice-fields, estuaries, coasts, reservoirs and rivers.

AMERICAN BLACK DUCK *Anas rubripes* <Migugori> Vag L 52cm. Large, blackish-brown duck with paler head, yellowish bill and orange legs; in flight, shows blue or purplish speculum, no white on upper wing, but conspicuous white underwing; crown darker with narrow dark eyeline. **Male:** bill yellowish. **Female:** as male but bill dull greenish, head less contrasting, body more streaked. **Similar species:** Spot-billed Duck, Mallard and hybrids. **Habitat:** as Mallard.

NORTHERN SHOVELER *Anas clypeata* <Neop-jeokburi> WV/c L 50cm. Short-necked duck with diagnostic, large, shovel-shaped bill; in flight, shows bluish-grey upper forewing, white wing bar and green speculum. **Male:** green-glossed head breast, body white with rufous sides, flanks and belly; iris yellow; tail coverts and centre black; tail edged white. **Female:** brown marked darker; upperwing duller than male; bill often yellowish; iris black. **Habitat:** reservoirs, estuaries, rivers.

Marsh Ducks

Feeding

♂ eclipse

Mallard

Spot-billed Duck

American Black Duck

♂ eclipse

Northern Shoveler

81

COMMON TEAL [Green-winged Teal] *Anas crecca* <Soe-ori> WV/c L 38cm. Small duck with rapid flight, upperwing showing white wing bar and trailing edge with metallic-green speculum; blackish bill and legs. **Male:** chestnut-brown head, with green head stripe from eye outlined with yellowish-buff; vermiculated grey body has white scapular line. On vent, cream yellow patches bordered with black. North American subspecies, *A.c.carolinensis*, a vagrant in Korea has vertical white line at side of breast, lacks white scapular line, has indistinct buff lines on head. **Female:** pale brown marked darker, especially above; narrow dark eyeline; white wing bars of upperwing narrower. **Habitat:** lakes, reservoirs, rivers, pools.

BAIKAL TEAL *Anas formosa* <Gachang-ori> WV/c L 40cm. Often in huge, compact flocks, roosting in daytime on open water, or in reedbeds, and feeding at night in rice-fields. **Male:** unique head pattern of cream, metallic green and black; vermiculated grey body has vertical, white stripe at side of breast and at vent; elongated, striped scapulars and tertials. **Female:** brown marked darker; small white spot at base of bill; white stripe from throat to below eye. **Habitat:** lakes, rivers, reservoirs, reclamation fields, coasts, rice-fields. **Status:** most of population of the world are wintering in Korea.

FALCATED TEAL *Anas falcata* <Cheongmeoriori> WV/c L 48cm. Bill and legs blackish. **Male:** glossy green sides to maned head with chestnut from forehead to nape; white chin and throat, and black collar; vermiculated grey body scaled black on breast; undertail coverts buff; tertials long, drooping over tail. **Female:** brown marked darker, greyer on plain head with darkish eye-ring. **Habitat:** lakes, estuaries, rivers, coasts.

GARGANEY *Anas querquedula* <Balguji> PM/uc・ WV/r L 38cm. Dark bill. **Male:** conspicuous white supercilium extends to nape and contrasts with dark crown and speckled brown face, neck and breast; upperwing-coverts blue-grey. **Female:** distinct dark eyestripe and gape line enclose small pale oval patch at base of bill; upperwing-coverts grey-brown. **Habitat:** lakes, marshes, rivers, estuaries, reservoirs, rice-fields of coasts.

Marsh Ducks

Common Teal

♂

subsp. *carolinensis*

♂

♀

♀ ♂ eclipse

Baikal Teal

♂

♂ eclipse

♀

Falcated Teal

♂

♂ eclipse

♀

Garganey

♂

♂ eclipse

♀

83

GADWALL *Anas strepera* <Allagori> WV/c L 50cm. Grey, brownish and black with white of belly. **Male:** black bill, speckled brownish head, vermiculated grey body with elongated scapulars and black rear-end. **Female:** brown, marked darker, with dark brown markings. **Male eclipse:** as female, including bill, but unstreaked above and wing as male Br. **Habitat:** wetlands with submerged plants; open lakes, marshes, rivers in lowlands.

EURASIAN WIGEON *Anas penelope* <Hong-meoriori> WV/c L 49cm. Medium-sized, variably rusty-brown and grey with shortish neck, and small blue-grey bill tipped black. **Male:** head and neck chestnut with yellowish forehead and crown; white flanks and black undertail-coverts. **Female:** rusty brown, darker on speckled head; wing-coverts grey-brown, with marrow white bar in front of green speculum. **Male eclipse:** as female but more chestnut, keeps white wing-coverts. **Habitat:** wetlands, grazing on wetland grasses and seaweeds.

AMERICAN WIGEON *Anas americana* <Amerika-hongmeoriori> WV/r L 48cm. White axillaries and median underwing-coverts make more contrasting underwings. **Male:** mostly grey face with whitish crown and forehead, and dark, glossy green stripe from eye to nape; breast and flanks pinkish rufous-brown. **Female/male eclipse:** plumages as Eurasian Wigeon, but head greyer. **Similar species:** Eurasian Wigeon. **Habitat:** rivers, estuaries, reservoirs, lakes, coasts.

PINTAIL *Anas acuta* <Gobang-ori> WV/c L ♂ 75cm/♀ 53cm. **Male:** head and hindneck dark brown, with white neck line, breast and belly; back and flanks grey; scapulars black broadly edged grey; tail-coverts and long tail black. **Female:** finely streaked, rather plain head and neck, with grey bill diagnostic; body brown, scaled darker. **Male eclipse:** like female, but bill and upperwing as male Br. body scaling more regular, scapulars longer and greyer. **Similar species:** female Falcated Teal has black bill. Female Mallard has black bill with orange sides. **Habitat:** lakes, marshes, rivers; often grazes in rice-fields.

Marsh Ducks

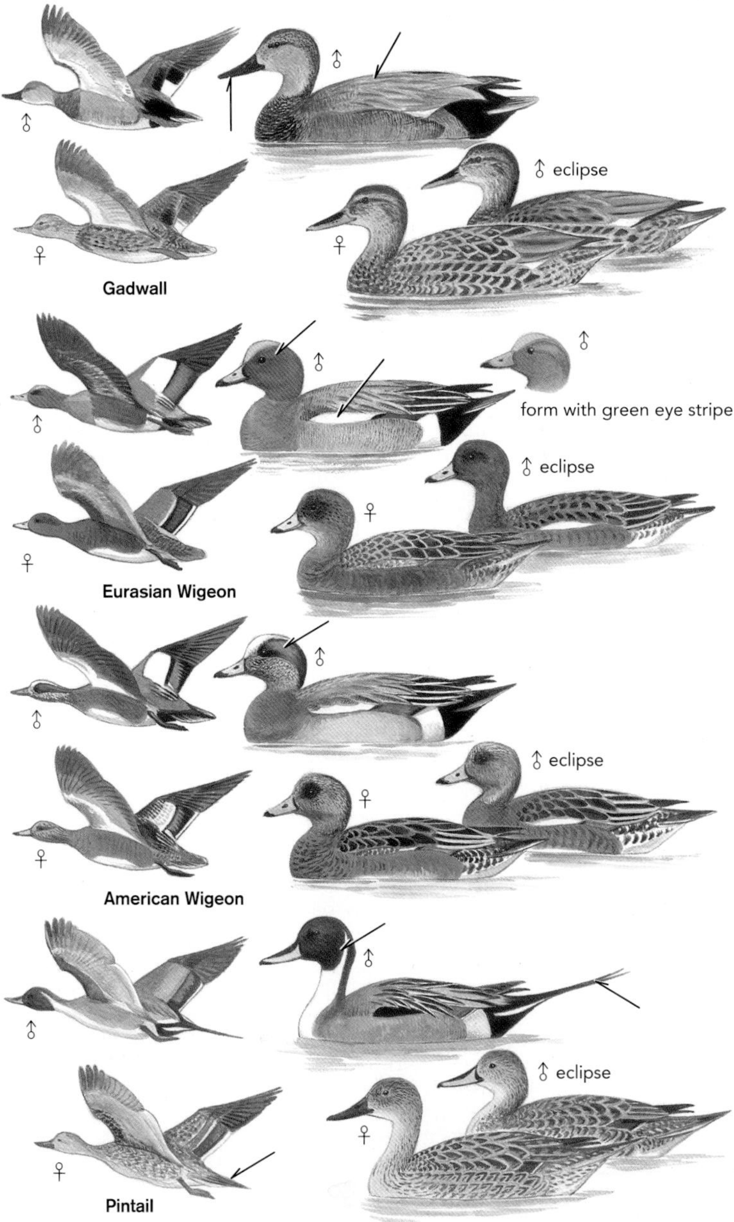

♂

♀

Gadwall

♀   ♂ eclipse

♂

♀

Eurasian Wigeon

♂   ♂ form with green eye stripe

♀   ♂ eclipse

♂

♀

American Wigeon

♀   ♂ eclipse

♂

♀

Pintail

♂

♀   ♂ eclipse

85

Diving Ducks

(Korea: 13 species) Diving and swimming underwater to feed on small bivalves, fishes and aquatic plants. Small and sharp wings than marsh ducks. Flight is attained by running for take off and rapid flutter.

RED-CRESTED POCHARD *Netta rufina* <Bulgeunburihuinjukji> Vag L 50cm. **Male Ad:** orange-brown head with brighter crown; tail and back grey-brown; iris, bill and legs red. **Female:** underparts grey-brown with some barring; iris brown; dark bill edged and tipped with pink. **Male eclipse:** resembles female, but iris and bill red. **Habitat:** lakes, marshes, inlets.

POCHARD *Aythya ferina* <Huinjukji> WV/c L 45cm. **Male:** grey body with chestnut head and neck, and black breast and tail-coverts; iris red; bill black with pale-grey band near tip. **Female:** head and neck brown; paler eye-ring and line behind eye; iris brown; body grey-brown; upperwing-coverts brown. **Male eclipse:** as male Br., but duller. **Habitat:** lakes, large rivers, bays and estuaries.

REDHEAD *Aythya americana* <Migukhuinjukji> Vag L 49cm. Very similar to Common Pochard but head round, with steeper forehead. **Male:** body grey; bill blue-grey with narrow white band bordering square-cut black tip; iris pale orange. **Female:** undertail-coverts often contrastingly whitish; bill tip and head shape also differ. **Habitat:** ponds with other diving ducks, brackish lakes, bays.

CANVASBACK *Aythya valisineria* <Keunhuinjukji> Vag L 55cm. Large duck, similar to Common Pochard, but head slopes from crown to tip of long, thin-tipped, blackish bill. **Male:** neck and head chestunt; breast and tail coverts black; body greyish white. **Female:** brownish grey body. **Male eclipse:** rusty brown head with pale brown breast. **Habitat:** lakes and bays.

BAER'S POCHARD *Aythya baeri* <Bulgeun-gaseumhuinjukji> WV/r L 45cm. Round head; longish, grey bill with black oval nail. In flight, shows distinct white wing-bar. **Male:** greenish glossed head; chestnut breast; rusty-brown flanks; dark brown upperparts; white undertail-coverts; whitish iris. **Female:** head, breast, upperparts dark-brown; oval patch at base of bill is less dark; flanks brown; iris brown. **Male eclipse:** as female, but iris whitish. **Habitat:** well-vegetated shallow lakes.

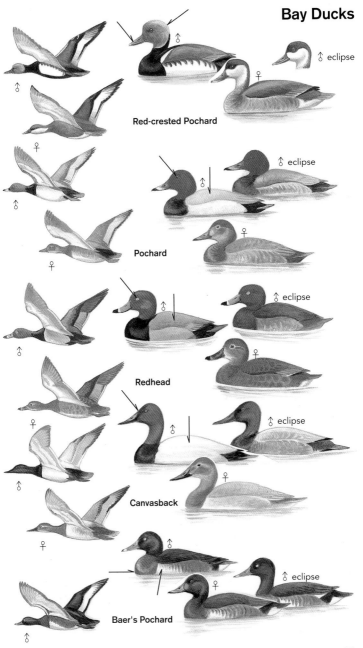

Bay Ducks

Red-crested Pochard

♂

↑ eclipse

♀

Pochard

↑ eclipse

♂

♀

Redhead

↑ eclipse

♂

♀

Canvasback

↑ eclipse

♂

♀

Baer's Pochard

♂

♀

↑ eclipse

TUFTED DUCK *Aythya fuligula* <Daenggihuinjukji> WV/c L 40cm. Bill blue-grey, paler before thick black tip; iris usually yellow. **Male:** black with white flanks and belly, purple glossed head with long, drroping crest. **Female:** variable; head and upperparts dark-brown; belly white; flanks variably mottled pale; usually has white patch at base of bill. **Male eclipse:** as male Br. but browner, and darker on flanks. **Juv:** as female but paler, upperparts fringed buff. **Similar species:** female Greater Scaup is larger, with larger white patch at bill base, lacks crest; female Baer's Pochard is browner overall. **Habitat:** in winter, lakes, large rivers, sometimes estuaries and bays.

GREATER SCAUP *Aythya marila* <Geomeun-meorihuinjukji> WV/c L 45cm. Rather large, rounded head with yellow iris and large, grey bill tipped with small, black, triangular nail. **Male:** greenish glossed head and black breast and rear; pale grey, vermiculated back with white flanks and belly. **Female:** dark-brown head has large white patch around bill base; breast and flanks brown with rusty wash; upperparts brown with geryish vermiculations; belly white. **Male eclipse:** as Br. male but browner; belly and flanks grey-brown; some white at bill base. **Habitat:** sheltered bays, estuaries, occasionally inland lakes.

BLACK SCOTER [Common Scoter] *Melanitta nigra* <Geomdung-ori> WV/c L 48cm. Dark sea duck showing no white in flight. **Male:** all black; with large, sloping, dark yellow knob on upper mandible of black bill. **Female:** mostly dark brown; dark brown crown contrasts with paler cheeks, throat and sides of neck; black bill lacks knob. **Habitat:** large estuaries, wide bays, open sea

VELVET SCOTER [White-winged Scoter] *Melanitta fusca* <Geomdung-orisachon> WV/c L 55cm. Dark sea duck with conspicuous white secondaries in flight. **Male:** black with white mark curving up from below eye, and orange bill with black knob at base. **Male eclipse:** browner, unglossed. **Female:** dark brown with two pale patches on ear coverts and lores. **Habitat:** large estuaries, wide bays, open sea. **Status:** sometimes flock together with Black Scoters.

Bay Ducks, Sea Ducks

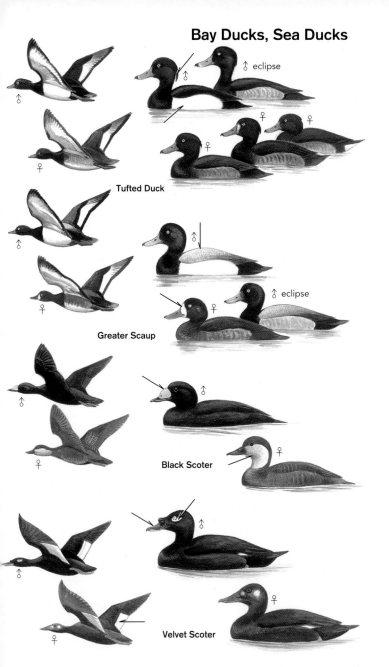

♂ eclipse

Tufted Duck

Greater Scaup

♂ eclipse

Black Scoter

Velvet Scoter

HARLEQUIN DUCK *Histrionicus histrionicus*
<Huinjulbagiori> WV/sc L 43cm. **Male:** largely
dark blue with chestnut flanks and contrasting
white bars and patches on head, breast, and back.
Male eclipse/1stW male: darker and duller, with
white head pattern of male. **Female:** sooty brown
with white spots above and below eye, and one
on ear coverts; lacks wing patch. **Similar species:**
see female Scoters. **Habitat:** rocky seacoasts,
sheltered harbours.

OLDSQUAW [Long-tailed Duck] *Clangula hyemalis*
<Bada-kkwong> WV/r L ♂ 59cm/♀ 38cm.
Brown, white and black seaduck with rounded
head and short bill; wings black. **Male:** long
pointed tail; **winter:** largely white, including
scapulars; creamy face with white eye-ring; dark
brown patch on upper neck; bill black with pink
band; **summer:** head, neck, breast, upperparts
blackish-brown with large white patch on face;
Female: tail pointed, not elongated; bill, legs and
feet dark greyish-blue; **winter:** belly, face and
neck white, with crown and upper neck patch,
breast, upperparts and tail blackish-brown;
summer: whitish around eye. **Habitat:** sheltered
bays, rocky coasts.

COMMON GOLDENEYE *Bucephala clangula*
<Huinppyamori> WV/c L 45cm. Peaked crown
gives triangular head shape. **Male:** head with dark-
greenish gloss; distinct white oval patch near base
of bill. **Male eclipse:** resembles female but has
touch of white on cheeks. **Female:** head greyish-
brown with white collar; black bill with yellow
band at tip; body grey. **Similar species:** Barrow's
Goldeneye. **Habitat:** open areas of inland and
coastal waters.

BARROW'S GOLDENEYE *Bucephala islandica*
<Bukbanghuinppyamori> Vag L 46cm. Similar to
Common Goldeneye but has very steep forehead
above shorter, thicker bill. **Male:** head with dark-
purple gloss; crescent-shaped white patch at bill
base reaches above eye; slightly narrower panel of
white on upperwing. **Female:** bill usually yellow,
blackish at base; sometimes wholly yellow; brown
extends further down neck than Common.
Habitat: estuaries, lakes, and rivers along the
coasts. **Status:** One record at Nakdonggang

Sea Ducks, Bay Ducks

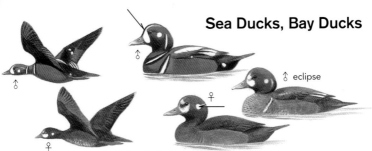

♂

♂

♀

↑ eclipse

♀

Harlequin Duck

♂ winter

♂ summer

♂

♀

♀ summer

♀ winter

Oldsquaw

♂

♂

♀

♀

↑ eclipse

Common Goldeneye

♂

♂

♀

↑ eclipse

Barrow's Goldeneye

91

Mergansers

(Korea : 4 species) Mergansers feeding mainly on fish, caught with long, slender, saw-edged bills with slightly hooked tips. Most species have crests. Patter along the surface of the water with their feet before taking flight. Fly rapidly with necks and legs outstretched. Mostly breed in holes in trees by rivers in forest zones; outside breeding season on lakes, rivers, bays etc.

SMEW *Mergus albellus* <Huinbiori> WV/c L 42cm. Small, compact, short-billed sawbill. **Male:** strikingly white, with black loral patch, back, and primaries. **Female/Imm:** chestnut cap and hindneck; white cheek and throat; (may be confused with a grebe at great distance). **Male eclipse:** as female but has darker back; sometimes with white spots on chestnut cap. **Voice:** throaty 'gorrr'; usually silent. **Habitat:** large rivers, lakes.

RED-BREASTED MERGANSER *Mergus serrator* <Badabiori> WV/c L 55cm. Divided shaggy crest; red iris. **Male:** Glossy, greenish-black head with white collar, and chestnut breast with dark spots. **Female:** Chestnut head with ill-defined white collar. **Male eclipse:** as female but back darker. **Similar species:** male Common Merganser has white breast and body; female has clear-white collar. **Habitat:** coasts, bays, estuaries.

CHINESE MERGANSER [Scaly-sided Merganser] *Mergus squamatus* <Hosabiori> WV/r L 57cm. Distinct scaling on flanks; diagnostic yellow tip to bill difficult to see at distance. **Male:** head greenish-black with long shaggy crest; white breast; black iris. **Female:** chestnut head with slightly shorter crest; has straighter, pale-tipped bill and with nostril midway. **Habitat:** freshwater lakes and rivers.

COMMON MERGANSER [Goosander] *Mergus merganser* <Biori> WV/c・Res/r L 65cm. Large, freshwater merganser with brown iris and red bill that thickens at base and has darker. **Male:** crestless, greenish-black head; white breast and flanks. **Male eclipse:** resembles female but has shorter crest; sometimes with white line from lores to bill which is seldom visible in field. **Female:** similar to female Red-breasted Merganser, but larger with thicker neck, brighter chestnut head sharply demarcated from white on neck; chin usually more clearly white. **Habitat:** rivers, lakes.

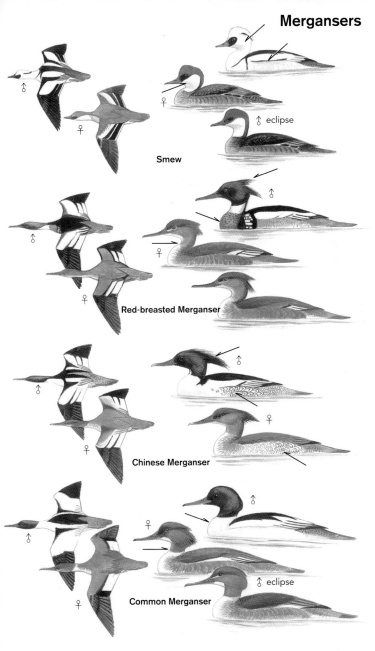

Mergansers

♂

♀

Smew

♀

♂ eclipse

♂

♂

♀

Red-breasted Merganser

♂

♀

♂

♀

Chinese Merganser

♂

♀

♂

♀

♂ eclipse

Common Merganser

93

Hawks, Eagles, and Vultures

Family Accipitridae (World : 226 species, Korea : 24 species) Diurnal birds of prey with good eyesight and powerful hooked bills and claws. Most species take live prey, but some eat carrion. Sexes usually alike, but females are larger.

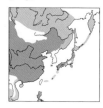

OSPREY *Pandion haliaetus* <Mulsuri> PM/r • WV/r L ♂ 58cm/♀ 60cm • W 147~169cm. Upperparts brown with white crown and underparts; broad dark eyestripe, brownish breastband (more marked on female) clear white belly and underwing-coverts, with dark wrist marks and primaries which show four fingers. **Ad:** dark terminal tail band; black band along underwing-coverts. **Imm:** lacks these bands; has pale tips to feathers of upperparts. **Habitat:** coasts, estuaries, rivers, reservoirs.

ORIENTAL HONEY BUZZARD *Pernis ptilorhynchus* <Beolmae> PM/uc L ♂ 57cm/♀ 60.5cm • W 121~135cm. Longish-necked and rather pigeon-headed, with white throat and dark mesial line. Typically dark greyish-brown above, pale below, with dark trailing edge to wing and tail; breast, belly and underwing-coverts usually buff; lacking a dark carpal patch; tail usually pale below with dark terminal and central bars and often another at the base. Underpart coloration is highly variable. **Habitat:** open lands, coasts.

BLACK KITE *Milvus migrans* <Solgae> WV/uc • Res/r L ♂ 58.5cm/♀ 68.5cm • W 157~162cm. Long, fingered wings showing pale patches at base of primaries; tail deeply forked when folded, but can appear triangular in flight; unstreaked, dark brown ear coverts. **Juv:** streaked with buff. **Habitat:** coasts, estuaries, rivers, open lands, farmlands.

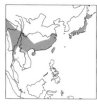

MOUNTAIN HAWK-EAGLE *Spizaetus nipalensis* <Ppulmae> Vag L ♂ 72cm/♀ 80cm • W 140~165cm. **Ad:** dark brown above; pale throat with dark mesial; breast streaked, belly and undertail coverts barred; crown, short crest, and nape boldly streaked with black; broad wings barred below, appearing strongly incut at body; longish tail shows 4 dark bars. **Juv:** whitish underparts with brown streaking on head. **Habitat:** forested mountains.

Ospreys, Honey Buzzards, Kites, Eagles

Osprey

imm.

light phase

dark phase

brown phase

Oriental Honey Buzzard

juv.

Black Kite

juv.

juv.

Mountain Hawk Eagle

WHITE-TAILED SEA EAGLE *Haliaeetus albicilla* <Huinkkorisuri> WV/sc • Res/r L ♂ 84cm/♀ 94cm • W 199~228cm. **Ad:** body and wings brown, paler on mantle and head; tail white, wedge-shaped, shorter than Steller's; bill very large, pale yellow; leading and trailing edges of wing almost straight, wingtips rather square-ended but fingered, giving door-shaped silhouette. Wingbeats often sluggish. **Juv:** dark brown body and wing-coverts, mottled paler, contrast with dark flight feathers of upper wing; breast and belly same tone; narrow whitish band along underwing-coverts; bill and eye dark. **Imm:** brown body and wing-coverts heavily marked with white. **2nd W:** cere and eye pale. Feeds mainly on fish and birds. **Similar species:** Steller's Sea Eagle. **Habitat:** coasts, estuaries, rivers, reservoirs.

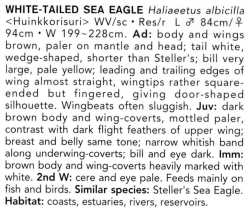

STELLER'S SEA EAGLE *Haliaeetus pelagicus* <Chamsuri> WV/r L ♂ 88cm/♀ 102cm • W 221~244cm. Massive bill and very dark plumage. **Ad:** unmistakable with large white area on leading edge of wing formed by lesser and median coverts, large, white diamond-shaped tail, and enormous bright orange-yellow bill; forehead, rump and tail coverts, are also white; trailing edge of wing bulges out at outer secondaries. **Imm:** body and wing-coverts heavily marked with inner primaries noticeably white into 2Y; dark terminal tail band. **Similar species:** White-tailed Sea Eagle. **Habitat:** coasts, estuaries, rivers, reservoirs.

GOLDEN EAGLE *Aquila chrysaetos* <Geomdoksuri> Res/r • WV/r L ♂ 81.5cm/♀ 89cm • W 167~213cm. **Ad:** large, blackish-brown eagle with diagnostic golden nape, and buffy wing-coverts which form wing bars, and long, rounded tail; flight feathers and tail show irregular greyish bars from above and below, if seen well; bill dark-tipped with yellow cere and gape. **Juv:** much darker brown though nape pale as adult; variable amount of white at base of flight feathers; tail white with dark terminal band. **Imm:** body and wings mottled; buffy wing bars; tail less clearly white. In flight, wings are held above the horizontal with the leading primaries spread and upturned. **Similar species:** Emperial Eagle. **Habitat:** rocky mountains.

SeaEagles, Eagle

imm.

imm.

White-tailed Sea Eagle

imm.

imm.

Steller's Sea Eagle

imm.

Golden Eagle

imm.

97

CRESTED SERPENT EAGLE *Spilornis cheela* <Gwansuri> Vag L 54cm • W 120cm. Large head and short, thick, blackish crest; prominent yellow facial skin and cere. **Ad:** chocolate brown underparts finely spotted with white on breast, barred on belly and undertail coverts. In flight, broad, rounded, wings are fingered and held in a shallow V, showing diagnostic pattern of black-and-white bands on underside; blackish tail has broad white bar and black tip. **Imm:** much paler, whitish below with some streaking, lacking Ad. underwing pattern; head mottled with white, contrasting dark ear patch. Feeds on snakes, frogs, and other small prey. **Habitat:** forests, farmlands near from forest, grassy wetlands, open lands. **Status:** two records in Gimhae, Gyeongsangnam-do and Busan.

CINEREOUS VULTURE [Black Vulture] *Aegypius monachus* <Doksuri> WV/sc L 100~112cm • W 250~295cm. Huge. Rather uniform sooty-brown plumage looks black at a distance; wings rather evenly broad, pointed secondaries giving saw-toothed rear edge to wing; primaries long and 'fingered'; tail short, slightly wedge-shaped or rounded. Shape in flight similar to eagles but outer two primaries bend upwards more than eagles, and head is noticeably smaller compared with the wings; legs and feet greyish-white. **Ad:** head and ruff pale brownish. **Imm:** head and neck blackish. Feeds on carrion. **Habitat:** rivers, estuaries, open lands, farmlands.

LAMMERGEIER [Bearded Vulture] *Gypaetus barbatus* <Suyeomsuri> Vag L 110cm • W 260cm. Huge. Long, pointed wings with long, wedge-shaped tail; tail is longer than the width of the wing. Sexes similar though females may have slightly bulging trailing edge to wing. **Ad:** head and underparts whitish or buffy; underwing-coverts black; rest of underwing, tail and upperparts bluish-grey. **Imm:** dull brownish-grey with darker head and breast, whitish triangle on mantle, and pale patch at carpal bend; rather shorter tail and less pointed wings. **Habitat:** high mountains. **Status:** three captured records in winter at Hamgyeongnam-do and Gangwon-do.

Eagles, Vultures

juv.

imm.

Crested Serpent Eagle

Cinereous Vulture

imm.

imm.

imm.

Lammergeier

GREATER SPOTTED EAGLE *Aquila clanga*
<Hangnameorigeomdoksuri> WV/r L ♂ 67.5cm/
♀ 70cm • W 158~182cm. Arm of wing short;
upperwing-coverts and flight feathers brown,
underwing-coverts usually darker; single, small
white patch on wing due to white bases of long-
fingered primaries; flight feathers below usually
sparsely and finely barred black, less towards tips;
tail rounded; cere and feet yellow; gape extends
to below eye; round nostril; bill black becoming
greyer with age. **Ad:** (5-6 years) dark brown. **Imm:**
blackish-brown with purplish sheen. Even, white
trailing edge to wing; typically has large, pale
spots on wing-coverts, which form rows in flight
and spotting on scapulars; uppertail coverts form
whitish U on uppertail; underparts streaked with
buff; pale vent. Some juveniles are dark. **Habitat:**
rivers, reservoirs, farmlands.

STEPPE EAGLE *Aquila nipalensis* <Chowonsuri>
Vag L 65~77cm • W 174~260cm. Soars on
flexible, long, level wings, drooping at wrist;
yellow gape extends to rear edge of eye; iris
always brown; oval nostril. **Ad:** dark-brown, usually
with greyish barring on flight feathers that have a
narrow dark trailing edge; tail indistinctly barred
with dark terminal band; paler throat and darker
carpals; indistinct rusty nape-patch. **Imm:** pale
band along underwing becomes browner year by
year; whitish trailing edge to wing is lost with
feather wear. **Similar species:** Greater Spotted
Eagle. **Habitat:** open land, rice-fields.

IMPERIAL EAGLE *Aquila heliaca* <Huinjukjisuri>
WV/r L ♂ 77.5cm/♀ 83cm • W 190~211cm.
Wings held level, slightly arched. **Ad:** blackish-
brown; large head with pale crown, nape and
cheeks which contast with throat; some white
feathers on scapulars; undertail coverts pale, tail
with fine greyish bars and dark tip. **Imm:** Pale
brown, streaked below; dark outer primaries and
secondaries contrast with wing-coverts and much
paler inner primaries; pale edge to greater
upperwing-coverts forms wing bar; whitish rump.
Similar species: Golden Eagle. **Habitat:**
farmlands, open lands, estuaries, reservoirs.

Eagles

Greater Spotted Eagle

imm.

imm.

Steppe Eagle

imm.

imm.

Imperial Eagle

imm.

imm.

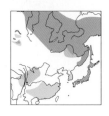

GOSHAWK [Northern Goshawk] *Accipiter gentilis* <Chammae> WV/uc L ♂ 50cm/♀ 56cm • W 106~131cm. Medium-sized and bulky with broad, rounded wings. **Ad:** broad, white supercilium from bill; dark grey back; short; finely barred whitish underwings; long tail with dark bars. **Male:** whitish underparts finely, often indistinctly, barred to belly. **Female:** more distinctly barred below. **Juv:** Brown above, mottled with buff and white, very streaked on head; pale buffy-brown underparts streaked with dark brown. **Similar species:** Eurasian Sparrow Hawk. **Habitat:** forests, farmlands, rivers.

CHINESE SPARROWHAWK *Accipiter soloensis* <Bulgeunbaesaemae> SV/c L ♂ 30cm/♀ 33cm. Small. **Ad:** pale rufous breast and underwings, whiter on belly, often with light barring; black-tipped primaries; indistinct mesial; lacks yellow eye-ring. **Male:** red cere; dark red eye. **Female:** yellow eye. **Juv/Imm:** distinct mesial; broad brown streaks on breast, broad bars on belly and flight feathers; pale supercilium; pale buff fringes on dark brown upperparts; lacks black wing tips, barring on wing linings indistinct. **Habitat:** low mountains, forests, rice-field near from forest, open lands.

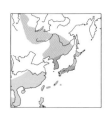

JAPANESE LESSER SPARROWHAWK *Accipiter gularis* <Jorong-i> Res/uc L ♂ 27cm/♀ 30cm • W 51~63cm. Throat white with thin dark mesial; lacks black wing tips. **Male:** blue-grey above; pale rufous-buff breast and belly, often barred white; red iris with narrow yellow eye-ring and cere. **Female:** grey-brown above; white underparts and underwings with distinct bars; yellow iris. **Juv:** as Chinese Sparrowhawk but barred across all of underwing. **Habitat:** low mountains, forests, open lands.

EURASIAN SPARROWHAWK *Accipiter nisus* <Saemae> Res/uc L ♂ 32cm/♀ 39cm • W 61~79cm. Small hawk, similar to Goshawk but with less prominent white supercilium. Deep-chested, with usually obvious bulge on outer secondaries. **Male:** Bluish-grey upperparts; pale rufous-buff cheeks and finely barred breast above white belly; underwing with fine barring on lining, broader on flight feathers; long tail with dark bars. **Female:** grey-brown upperparts; white underparts closely barred with dark brown. **Habitat:** forests, open lands, farmlands, rivers.

Accipiters

juv.

Goshawk

subs.*albidus*

Chinese Sparrowhawk

juv.

Jepanese Lesser Sparrowhawk

Eurasian Sparrowhawk

ROUGH-LEGGED BUZZARD *Buteo lagopus* <Teolbalmalttonggari> WV/sc L ♂ 55.5cm/♀ 58.5cm • W 129~143cm. Plumage variable; small bill and darkish eyeline; whitish legs feathered to toes. **Ad:** whitish underwings with dark carpal patches and primary tips. **Male:** dark head, upper breast more streaked with brown than belly, flanks barred; two or more dark bands on tail; dark face; orange toes. **Female:** pale head, dark brown lower breast, belly and unbarred flanks; tail with single dark band; leg feathers barred. **Habitat:** farmlands, open lands, grassy wetlands, rivers.

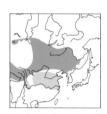

UPLAND BUZZARD *Buteo hemilasius* <Keunmalttonggari> WV/r L ♂ 61cm/♀ 72cm • W 158cm. Wings and tail longer than other buzzards; resembling eagle; holds wings in slightly deeper V and often hovers. Plumage is variable; typical pale morph; whitish head with pale streaked brown underparts; brown on thighs forms a U in flight; upperwing has dark carpal patches and large white patch at base of primaries; pale greyish-brown tail, finely barred towards tip, contrasts with dark rump. **Habitat:** farmlands, open lands, grassy wetlands, rivers.

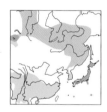

COMMON BUZZARD *Buteo buteo* <Malttonggari> WV/c L ♂ 52cm/♀ 56cm • W 122~137cm. Compact and short-necked with broad rounded wings and tail. Plumage is variable; pale head and underparts variably streaked with brown; dark brown flanks and upper belly patch contrast with whitish lower belly and undertail coverts; wings have black tips to primaries and black, usually distinct, carpal patches. **Habitat:** farmlands, open lands, grassy wetlands, rivers.

GREY-FACED BUZZARD *Butastur indicus* <Wangsaemae> PM/uc • SV/r L ♂ 47cm/♀ 51cm · W 102~115cm. Plumage is variable, but wings are distinctly long and narrow. **Ad:** greyish cheeks, whitish supercilium, white throat outlined by black submoustachials and with black central (mesial) stripe; brown back and wings and uppertail; pale underwings with fine bars, tail with three dark bands; yellow cere and eye. **Male:** breast almost solid brown, belly barred. **Female:** breast mottled white, belly less heavily marked. **Juv:** Underparts streaked. **Habitat:** forests, farmlands, open lands.

Buzzards

Rough-legged Buzzard

imm.

Upland Buzzard

Common Buzzard

dark phase

juv.

juv.

Grey-faced Buzzard

HEN HARRIER *Circus cyaneus* <Jaetbit-gaegurimae> WV/c L ♂ 45cm/♀ 51cm • W 99~123cm. **Male:** Pale grey with black primaries and dark trailing edge to underwing, white from upper breast to undertail coverts. **Female:** Upperparts dark brown with streaking on neck and crown, and distinctive face pattern; belly streaked brown; tail and flight feathers of underwing clearly barred. **Imm:** as female but barring less distinct, secondaries dark brown, belly less streaked. **Similar species:** see female Pied Harrier, Rough-legged Buzzard. **Habitat:** reedbeds, grassy wetlands, farmlands.

PIED HARRIER *Circus melanoleucos* <Allak-gaegurimae> SV/r • PM/r L ♂ 42.5cm/♀ 45.5cm · W 104~115cm. **Male:** Clear 'black-and-white' upperpart pattern; pale grey wings and tail, white lesser wing coverts and uppertail coverts, with unstreaked black head, back, upper breast, median wing-coverts and primaries; underparts white. **Female:** Head and upperparts dark brown; white leading edge of lesser wing-coverts flight feathers mostly grey with dark bars; underparts white, streaked with dark brown; white uppertail covert band. **Imm:** dark rufous-brown wing linings and underparts. **Similar species:** Hen Harrier, Eastern Marsh Harrier. **Habitat:** reedbeds, grassy wetlands, farmlands.

EASTERN MARSH HARRIER *Circus spilonotus* <Gaegurimae> WV/uc L ♂ 48cm/♀ 58cm • W 113~137cm. The biggest and bulkiest harrier, lacking strongly barred flight feathers in all plumages. Small head, long rounded wings, long tail. **Male:** variable; typical morphs have greyish head and brown upperparts streaked darker; pale brown below with streaking, and dark tail; or pattern similar to Pied Harrier but less clean-looking, pale grey with black head, throat, breast, back, upperwings and wing-tips. **Female:** dark brown paler on head, breast, and under wing-coverts; rump may be whitish, or lack contrast. Glides low over vegetation with wings held in V. **Similar species:** Male Pied Harrier; females of other harriers have barred wings. **Habitat:** reedbeds, grassy wetlands, farmlands.

Harriers

Hen Harrier

Pied Harrier

imm.

Eastern Marsh Harrier

imm.

imm.

Falcons

Family Falconidae (World : 60 species, Korea : 6 species) Small to medium-sized, streamlined birds of prey with long pointed wings and long tapered tails. Direct powerful flight with rapid but shallow wingbeats.

PEREGRINE FALCON *Falco peregrinus* <Mae> Res/sc L ♂ 42cm/♀ 49cm • W 84~120cm. Dark grey upperparts contrast with pale underparts. White throat and broad black moustaches. **Ad:** underparts narrowly barred. **Juv:** browner above with buff fringes, underparts streaked. **Similar species:** Eurasian Hobby is smaller, with longer, narrower, more pointed wings and chestnut thighs and under tail coverts. **Status:** locally common winter visitor and breeder, especially on coastal islands.

SAKER FALCON *Falco cherrug* <Hendasonmae> Vag L 48~57cm • W 110~125cm. A Buzzard-sized falcon with brown upperparts, and contrasting pale head with rather indistinct moustache; underparts not barred, but variably streaked and spotted; wing-tips do not reach tail-tip when seen at rest. **Similar species:** Juv. Peregrine has uniform underwing, rump and base of tail usually paler than end of tail. **Habitat:** open fields, farmlands, grassy wetlands.

EURASIAN HOBBY *Falco subbuteo* <Saeholligi> SV/uc L ♂ 33.5cm/♀ 35cm • W 72~84cm. At a distance looks dark with white throat. Resembles Peregrine but much smaller, with narrower moustaches; has longer, narrower, more pointed wings and tail is slightly shorter; breast and belly heavily streaked, not barred; wings longer than tail when perched. **Ad:** dark grey above with chestnut thighs and undertail coverts. **Juv:** Browner upperparts, more heavily streaked underparts; thighs and under tail coverts lack chestnut. **Similar species:** see Peregrine Falcon. Kestrel is paler below with slightly longer black-tipped tail, and less rapid flight. **Habitat:** forest, open field, farmlands,urban area.

Falcons

Peregrine Falcon

juv.

juv.

Saker Falcon

juv.

juv.

Eurasian Hobby

juv.

juv.

MERLIN *Falco columbarius* <Soehwangjorong-i>
WV/uc L ♂ 29cm/♀ 33cm • W 64~73.5cm. Shape
similar to Peregrine with rather broad, pointed
wings, but flight more agile with much faster
wingbeat, slate-grey tail has narrow white tip and
broad black subterminal band. **Male:** crown, ear
coverts slaty-blue with whitish brow and indistinct
dark moustache; upperparts slaty-blue with
blackish wing tips; throat white; neck, wing linings
and underparts pale buffy-orange below with
black streaks; undertail with broad black and
white bands. **Female:** Brown above, spotted and
marked with paler brown, whitish below with dark
brown streaks. **Similar species:** female Common
Kestrel has has longer wings, paler underparts,
more rufous back, different tail pattern and hovers
more frequently. **Habitat:** farmlands, open fields.

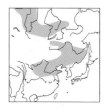

AMUR FALCON *Falco amurensis* <Bidulgijorong-i>
PM/r L 29cm • W 70~72cm. Wings long,
resembling Eurasian Hobby, extending beyond
long tail when perched. Cere and feet reddish-
orange. **Male:** Dark slaty grey with paler throat
and cheeks and dark moustache; lower belly,
thighs and under tail coverts reddish-brown;
Female: grey upperparts barred darker, more
broadly on tail, with subterminal band broadest;
underwing finely barred with dark trailing edge;
buffy white thighs and vent; white throat with
short black moustache. **Juv:** much buff fringing on
upperparts, paler on head; subterminal tail band
not broad; cere and legs yellowish. **Similar
species:** Eurasian Hobby lacks upper tail barring.
Habitat: open field, farmlands, grassland. **Status:**
recorded at Mangyeonggang and Dongjingang.

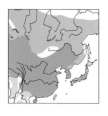

COMMON KESTREL *Falco tinnunculus* <Hwang-
jorong-i> Res/c L ♂ 33cm/♀ 38.5cm • W
68~76cm Widespread in open country, often near
towns. Often hovers with tail spread. Pointed
wings do not reach tip of tail when perched. Black
claws. **Male:** rufous back and pale buff underparts
spotted with black; grey head and rump; grey tail
has black subterminal band and white tip. **Female:**
upperparts with triangular black spots and tail.
Habitat: forests, open field, farmlands, urban area.

Merlin

Amur Falcon

hovering   Common Kestrel

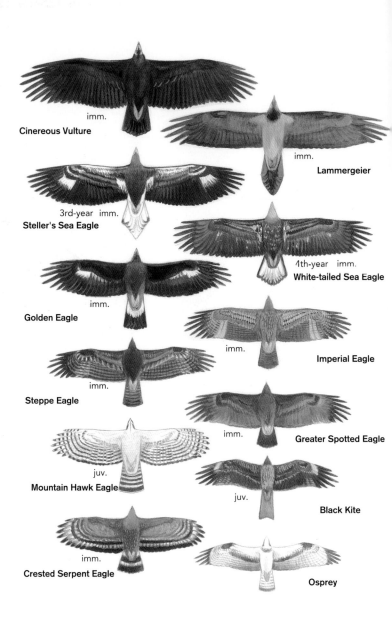

Cinereous Vulture imm.

Lammergeier imm.

Steller's Sea Eagle 3rd-year imm.

White-tailed Sea Eagle 4th-year imm.

Golden Eagle imm.

Imperial Eagle imm.

Steppe Eagle imm.

Greater Spotted Eagle imm.

Mountain Hawk Eagle juv.

Black Kite juv.

Crested Serpent Eagle imm.

Osprey

Birds of Prey, Overhead

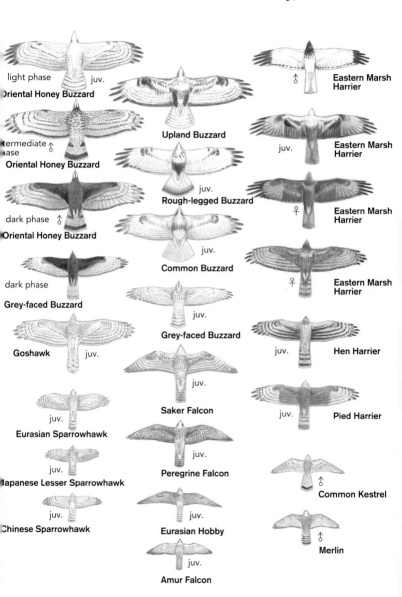

light phase   juv.
Oriental Honey Buzzard

intermediate
phase
Oriental Honey Buzzard

dark phase
Oriental Honey Buzzard

dark phase
Grey-faced Buzzard

Goshawk   juv.

juv.
Eurasian Sparrowhawk

juv.
Japanese Lesser Sparrowhawk

juv.
Chinese Sparrowhawk

Upland Buzzard

juv.
Rough-legged Buzzard

juv.
Common Buzzard

juv.
Grey-faced Buzzard

juv.
Saker Falcon

juv.
Peregrine Falcon

juv.
Eurasian Hobby

juv.
Amur Falcon

Eastern Marsh Harrier

juv.
Eastern Marsh Harrier

♀
Eastern Marsh Harrier

♀
Eastern Marsh Harrier

juv.
Hen Harrier

juv.
Pied Harrier

Common Kestrel

Merlin

Grouse
Family Tetraonidae (World : 17 species, Korea : 2 species) Primarily ground dwelling, but partly tree dwelling. Short bills, legs, and wings. They walk more than fly, but flight is swift and direct. Nest and breed on the ground. Feed on seeds, berries, buds, roots and insects.

BLACK GROUSE *Tetrao tetrix* <Metdak> Res/r(n) L ♂ 53cm/♀ 41cm. A small headed grouse of high mountains. Form flocks in winter, displaying in 'leks' in spring. **Male:** glossy dark blue with red 'eyebrows'; white wing bars and underwings, and white undertail coverts which are displayed during lekking; strange curled tail looks long in flight. **Female:** barred greyish-brown including throat and breast; tail squarish or slightly forked; narrow whitish wing bar. **Similar species :** female Ring-necked Pheasant is larger, paler and spotted, with longer, pointed tail. **Habitat:** open areas on high mountains, in forest clearings.

HAZEL GROUSE *Bonasa bonasia* <Deulkkwong> Res/c L 36cm. Secretive but sometimes confiding, grey-brown grouse of mixed forest. Browner on wings, finely patterned with white and brown spots and bars, and with chestnut markings on sides; whitish-tipped greyish tail with dark subterminal band is obvious in flight. **Male:** head with short crest, small red supercilium, and conspicuous black throat with whitish edging; also has white scapular lines. **Female:** throat brown speckled with white. Often occurs in pairs or in family groups. **Chick:** unspotted with small black facial marks, reminiscent of Little Ringed Plover. **Habitat:** forests.

Pheasants and Quails
Family Phasianidae (World : 194 species, Korea : 2 species) Ground-dwelling birds with short bills and legs. Often run from danger rather than fly. Flight with rapid wingbeats of short rounded wings. Nest on the ground. Mainly feed on seeds, berries, and insects.

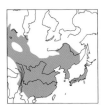

RING-NECKED PHEASANT *Phasianus colchicus* <Kkwong> Res/ab L ♂ 80cm/♀ 60cm. Unmistakable large ground-dwelling bird with a long, pointed, barred tail. Bursts into flight from underfoot. **Male:** white neck-ring and chestnut underparts. **Female:** pale brown heavily spotted darker on body, and barred on tail; small white crescent below eye. **Voice:** resonant 'korrk-korrk'. **Habitat:** low mountains, grasslands, parks, edge of forest and cultivated fields.

Grouses, Pheasants

♂
♀

Black Grouse

♂
♀

♂

♂
♀

Hazel Grouse

♂

♀

♂

chick

Ring-necked Pheasant

JAPANESE QUAIL *Coturnix japonica* <Mechuragi> WV/c L 20cm. A small, plump, brownish bird with short tail, usually seen in brief, explosive escape flight low across rice-fields. Yellow-brown body with distinct long creamy-white supercilium reaching neck, and many white streaks. **Male Br:** neck reddish-brown. **Non-Br:** similar to female. **Female:** whitish neck. **Similar Species:** Yellow-legged Buttonquail. **Habitat:** grasslands and cultivated fields.

Buttonquail

Family Turnicidae (World : 15 species, Korea : 1 species) Small terrestrial birds with rounded, short tails, which can easily be mistaken for true quail. Differ in having only 3 toes, lacking the hind toe. Polyandrous. In flight, dark scapulars contrast with paler flight feathers. Females are slightly larger and brighter than the males, which incubate eggs and rear the young.

YELLOW-LEGGED BUTTONQUAIL *Turnix tanki* <Segarangmechuragi> PM/sc L 13cm. Similar to Common Quail, but very much smaller with longer bill, no white supercilium; spotted or barred wing-coverts and scapulars, with spotting on sides of breast. Female has rufous patch on shoulders. Feet is yellow. **Similar species:** Common Quail, Swinhoe's Crake. **Habitat:** grass, scrub, and cultivated fields.

Rails, Crakes and Coots

Family Rallidae (World : 127 species, Korea : 9 species) Small to medium-sized marsh waders with small heads, stout bodies, short rounded wings, short tails, and long toes. The smaller rails are very shy and skulking, and usually difficult to observe except at dawn and dusk. Fly weakly with legs trailing. All nest on or near the ground, some on floating vegetation. Sexes alike in most species.

SWINHOE'S RAIL *Coturnicops exquisitus* <Allaktteumbugi> PM/r L 13cm. Smallest rail. Tiny size distinct. Chestnut brown upperparts with bold dark-brown streaks and fine white bars. Throat and face finely spotted white with indistinct brownish eyeline; belly white. Brownish legs. White secondaries are conspicuous in flight. **Similar species:** Yellow-legged Buttonquail. **Voice:** 'kyo! kyoro, rurururu' accelerating in tempo, following call being quieter. **Habitat:** wet marshes and rice-fields.

Quails, Buttonquails, Rails

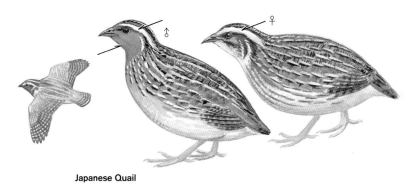

Japanese Quail

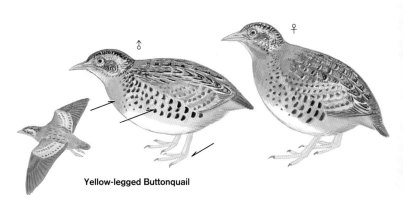

Yellow-legged Buttonquail

Swinhoe's Rail

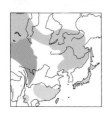

WATER RAIL *Rallus aquaticus* <Huinnun-sseoptteumbugi> WV/r • PM/sc L 29cm. Medium-sized rail. Comparatively long, slightly decurved, red bill with darker upper mandible; greyish-blue face and breast, with brownish eyeline; sides, belly, flanks, undertail coverts barred black and white; often looks all-dark at a distance. **Similar Species:** Baillon's Crake is smaller and has shorter, greenish yellow bill. **Voice:** many calls known, including a series of 'khru-i' notes given at 2 per sec; sharp 'kik'. **Habitat:** reedbeds, disused ricefields, and marshes with dense vegetation.

BAILLON'S CRAKE *Porzana pusilla* <Soe-tteumbugi> PM/sc L 20cm. Small crake with short greenish-yellow bill, showing no red; brown upperparts streaked narrowly and irregularly with white, and broadly with black; bluish-grey face with brown eyeline, bluish-grey throat and underparts with boldly barred flanks, vent and undertail coverts, red iris. **Juv:** brownish face and sides of breast with whitish throat and less distinct barring; dull brown iris. **Habitat:** marshes and ricefields.

RUDDY CRAKE [Ruddy-breasted Crake] *Porzana fusca* <Soetteumbugisachon> SV/uc L 22.5cm. Widespread dark crake often seen in rice-fields. Medium-sized with dark brown upperparts, chestnut head and underparts with whitish throat; black lower belly has narrow and inconspicuous white barring, but bird appears all-black at a distance. Distinct red legs. **Juv:** whitish chin; mostly sooty black, underparts finely barred whitish. **Similar species:** Band-bellied Crake. **Voice:** soft, repeated 'keek' turning into a long, wandering, mostly descending, trill. **Habitat:** wetlands, especially ricefields.

BAND-BELLIED CRAKE *Rallina paykullii* <Han-guktteumbugi> PM/r L 22cm. Similar to Ruddy Crake, but has broad, conspicuous black and white barring on belly, flanks, and undertail coverts. White barring on upperwing-coverts not always conspicuous and sometimes missing. Chin, throat. Bill blue-grey green at base, whitish front edge to wing visible in flight. **Juv:** darker than adult with dark bars on head and breast; belly whitish. **Habitat:** usually drier places than other crakes; marshes and rice-fields.

Rails, Crakes

Water Rail

Baillon's Crake

Ruddy Crake

chick

Band-bellied Crake

WHITE-BREASTED WATERHEN *Amaurornis phoenicurus* <Huinbaetteumbugi> PM/sc L 33cm. White face and underparts contrast with dark slate grey back; cinnamon vent and undertail coverts; yellow legs. **Non-Br:** duller legs. **Chick:** all black. **Juv:** browner with duller legs and bill; greyish face, throat and breast, becoming white with maturity. **Voice:** calls 'tok' at 3-4 per sec. Pairs call together with rising, bubbling 'kwarr'. **Habitat:** marshes, rice-fields, grasslands, and open areas.

MOORHEN [Common Gallinule] *Gallinula chloropus* <Soemuldak> SV/c • Res/sc(s) L 32.5cm. Blackish body, brownish above, tinged greyish on shoulders and below; red frontal shield and white lines along flanks diagnostic; white undertail coverts seen as 2 white patches when tail is cocked; yellowish-green legs. **Chick:** black with red and yellow bill. **Juv:** brownish with whitish face. Often swims but never dives; jerks tail when walking; jerks head back and forth when swimming. **Similar species:** Coot has white frontal shield and bill; Watercock. **Voice:** abrupt 'prruk'; nasal, repeated 'kwik' in alarm. **Habitat:** well-vegetated ponds, streams and wetlands.

WATERCOCK *Gallicrex cinerea* <Tteumbugi> SV/uc L ♂ 40cm/♀ 33cm. Now very scarce and difficult to see in Korea. **Male:** black body; red frontal shield which forms short crest; red legs; bright yellow bill; rear of body browner; undertail coverts barred with white. **Female/Non-Br Male:** buffy brown, finely barred underparts; broad dark feather centres give scalloped appearance to back and wings; crown dark brown; bills and legs greenish; female much smaller. **Voice:** throaty 'gok-gok-gok'. **Habitat:** nests in dense vegetation near edge of wet rice-fields.

COOT *Fulica atra* <Muldak> Res/uc • WV/c L 40cm. Hunched black bird usually seen swimming in open water. White frontal shield and pale pinkish-white bill diagnostic; narrow white trailing edge to secondaries; yellow legs and grey feet. Dives well. **Juv:** tinged brownish; throat and breast whitish; lacks white of sides and undertail of Moorhen. **Voice:** various calls - high-pitched, hiccoughing 'h-ip'; also loud, harsh 'kraw-kraw.' **Habitat:** wetlands with still open water and abundant plant.

Coots

White-breasted Waterhen

Moorhen

juv.

chick

Watercock

summer ♂

winter ♂

♀

Coot

juv.

chick

Cranes

Family Gruidae (World : 15 species, Korea : 7 species) Large, terrestrial wading birds with long bills, necks, and legs. Do not perch in trees as often depicted. Fly slowly with necks and legs outstretched. Some have large secondaries or tertials decurved over the short tail. Plumage is largely grey, white, black. Outside Br. season, tend to be gregarious; sometimes forming large flocks. Perform elaborate dancing courtship displays. Sexes similar, but females slightly smaller.

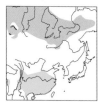

COMMON CRANE *Grus grus* <Geomeunmok-durumi> WV/r L 114cm. Often mixed in flocks of other cranes. Grey with red crown, distinct black chin and foreneck and white band from behind eye down sides of neck. In flight shows sharp contrast between black flight feathers and grey wing-coverts. **Juv:** entirely pale brownish grey. **Similar species:** Grey Heron flies with neck retracted; Sandhill Crane. **Habitat:** open rice-fields.

RED-CROWNED CRANE *Grus japonensis* <Du-rumi> WV/r L 140cm. Very large, white crane, well-known from cultural depictions. **Ad:** Red crown with rear of head and nape white; throat and neck black; long black tertials droop over tail; in flight also shows black secondaries and white tail. **Imm:** tinged brown and lacking red crown. **Juv:** brown head and neck. **Voice:** loud, piecing 'kurrk'. **Habitat:** open rice-fields, mud-flats and river basins.

WHITE-NAPED CRANE *Grus vipio* <Jaedurumi> WV/r • PM/sc L 127cm. **Ad:** White head with large, round patch of bare, red skin around eye, white extending down hindneck; Underparts and foreneck dark-grey; with narrow tongues stretching up sides of neck. Wing-coverts pale bluish-grey, flight-feathers black; tertials long, white. **Juv:** pale grey, heavily marked with buffy-brown; white on hindneck. **Similar species:** Common Crane. **Habitat:** open rice-fields, mud-flats; reservoirs, estuaries.

HOODED CRANE *Grus monacha* <Heukdurumi> WV/r · PM/sc L 100cm. Smallish, rather dark, crane. **Ad:** white head and upper neck with entirely dark-grey body; bare red skin on forecrown; black forehead and lores. **Juv:** head and neck rusty; lacking black and red. Hybrids with Common Crane are known: throat and foreneck typically grey not black. **Similar species:** White-naped Crane has red skin around eye, body, especially rear, is paler grey. **Habitat:** farmlands, grasslands.

Cranes

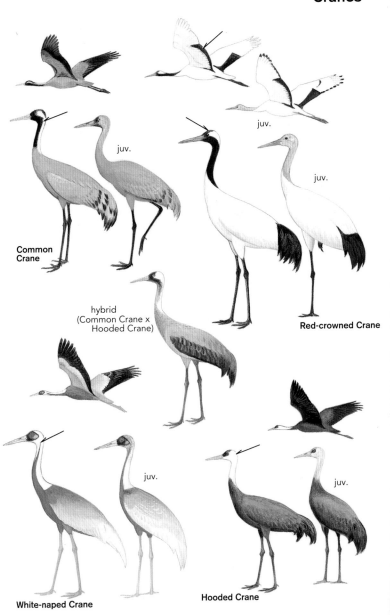

juv.

Common
Crane

juv.

juv.

Red-crowned Crane

hybrid
(Common Crane x
Hooded Crane)

juv.

White-naped Crane

juv.

Hooded Crane

SANDHILL CRANE *Grus canadensis* <Kaenada-durumi> Vag L 95cm. **Ad:** pale grey head and neck with whiter cheeks; grey body marked with rufous brown; bare red forehead; flight feathers and tail tipped blackish. **Juv:** more marked with brown, including head and neck. **Similar species:** Common Crane. **Habitat:** ricefields, riservoirs. **Status:** several records at Cheolwon, Gangwon-do and Daeseongdong, Gyeonggi-do.

DEMOISELLE CRANE *Anthropoides virgo* <Soejaedurumi> Vag L 95cm. Smallest crane with shortest neck and bill; black head and neck with grey crown and distinctive white ear tufts; black neck feathers are long and hang down over breast; ash-grey body and black tail. **Juv:** lacks white ear tufts. **Habitat:** open rice-fields, river basins. **Status:** records at Ganghwado, from 1940 to 1945.

SIBERIAN WHITE CRANE *Grus leucogeranus* <Siberiahuindurumi> Vag L 135cm. Large crane with all-white plumage and bare red skin on forehead. In flight shows distinctive black primaries and primary coverts, hidden at rest. Pink legs; long pinkish or yellowish bill. **Juv:** irregularly marked with pale rufous brown. **Similar species:** Red-crowned Crane. **Habitat:** open rice-fields and shallow wetlands. **Status:** rarely observed at Paju, Gyeonggi-do and Cheolwon, Gangwon-do.

Bustards Family Otididae (World : 22 species, Korea : 1 species)

Large terrestrial birds. They have long necks, strong legs and stout bodies. Gait stately; very shy; crouch or run swiftly when alarmed. Flight on broad wings with neck extended is powerful.

GREAT BUSTARD *Otis tarda* <Neusi> WV/r L ♂ 100cm/♀ 75cm. Large, wary bird with stout body, resembling a turkey. Flies with slow, heavy wingbeats with stiffly held wings which show striking black and white pattern above. Greyish-white head with long neck, rufous chestnut at base and around breast; back and shoulders yellowish brown narrowly barred with black. **Male Br:** white facial whiskers; broad breast band. **Non Br:** lacks whiskers, breast band narrower. **Female:** much smaller; lacks chestnut breast band and white moustache. In flight, white wing panel contrasts strikingly with black trailing edge. **Habitat:** open fields and rice-fields.

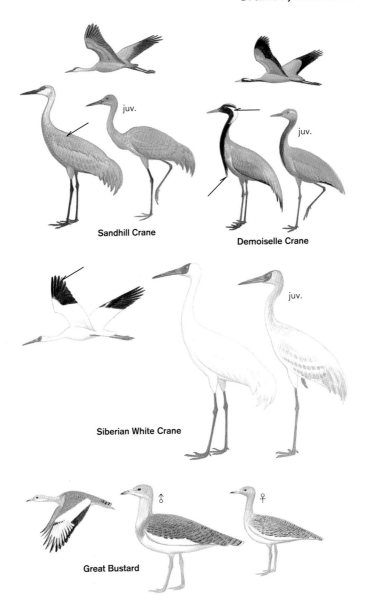

Sandhill Crane

juv.

Demoiselle Crane

juv.

Siberian White Crane

juv.

Great Bustard

Plovers

Family Charadriidae (World : 66 species, Korea : 11 species)
Plovers are small to medium-sized shorebirds with characteristic large heads, large eyes, short neck and short bills. In most species sexes are similar. 3 species breeds in Korea.

COMMON RINGED PLOVER *Charadrius hiaticula* <Huinjukji-kkomamulttesae> Vag L 19cm. Compact and deep-chested. In flight, shows clear white wingbar. Orange legs. **Br:** strongly contrasting black, white and brown; broad black band above stout bill; bill orange, tipped black. **Non-Br:** less contrasting; black on head and breast is replaced by brown; blackish bill. **Juv:** lacks black lines on head; brown feathers of upperparts show pale buffish fringes. **Habitat:** mudflats, estuaries.

LITTLE RINGED PLOVER *Charadrius dubius* <Kkomamulttesae> SV/c L 16cm. Distinctive bold, yellow eyering; shows no wingbar in flight. **Br:** black bar across crown bordered by white to rear; black breast band. **Non-Br:** black of head and breast is replaced by brown; white on head washed buffy; lacks black crown bar. **Juv:** scapulars and coverts show narrow buff fringes. **Voice:** loud 'kiu' or 'peeu'. **Habitat:** stony riverbeds, coasts, lakes, rice-fields.

LONG-BILLED PLOVER *Charadrius placidus* <Huinmongmulttesae> Res/uc L 21cm. Elongated shape, with long wings, legs and bill. Faint yellow eye-ring. **Br:** ear-coverts, eye-stripe and narrowish breast band all washed with brown, especially female; bill largely blackish. **Non-Br:** head and breast band even duller. **Juv:** like adults, legs yellowish. Black line on head is lacking. Buff tone to supercilium, and buff fringes on upperparts. **Voice:** clear sharp 'piwee'. **Habitat:** stony riverbeds.

KENTISH PLOVER *Charadrius alexandrinus* <Huinmulttesae> PM/c • Res/uc L 17cm. Incomplete breast band; all black bill with variable leg colour, usually dull In flight, shows broad white wingbar. **Male:** white forehead and supercilium. **Br:** rufous crown. **Female:** black areas of male are brown; lacks rufous on crown. **Juv:** scapulars and coverts show narrow buff fringes. **Voice:** soft 'pit' or 'twit'. Alarm call, hard 'prrr'. **Habitat:** sandy beaches, mudflats, estuaries.

Plovers

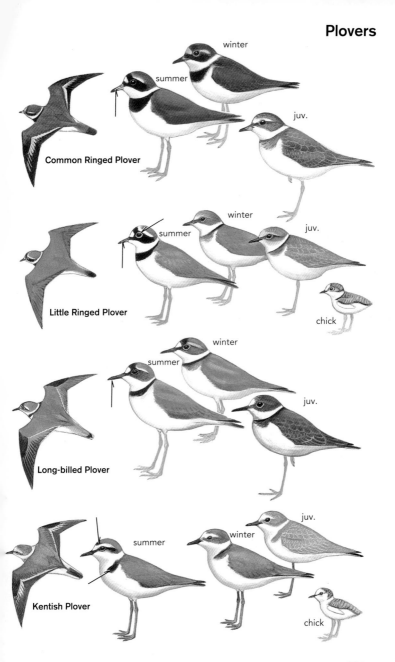

Common Ringed Plover

summer
winter
juv.

Little Ringed Plover

summer
winter
juv.
chick

Long-billed Plover

summer
winter
juv.

Kentish Plover

summer
winter
juv.
chick

MONGOLIAN PLOVER [Lesser Sand Plover] *Charadrius mongolus* <Wangnunmulttesae> PM/c L 20cm. Compared with Greater Sand Plover, generally has smaller bill and shorter, darker legs. In flight, shows narrow wing bar; has quicker movements. **Male Br:** narrow black line between white throat and orange breast band (not always visible), and white forehead with a central dividing black line. **Female Br:** black of male is replaced by brown, rufous breast band is duller. **Non-Br:** black and orange of head and breast are replaced by brown; white forehad and supercilium. **Voice:** well-pronounced 'kiripp'. **Habitat:** mudflats, estuaries.

GREATER SAND PLOVER *Charadrius leschenaultii* <Keunwangnunmulttesae> PM/r L 24cm. Larger and paler than Lesser Sand, with longer, yellower legs, and longer heavier bill, not wider at tip; more obvious wing bar. **Br:** black and orange areas are usually narrower than Lesser Sand Plover; lacks white forehead; breast-band is less clear-cut, lacking black line at upper edge. **Non-Br:** black and orange on head and breast are replaced by brown. **Voice:** short, indistinct trill 'trrri'. **Habitat:** mudflats, estuaries. **Status:** recorded at Ganghwado, Mangyeonggang, Dongjingang, and Nakdonggang.

ORIENTAL PLOVER *Charadrius veredus* <Keunmulttesae> PM/r L 24cm. Long, yellowish or pinkish legs; brown underwing contrasting with white belly. **Male Br:** face and neck are white, shading into chestnut-orange breast-band bordered below by black. **Female Br:** browner breast-band and duller head showing some contrast on ear-coverts. **Non-Br:** as female, but face and neck are pale buffy-brown, with darker crown. **Juv:** upperparts show pale buff fringes. **Voice:** sharp whistle 'chip-chip-chip'. **Habitat:** dry grasslands. **Status:** recorded at Yeongjongdo, Mangyeonggang, and Jeju-do.

Plovers

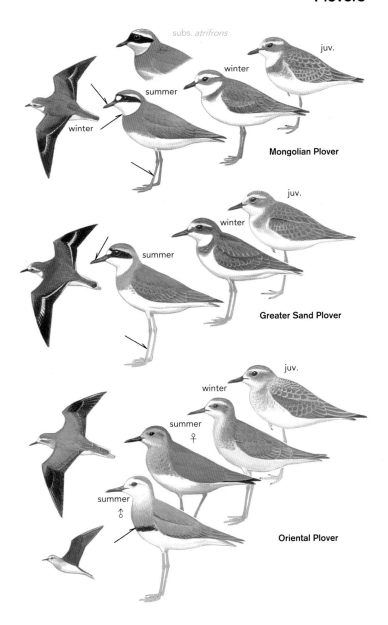

subs. *atrifrons*

winter

summer

winter

juv.

Mongolian Plover

juv.

winter

summer

Greater Sand Plover

juv.

winter

summer
♀

summer
♂

Oriental Plover

PACIFIC GOLDEN PLOVER *Pluvialis fulva* <Geomeun-gaseummulttesae> PM/uc L 24cm. Smallish head, with longish neck and legs; sharp pointed spots on upperparts and sides. In flight shows dark rump and faint wing-bar. **Br:** upperparts with pied spots, washed with yellow; underparts black with white stripe from forehead to breast sides only. **Non-Br:** greyish-brown underparts, with yellowish tone to face and upperparts; smudgy dark eyeline and pale supercilium. **Juv:** like non-Br, but more speckled above, lacks distinct eyeline; flanks finely barred. **Voice:** far-carrying 'chuwit' or 'tu-ee'. **Habitat:** mudflats, rice-fields, grasslands.

GREY PLOVER *Pluvialis squatarola* <Gae-kkwong> PM/c • WV/c L 29cm. In flight shows distinctive white underwing with black axillaries and white wingbar and rump. **Br:** black underparts contrast with white line from forehead to vent; upperparts silvery with black spotting on back. **Non-Br:** finely streaked and spotted, appearing all grey, with darker upper and paler underparts, whiter towards vent. **Juv:** like non Br., but upperparts and coverts greyish-brown, with margins spotted yellowish-white. **Voice:** loud, sad whistle 'tuuooee'. **Habitat:** mudflats, estuaries, sandy beaches.

GREY-HEADED LAPWING *Vanellus cinereus* <Mindaenggimulttesae> PM/r L 36cm. Striking black, white and brown pattern in flight. Long, bright yellow legs and yellow bill with black tip. **Ad:** head and neck grey; black band on lower breast. Red eyes. **Juv:** head and breast brownish, lacking breast band. **Habitat:** rice-fields, wet grasslands, rivers.

NORTHERN LAPWING *Vanellus vanellus* <Daeng-gimulttesae> WV/c L 30cm. Distinctive long, black crest and black facial marks. Upperparts dark glossy green. Black breast band. In flight, shows white wing tips to broad rounded wings, white rump and black tail band. **Juv:** dull head with short crest, and buff fringes on upperparts. **Voice:** slow, nasal 'pee-wit'. **Habitat:** rice-fields, marshes, lakes, rivers, sometimes tidal-flats.

Plovers, Lapwings

Pacific Golden Plover — winter, juv., summer

Grey Plover — winter, juv., summer

Grey-headed Lapwing — juv., summer

Northern Lapwing — juv., winter, summer

Painted Snipes
Family Rostratulidae (World : 2 species, Korea : 1 species) Short and decurved bill. Shows extensive sexual dimorphism. Polyandrous; male attends to nest and rears young.

PAINTED SNIPE *Rostratula benghalensis* <Hosadoyo> PM/r • WV/r L 24cm. Shy, rather solitary wader with white underparts and sides to breast, and yellowish lines down mantle; slightly down-curved long bill. **Female:** more brightly coloured than male; distinctive white eye-patch, with rufous face and neck merging into black breast patch. **Male:** plumage much duller, lacking rufous; yellow eye-patch and spots on upperwing. **Habitat:** rice-fields, riverbanks, swampy areas.

Oystercatchers
Family Haematopodidae (World : 11 species, Korea : 1 species) Contrast with black and white in body colour and long red bill. Mainly coastal, living on rocky shores feeding largely on bivalve molluscs. Sexes similar, but female has longer and thinner bill.

EURASIAN OYSTERCATCHER *Haematopus ostralegus* <Geomeunmeorimulttesae> Res/sc L 45cm. A large black-and-white wader with a long orange-red bill, and red iris. In flight, adult shows white wingbar, rump and tail with black tip, and white underwing. **Juv:** upperparts and wing-coverts brownish-black with faint brownish-buff fringes; iris reddish-brown **Voice:** high, sharp 'kleep' or 'pik'. **Habitat:** coasts, mudflats, estuaries.

Jacanas
Family Jacanidae (World : 8 species, Korea : 1 species) Small to medium-sized wading birds with long spur. Short and rounded wings, and short tail. Huge feet with very long toes and claws enable them to walk on floating vegatation. Polyandrous; male attends to nest and rears young.

PHEASANT-TAILED JACANA *Hydrophasianus chirurgus* <Mulkkwong> Vag L 39~58cm. Elongated, white-winged waterbird with very long toes, usually seen walking on floating vegetation of lakes. **Br:** black body and very long, black tail; white head and foreneck with yellow hindneck bordered black. **Non-Br:** white throat bordered by blackish stripe through eye and neck; yellowish supercilium and rear sides of neck; crown usually rusty with dark eyestripe; underparts white; shortish tail. **Habitat:** lakes and ponds with floating vegetation.

Painted Snipes, Oystercatchers, Jacanas

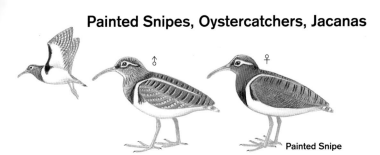

♂ ♀

Painted Snipe

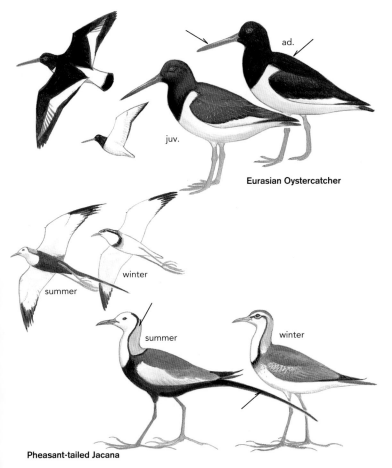

ad.

juv.

Eurasian Oystercatcher

summer

winter

summer

winter

Pheasant-tailed Jacana

Sandpipers

Family Scolopacidae (World : 86 species, Korea : 45 species) Size and shape of bill vary. Long legs. Most species are strongly migratory. Gregarious in Non-Br. season. Sexes usually similar. Feed on mainly invertebrate.

RED-NECKED STINT *Calidris ruficollis* <Jomdoyo> PM/c L 15cm. Dumpy, with shorter legs and slightly thicker bill than very similar Little Stint. **Br:** head, neck, upper breast rufous, streaked on crown; upperparts largely rufous-chestnut and black with contrastingly pale brownish-grey lower coverts and edges to tertials. **Non-Br:** upperparts grey-brown with narrow dark shafts. **Juv:** mantle dark brown fringed deep rufous with whitish on outer edges of lateral feathers; wing-coverts and tertials grey-brown. **Voice:** 'chit' or 'chiriri'. **Habitat:** mudflats, estuaries, saltpans, rice-fields.

LITTLE STINT *Calidris minuta* <Jageundoyo> Vag L 14cm. More active, and with longer, dark grey legs than Red-necked Stint. **Br:** sides of head and neck chestnut, streaked darker; wing-coverts and tertials with blackish centres and chestnut fringes. **Non-Br:** Dark shafts of scapulars usually broad. **Juv:** has white mantle lines, rufous and white edges to dark scapulars and coverts; and dark tertials with broad rufous fringes. **Voice:** short and incisive 'tit' or 'chit'. **Habitat:** mudflats, estuaries, saltpans, rice-fields.

LONG-TOED STINT *Calidris subminuta* <Jong-daldoyo> PM/uc L 15cm. Whitish supercilium outlines dark streaked brown crown as distinct cap, which usually extends down to base of bill; has yellow-green legs and with very long central toe; sides of breast rather heavily streaked. **Br:** crown rufous; upperparts scaly with blackish centred feathers fringed rufous. **Non-Br:** breast and upperparts grey-brown. **Juv:** bright, with striking white lines on mantle. **Voice:** short, soft 'prrt' or 'chrrup'. **Habitat:** freshwater wetlands.

TEMMINCK'S STINT *Calidris temminckii* <Huink-kkorijomdoyo> PM/uc L 14cm. Small, dull-coloured and easily overlooked stint with pale greenish-grey/yellow legs. **Br:** shows some contrast above with dark-centred scapulars fringed pale chestnut. **Non-Br:** upperparts and breast dark grey-brown. **Juv:** mantle, scapulars, tertials and wing-coverts show a clear dark submarginal line and pale fringe. **Voice:** rapid trilling 'tiririririr' or 'tirr'. **Habitat:** freshwater wetlands.

Small Sandpipers

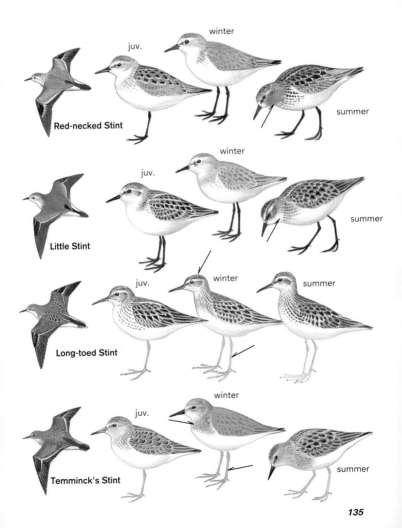

Red-necked Stint

juv.

winter

summer

Little Stint

juv.

winter

summer

Long-toed Stint

juv.

winter

summer

Temminck's Stint

juv.

winter

summer

PECTORAL SANDPIPER *Calidris melanotos*
<Amerikamechuragidoyo> PM/r L 22cm. Streaks
on breast sharply demarcated from unmarked
white belly in all plumages. Weaker supercilium
and eye-ring and less rufous on crown than Sharp-
tailed Sandpiper, also more upright stance. **Juv:**
clear double white lines on blackish-brown
upperparts. **Voice:** loud, reedy 'churk' or 'trrit'.
Habitat: rice-fields, grassy lake edges, sometimes
tidal-flats.

SHARP-TAILED SANDPIPER *Calidris acuminata*
<Mechuragidoyo> PM/c L 21cm. Lacks
demarcation on lower breast; prominent white
eye-ring. **Br:** rufous upperparts, especially distinct
crown; neck and breast heavily spotted brown;
broad, dark V's on lower breast, belly and flanks.
Non-Br: distinct rufous crown; upperparts duller.
Juv: bright buff breast with fine streaks. **Voice:**
'wheep' or 'pleep'. **Habitat:** rice-fields, lake
edges, mudflats.

DUNLIN *Calidris alpina* <Minmuldoyo> PM/c ·
WV/c L 19cm. Active; flocks often raise heads and
run when feeding; shows white wing-bar in flight.
Slightly decurved bill, usually shorter than Curlew
Sandpiper's. **Br:** large black patch on belly; rufous-
brown upperparts, especially scapulars; black
streaks on breast. **Non-Br:** dull, grey-brown
upperparts; white underparts. **Juv:** buffy, with
whitish mantle lines, and diffuse streaking on
underparts; mantle and scapulars blackish-brown
with buff fringes; brown streaks on breast. **Similar
species:** see Broad-billed, Curlew Sandpipers.
Voice: reedy 'kreee' or 'treeep'. **Habitat:**
mudflats, estuaries, saltpans, sometimes
freshwater wetlands.

CURLEW SANDPIPER *Calidris ferruginea*
<Bulgeun-gaetdoyo> PM/uc L 19cm. Elegant,
with longish legs and long, clearly decurved bill. In
flight, shows characteristic white rump and black
tail. **Br:** chestnut-red head and underparts. **Non-
Br:** upperparts grey-brown with darker shaft-
streaks; white supercilium and underparts, wing-
coverts grey, fringed whitish. **Juv:** largely
unstreaked buff head and breast with narrow
whitish supercilium; golden fringes on upperparts.
Voice: soft 'chirrup'. **Habitat:** mudflats, estuaries,
sometimes rice-fields, freshwater wetlands,
saltpans.

Small Sandpipers

Pectoral Sandpiper

juv.

winter

summer

Sharp-tailed Sandpiper

juv.

winter

summer

Dunlin

juv.

winter

summer

Curlew Sandpiper

juv.

winter

summer

RED KNOT *Calidris canutus* <Bulgeungaseumdoyo> PM/c L 24cm. Stocky wader with thickish, dark bill usually shorter than head length; legs shorter and greener than Great Knot. **Br:** rich rufous face and underparts. **Non-Br:** pale-greyish with whitish supercilium; breast patches indistinct or lacking; fine black shafts on grey back In flight, shows narrow wing-bar and less contrasting, scaly rump. **Juv:** dark sub-marginal lines and buff fringes on scapulars and coverts, giving a scaly appearance. **Voice:** 'knutt'. **Habitat:** mudflats, estuaries. **Status:** usually in flocks of Great Knot.

GREAT KNOT *Calidris tenuirostris* <Bulgeuneokkaedoyo> PM/c L 29cm. Rather large with longish bill (length usually longer than head length) and dull, greyish legs, wings projecting beyond tail tip. In flight, shows white underwings and rump. **Br:** dark, heavily streaked on head and neck, spotted black on breast, and on white belly and flanks; line of rufous spots on scapulars. **Non-Br:** dark-greyish upperparts with streaky breast patches. **Juv:** more streaked with dark brown spots on buffish breast and flanks, and dark-brown scapulars with pale scaling. Feed slowly and deliberately in long lines. **Voice:** hard, chattering 'chott-chott' from flocks. 'kit-kit'. **Habitat:** often in huge compact flocks which look all dark at distance, on mudflats, estuaries. **Status:** one of the commonest wader in Korea. Huge flocks are found in Mankyung and Dongjin Estuary.

RUDDY TURNSTONE *Arenaria interpres* <Kkokkadoyo> PM/c L 22cm. Distinctive wader with characteristic black, brown and white facial markings, short, orange-red legs, and short, slightly upturned, black bill. **Br:** In flight, shows diagnostic black, white and chestnut-red pattern. **Male:** chestnut and black upperparts, pied head and black breast. **Female:** duller than male, browner and more streaked on head. **Non-Br:** blackish-brown above, small white patches on throat and face; in flight, shows diagnostic white back and wingbars. **Juv:** like non-Br., but scapulars and coverts have buff fringes. **Voice:** clear rapid 'trik-tuk-tuk-tuk'. **Habitat:** rocky coasts, sandy beaches, mudflats, estuaries.

Sandpipers

Red knot

juv.

winter

summer

Great Knot

juv.

winter

summer

Ruddy Turnstone

winter

juv.

♀ summer

summer ♂

SANDERLING *Calidris alba* <Segarakdoyo> PM/uc • WV/uc L 20cm. Thickish black bill. In flight, shows broad white wing-bar. **Br:** head, breast and upperparts dark chestnut with dark brown streaks and speckles. **Non-Br:** very pale, with pale grey upperparts and white underparts; blackish lesser coverts often shows as distinctive black patch at bend of closed wing. **Juv:** crisp white and yellow fringes to blackish upperparts and sides of nec; crown dark brown, fringed buff with broken white supercilium. **Voice:** rather quiet 'twick' or 'kip'; short trills 'quiriri-quiriri'. **Habitat:** sandy beaches, estuaries

SPOON-BILLED SANDPIPER *Eurynorhynchus pygmeus* <Neopjeokburidoyo> PM/r L 15cm. Characteristic spatulate bill tip. **Br:** rich rufous head and breast; chestnut fringes on blackish wing-coverts. **Non-Br:** brownish-grey upperparts with strong dark eyestripe, white supercilium and underparts. **Juv:** upperparts blackish-brown with whitish and buffish fringes; dark ear-coverts, eye-stripe and crown contrast with white supercilium and pale hind-neck; buffish fringes on upperparts. **Voice:** quiet trill 'preep'. **Habitat:** mudflats, estuaries, saltpans.

BUFF-BREASTED SANDPIPER *Tryngites subruficollis* <Nureundoyo> Vag L 19cm. Scaly above, with buff face and underparts in all plumages. Can be confused with larger juvenile Ruff, but lacks white tail sides, has yellower legs, rounder head, and shorter neck; black bill is shorter than Ruff's, black eye more striking in bland face. In flight, shows white underwing, with dark markings. **Juv:** as adult, but with browner centres to feathers on upperparts. **Voice:** Usually silent, sometimes soft trill 'kirrr' **Habitat:** grasslands.

BROAD-BILLED SANDPIPER *Limicola falcinellus* <Songgotburidoyo> PM/c L 17cm. Long bill with sharp downward angle near tip, greenish grey legs shorter than Dunlin's; has double supercilium in all plumages. **Br:** deep brown above with rufous scaling, heavily streaked on head, breast and sides. **Non-Br:** pale grey upperparts show dark shaft-streaks and dark centres. **Juv:** like Br, but breast pale buff-brown, more lightly streaked; streaking absent on flanks and vent. **Voice:** rolling 'chureet'. **Similar species:** Dunlin. **Habitat:** mudflats, estuaries, muddy wetlands.

Small Sandpipers

Sanderling
juv.
winter
summer

Spoon-billed Sandpiper
juv.
winter
summer

Buff-breasted Sandpiper
juv.
ad.

Broad-billed Sandpiper
juv.
winter
summer

GREY PHALAROPE [Red Phalarope] *Phalaropus fulicarius* <Bulgeunbaejineureomibaldoyo> Vag L 21cm. Compared with Red-necked Phalarope, larger with heavier, broader bill. **Br:** unmistakable, rufous underparts, white face, and yellow bill with black bill tip; in flight, shows broad, white wing-bar and rufous rump; male is duller than female. **Non-Br:** unstreaked grey upperparts (sometimes with black marks on mantle) are usually paler than Red-necked Phalarope; bill black; in flight, grey rump and back, narrow wingbar. **Voice:** hard, sharp 'pik' or 'kit', also a softer 'dreet'. **Habitat:** seas, coasts, estuaries. **Status:** one record at Nakdonggang, Gyeongsangnam-do on May 1994.

RED-NECKED PHALAROPE *Phalaropus lobatus* <Jineureomibaldoyo> PM/c L 19cm. Usually seen swimming at sea or in bays, or in flight when flushed by boat. Distinctive thin and pointed bill. In flight, shows white patches on sides of black rump and white wingbar. **Br:** reddish band on neck and broad, pale rufous stripes on upperparts; male is duller than female. **Non-Br:** long, dark eye patch, drooping to rear; white fringes and dark feather centres on upperparts. **Juv:** as Non Br. but darker above, with yellow mantle lines. **Voice:** short, hard 'kitt' or 'kirrik'. **Habitat:** seas, coasts, estuaries.

WILSON'S PHALAROPE *Phalaropus tricolor* <Keunjineureomibaldoyo> Vag L 23cm. Large phalarope with longish, needle-shaped bill, small head and long neck with pot belly. Swims or walks rapidly. In flight, shows white rump, dark tail and no wing bar. **Br:** short, white supercilium; legs black. **Female:** pale-grey crown and hindneck, with black band from bill through eye and down sides of neck contrasting with greyer hindneck; chestnut and grey V-patterns on mantle. **Male:** dark-brown crown, eyeline and hindneck, less contrasting plumage. **Non-Br:** upperparts pale-grey, supercilium and underparts white; legs yellow. **Habitat:** seas, coasts, estuaries. often on muddy shores and in shallow water. **Status:** one record at Nakdonggang, Gyeongsangnam-do.

Phalaropes

Grey Phalarope

winter · juv. · winter · summer ♀ · ♂ · summer

Red-necked Phalarope

winter · juv. · winter · summer ♀ · summer ♂

Wilson's Phalarope

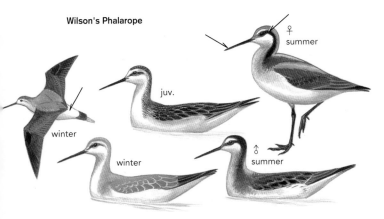

winter · juv. · winter · summer ♀ · summer ♂

143

RUFF *Philomachus pugnax* <Mokdoridoyo> PM/r L ♂ 30cm/ ♀ 25cm. Distinctive shape, with small flat head, long neck. Short and slightly down-curved bill; longish legs vary from green, yellow to orange. In flight, shows distinctive tail pattern, with dark central bar separating large, white patches on each side of rump, and narrow white wing-bar. **Male Br:** unmistakable with wide variably-coloured (often chestnut or black) ruffs and ear-tufts. **Female:** smaller, lacking ruff and tufts; black-centred feathers on upperparts fringed paler. **Non-Br:** upperparts blackish scaled with buff, crown finely streaked, face and underparts unstreaked pale buffy brown. **Juv:** like non-Br, but underparts pale buff. **Habitat:** freshwater wetlands, mudflats.

SPOTTED REDSHANK *Tringa erythropus* <Hakdoyo> PM/c L 30cm. Long, red or orange-red legs and slender, black bill with red base of lower mandible. **Br:** Black, variably spotted white on upperparts; broken white eye-ring. **Non-Br:** Grey-brown upperparts, speckled with white, vermiculated on sides; dark eye-stripe and white supercilium. **Juv:** like non-Br., but upperparts generally browner, and legs paler. **Voice:** a sharp, rapid whistle 'chuwit'. **Habitat:** fresh or brackish water wetlands, rice-fields, mudflats.

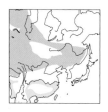

REDSHANK *Tringa totanus* <Bulgeunbaldoyo> PM/c L 28cm. Smaller with shorter legs, bill and neck than Spotted Redshank. Legs and entire bill-base orange-red. In flight shows diagnostic broad white trailing edge to wing. **Br:** strong dark brown streaks on head, neck and underparts. **Non-Br:** uniformly grey-brown above. **Juv:** rufous edges on upperparts; indistinct orange-red bill base. **Voice:** piping 'tew-hoo-hoo'. **Habitat:** all kinds of wetlands.

MARSH SANDPIPER *Tringa stagnatilis* <Soecheong-daridoyo> PM/uc L 24cm. Elegant wader with long, greenish legs and thin, straight, black bill. **Br:** upperparts show brown feathers with black centres; blackish-brown streaks or fine spots on head, neck and breast. **Non-Br:** upperparts pale brownish-grey with often striking dark eye-patch. **Juv:** upperparts generally browner with whitish fringing and few streaks on sides of neck, often looks long-necked and small-headed. **Voice:** 'pyu' or 'pi' often repeated. **Habitat:** estuaries, saltpans, freshwater wetlands.

Sandpipers

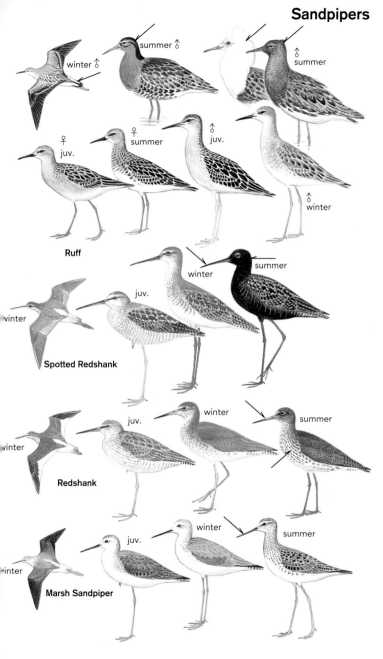

winter ♂

summer ♂

♂ summer

♀ juv.

♀ summer

♂ juv.

♂ winter

Ruff

winter

summer

winter

juv.

Spotted Redshank

winter

juv.

winter

summer

Redshank

winter

juv.

winter

summer

Marsh Sandpiper

145

GREENSHANK *Tringa nebularia* <Cheongdaridoyo>
PM/c L 35cm. Slightly upturned, thickish bill and
green legs. In flight, shows long white rump and
dark underwings. **Br:** greyish-brown head, neck
and upper breast heavily streaked. **Non-Br:** paler,
with fine streaking on head and neck. **Juv:** like
non-Br, but upperparts generally browner, with
buff fringes. **Voice:** loud and ringing 'tow' or 'tyu'
given 3 times when flushed. **Habitat:** Very
widespread in all kinds of wetlands; often solitary
or in small groups.

GREATER YELLOWLEGS *Tringa melanoleuca*
<Keunnorangbaldoyo> Vag L 30cm. Similar
structure and size to Greenshank. Bright orange or
yellow legs, and almost straight bill. Square white
rump, cut off sharply across lower back, is
diagnostic; heavily streaked on neck and breast in
all plumages and more spotted above than
Greenshank. **Voice:** loud clear 'teu-teu-teu', 'klee-
klee-klee'. **Habitat:** coastal wetlands.

SPOTTED GREENSHANK [Nordmann's Greenshank]
Tringa guttifer <Cheongdaridoyosachon> PM/r L
30cm. Stocky, with rather large head, and short,
thick, usually yellowish legs; thick, almost straight
bill can show pale base with darker terminal third.
In flight, shows whitish underwing-coverts. **Br:**
head and breast are heavily spotted black. **Non-
Br:** often strikingly pale and greyish above, much
less streaked than Greenshank. **Juv:** like non-Br,
but upperparts generally browner, rather finely
speckled. **Voice:** 'keyew' sharper than
Greenshank; also 'kiiii'; and 'gwark'. **Habitat:**
mudflats, estuaries. **Status:** often seen in
Namyangman, Asanman, and Mangyeonggang.

TEREK SANDPIPER *Xenus cinereus* <Dwitburi-
doyo> PM/c L 23cm. Distinctive, long, upcurved
bill. In flight, shows conspicuous white trailing
edge to wing. Legs yellow to yellowish orange. **Br:**
upperparts brownish-grey, with black feather-
centres particularly broad on scapulars. **Non-Br:**
lacks black scapular lines. **Juv:** as adult, but
upperparts darker and browner, with buffy fringes.
Voice: sharp, far-carrying 'twit-wit-wit-wit'.
Habitat: mudflats, estuaries, sometimes larger
rivers.

Sandpipers

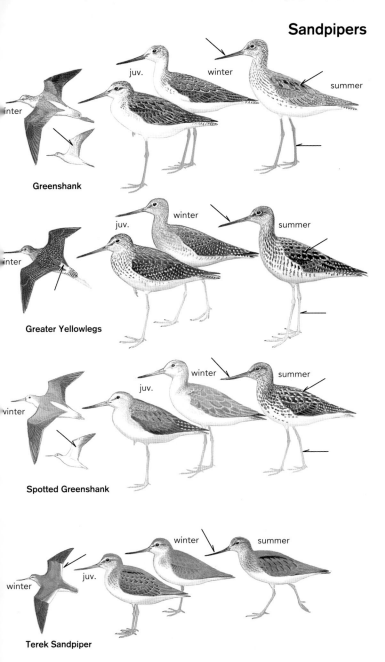

Greenshank

inter

juv. winter summer

Greater Yellowlegs

inter

juv. winter summer

Spotted Greenshank

winter

juv. winter summer

Terek Sandpiper

winter

juv. winter summer

147

GREEN SANDPIPER *Tringa ochropus* <Ppikppik-doyo> PM/uc • WV/uc L 23cm. Dark, stocky wader with greenish-brown upperparts, dark breast and clean white underparts; white fore-supercilium and eyering. In flight, shows uniformly dark underwing, strongly contrasting white rump; 2-3 broad black bars on tail. Legs greenish-grey. **Br:** head and breast strongly streaked with white; upperparts speckled white. **Non-Br:** plainer upperparts and breast. **Voice:** high pitched 'twit-wit-wit'. **Habitat:** inland freshwater wetlands, often small rivers.

WOOD SANDPIPER *Tringa glareola* <Allakdoyo> PM/c L 20cm. Elegant, grey-brown wader speckled with white, and with obvious supercilium; legs and neck longer than either Green or Common Sandpiper. In flight, shows white rump, pale underwing, dark brown barring on tail with feet extending beyond; legs yellowish. **Br:** upperparts boldly speckled. **Non-Br:** upperparts brownish, less clearly speckled. **Juv:** upperparts dark warm brown, spotted and fringed bright buff-brown; breast suffused with grey-brown. **Voice:** An anxious 'chip-chip-chip', 'chew-ew chew-ew'. **Habitat:** rice-fields and other freshwater wetlands.

GREY-TAILED TATTLER *Heteroscelus brevipes* <Norangbaldoyo> PM/uc L 25cm. Plain, dark grey upperparts, including entire wings and tail; well-defined white supercilium; dark brown lores; yellow legs. **Br:** narrow grey barring on breast and flanks, not on belly or vent. **Non-Br:** plain grey underparts, lacking barring. **Voice:** deeper than Terek, a piping 'tu-whip'. **Habitat:** mudflats, estuaries.

COMMON SANDPIPER *Actitis hypoleucos* <Kkapjakdoyo> SV/c L 20cm. Short greenish legs and elongated shape; white wedge between wing and dark breast sides. In flight, shows distinctive flickering wing-beats; white bar on upperwing and dark rump; also has whitish eye-ring and pale supercilium. **Br:** narrow, dark streaks on brown upperparts and on brown patches at sides of breast, which form breast-band. **Non-Br:** brown breast patches less distinct; upperparts plainer. **Juv:** like non-Br., but mantle, scapulars and wing-coverts have faint buff fringes. **Voice:** distinctive thin, high 'seep-seep- seep'. **Habitat:** rivers, lakes, marshes, saltpans.

Sandpipers

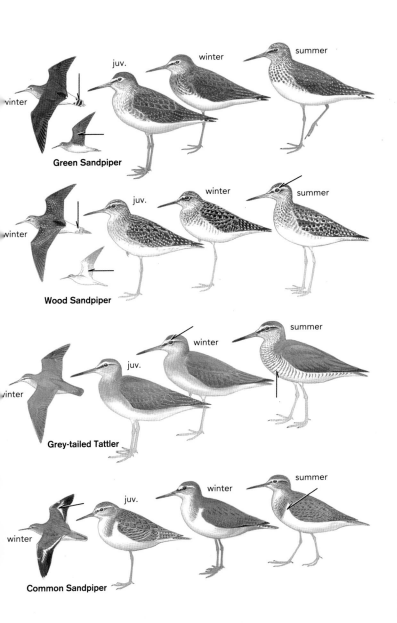

winter

juv. winter summer

Green Sandpiper

winter juv. winter summer

Wood Sandpiper

winter juv. winter summer

Grey-tailed Tattler

winter juv. winter summer

Common Sandpiper

BLACK-TAILED GODWIT *Limosa limosa* <Heuk-kkoridoyo> PM/c L 38cm. Elegant, with long straight pinkish bill with black tip. In flight, shows characteristic white wingbar and black tail. **Br:** rufous neck and breast, dark brown barring on breast and belly. **Non-Br:** gray-brown upperparts. **Juv:** neck and most of underparts buff; whitish-buff fringes on upperparts feathers. **Voice:** short 'kek'. **Habitat:** rice-fields, estuaries, mudflats, saltpans.

BAR-TAILED GODWIT *Limosa lapponica* <Keun-dwitburidoyo> PM/c L 39cm. Slightly upturned, pinkish bill with black tip; legs shorter than Black-tailed Godwit. **Br:** males; rich rufous head, unbarred, rufous neck and underparts, females; dark barring and light chestnut blotches on underparts. **Non-Br:** upperparts pale grey-brown streaked darker. In flight, paler brown wedge up back, barred rump and tail. **Juv:** upperparts and coverts dark brown fringed pale buff. **Voice:** 'kak-kak' or 'kirruc'. **Habitat:** mudflats, estuaries.

ASIATIC DOWITCHER [Asian Dowitcher] *Limnodromus semipalmatus* <Keunburidoyo> PM/r L 35cm. Smaller and more compact-looking than godwits, often feeding with prolonged 'sewing' action. Long, straight, thickish, black bill; black legs; white underwing. **Br:** rufous head lacking pale supercilium, but with dark lores and white spot at bill base. **Non-Br:** contrasting face pattern of dark lores and crown with whitish supercilium and cheeks. **Juv:** upperparts rich dark-brown with buff fringes, pinkish base to bill. **Voice:** yelping 'chop-chop'. **Similar species:** Long-Billed Dowitcher. **Habitat:** tidal mudflats.

LONG-BILLED DOWITCHER *Limnodromus scolopaceus* <Ginburidoyo> Vag L 29cm. Smaller than similar species, and lacks obvious pale fringes on upperparts; green legs. **Br:** all underparts rufous; foreneck densely spotted; upper breast barred. **Non-Br:** demarcation between grey breast and white belly relatively distinct. **Juv:** grey from head to neck; breast washed-buff. Plumage of upperparts narrowly edged dull-chestnut. Tertials uniform dark-brown. **Voice:** highpitched 'zeekeekeek'. **Habitat:** prefers fresh or brackish water rather than intertidal mudflats. **Status:** records in Cheonsuman and Junam Lake.

Godwits, Dowitchers

inter

winter

summer

juv.

Black-tailed Godwit

winter

winter

summer

juv.

Bar-tailed Godwit

winter

juv.

winter

summer

Asiatic Dowitcher

winter

juv.

winter

summer

Long-billed Dowitcher

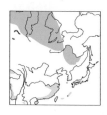

EURASIAN CURLEW *Numenius arquata* <Madoyo> PM/c • WV/c L 58cm. Long decurved bill (longest in adult female, shortest in small males and juveniles), with some pink at base; rear of crown rounded; grey toned plumage, especially on closed wing, with unstreaked white belly and vent making species often look pale at distance. In flight, shows white from back to tail. Underwing white. **Voice:** rising 'cour-lee'. **Habitat:** mudflats, estuaries.

FAR EASTERN CURLEW [Eastern Curlew] *Numenius madagascariensis* <Allak-kkorimadoyo> PM/c L 63cm. Very long decurved bill with pink base. Bill longest in adult female, shortest in small males and juveniles. Background colour of body buff or warm brown, streaking continuing to belly, so usually appear dark at distance. In flight, never shows any white on back and rump; underwing-coverts densely barred brown. **Voice:** 'cour-lee', flatter in tone than Eurasian curlew. **Habitat:** mudflats, estuaries.

WHIMBREL *Numenius phaeopus* <Jungburidoyo> PM/c L 43cm. A small, dark curlew, often seen running on drier part of tidal-flats. Crown has two dark lateral crown stripes; upperparts mainly dark brown, variably notched and fringed whitish; breast pale buff, heavily streaked brown. **Voice:** far-carrying trill 'pu hu hu hu hu'. **Juv:** short-billed and recalls Little Curlew but lacks golden tones and bright fringes on upperparts; in flight back is white. **Habitat:** mudflats, estuaries, rice-fields, grasslands.

LITTLE CURLEW *Numenius minutus* <Soeburidoyo> PM/r L 30cm. Tiny curlew with short, only slightly decurved bill with clear pink base; has two dark-brown, lateral crown-stripes, broad, pale, almost unstreaked supercilium and narrow eyeline; eye appears large, dominating the face; breast pale buff with dark brown streaks; upperparts dark brown, edged paler. **Voice:** sharp 'klu-ewu', rising 'twi-twi-twi-twi...', rising and accelerating series of 'kleew' kleew...'. soft whistle 'te-te-te'. **Similar species:** see Whimbrel. **Habitat:** grasslands, barley-fields, drier areas than Whimbrel.

Curlews

Eurasian Curlew

Far Eastern Curlew

Whimbrel

Little Curlew

COMMON SNIPE *Gallinago gallinago* <Kkakdoyo>
PM/c • WV/uc L 26cm. When flushed, bursts from
ground and is usually noisy; often flying high, zig-
zagging, showing white trailing-edge to wing, dark
and white areas on underwing, but little contrast
between coverts and flight feathers on upperwing.
On ground, shows clear tail extension beyond
primaries, and upperparts show buffy-yellow lines
with broader edges to outer edge of scapulars
than inner; supercilium width at base of bill usually
appears narrower than eye-stripe. **Voice:** when
flushed a harsh 'schiyip'. **Habitat:** rice-fields, lotus
ponds, marshes, riverbanks.

PINTAIL SNIPE *Gallinago stenura* <Baneulkkoridoyo>
PM/uc L 26cm. Flushes quickly but flight slower,
less zig-zag, and is more apt to land closeby than
Common; in flight, broader wings show thin,
greyish trailing edge, feet project further beyond
shorter tail. On ground, scapulars are usually more
rounded, edges of scapulars more equally fringed
yellowish-buff; dark eyestripe often broken in front
if the eye; occasionally shows diagnostic, pin-
shaped outer-tail feathers when preening. **Voice:**
when flushed, a wet 'shwik'. **Habitat:** rice-fields,
lotus ponds, marsh, riverbanks.

SWINHOE'S SNIPE *Gallinago megala* <Kkak-
doyosachon> PM/uc L 28cm. Larger and heavier
than Pintail and Common Snipe, most similar to
Latham's Snipe; flushes relatively slowly and
usually silently, short escape flight often direct
with relatively heavier wingbeats of longer wings,
feet less visible than Pintail, and lacking
contrasting underwing of Common Snipe. On
ground, shows slight primary extension beyond
tertials, and clear tail extension beyond primaries.
Voice: drier-sounding call than Pintail Snipe.
Habitat: often in well-vegetated wetlands, rice-
fields, grassland; often chooses drier habitat than
Common Snipe.

LATHAM'S SNIPE *Gallinago hardwickii* <Keun-
kkakdoyo> PM/r L 29cm. When flushed escape
flight strong and direct; pale panel across the
median coverts may be visible. On ground, tail
clearly extends beyond primaries, which are
usually completely covered by tertials. **Voice:**
when flushed, deep 'hwok' or 'shok'. **Habitat:**
often in dry grassland areas; also rice-fields and
other freshwater wetland.

Snipes

Common Snipe

Pintail Snipe

Swinhoe's Snipe

Latham's Snipe

SOLITARY SNIPE *Gallinago solitaria* <Cheong-doyo> PM/uc • WV/uc L 30cm. Large with distinctive gingery brown plumage; pale parts of feathers whitish rather than yellow, notably the crown stripe, and scapular and mantle fringes. When flushed, flies rather slowly and usually pitches down quickly, feet not projecting beyond tail, and lacking white on underwing and trailing edge. **Voice:** harsh 'kensh', rather deeper than Common Snipe. **Habitat:** mountain streams; on migration, may occur in rice-fields and marshes.

JACK SNIPE *Lymnocryptes minimus* <Kkoma-doyo> Vag L 18cm. A tiny, dark, very skulking snipe of well-vegetated wetlands. Smaller and shorter-billed (1.5x head length) than other snipes; lacks central crown line and supercilium encloses short dark line; dark crescent below eye; slight green metallic gloss to back; dark brown, wedge-shaped tail. Bouncing action when feeding; flushes at very close range with short escape flight. **Voice:** silent when flushed. **Habitat:** rice-fields, lotus ponds, marshes.

EURASIAN WOODCOCK *Scolopax rusticola* <Metdoyo> PM/uc L 34cm. A plump, warm-brown, woodland species, often nocturnal. Larger and heavier than snipes with distinctive broad black bars on rear crown and hindneck. In flight, shows broad, rounded wings and dark subterminal tail band. **Voice:** usually silent when flushed. **Habitat:** streamsides and wet areas in woods.

Tails of Snipes

Common Snipe

Pintail Snipe

Swinhoe's Snipe

Latham's Snipe

Jack Snipe

Solitary Snipe

Jack Snipe

Eurasian Woodcock

Stilts

Family Recurvirostridae (World : 13 species, Korea : 2 species) White and black waders with extremely long legs. All have slender necks, small heads, and very long, thin bills. sexes similar.

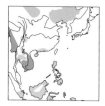

BLACK-WINGED STILT *Himantopus himantopus* <Jangdarimulttesae> PM/r • SV/r L 37cm. Unmistakable wader with thin black bill, long pink-legs. **Male:** black wings and white underparts; crown and nape variably black, white or greyish. **Female:** brownish above rather than black. **Juv:** brownish crown, nape and back, scaled with buff fringes which wear off by the first winter. **Voice:** sharp 'kek'. **Habitat:** rice-fields, estuaries, lakes. **Status:** rare but increasing migrant; recently started to nest at Cheonsuman, Chungcheongnam-do.

AVOCET *Recurvirostra avosetta* <Dwitburi-jangdarimulttesae> PM/r • WV/r L 43cm. Unmistakeable, elegant, pied wader with distinctive thin, strongly upcurved bill; black crown and hindneck; black-and-white pattern on wings visible both in flight and at rest. **Juv:** black of head and wings blackish-brown, white of upperparts suffused with brown. Feeds in water with sideways movements of head. **Voice:** clear 'kluit', 'pleet'. **Habitat:** estuaries, lakes.

Pratincoles

Family Glareolidae (World : 17 species, Korea : 1 species) Brown or olive above and lighter below, with short legs, long, pointed wings, and long forked tail. Often seen in flocks, hunt insects in flight.

ORIENTAL PRATINCOLE *Glareola maldivarum* <Jebimulttesae> PM/r L 24cm. In flight, appears dark with bright white rump and pale vent; black, forked tail looks very short compared to long, arced wings; blackish underwing with chestnut underwing-coverts. **Br:** red bill with black bill tip; creamy throat outlined neatly in black. **Non-Br:** black throat outline becomes streaked; lacks black lores and red bill base. **Juv:** upperparts appear frosted with pied fringes; throat buff lacking adult pattern, foreneck streaked. Has rapid wing beats, and often feeds in flight, like large swallow. **Voice:** 'chup-chup' and sharp 'kee-ark' reminiscent of Black-Headed Gull; sharp 'kyik' or 'chet'. **Habitat:** wetlands, farmlands, grasslands.

Stilts, Avocets, Pratincoles

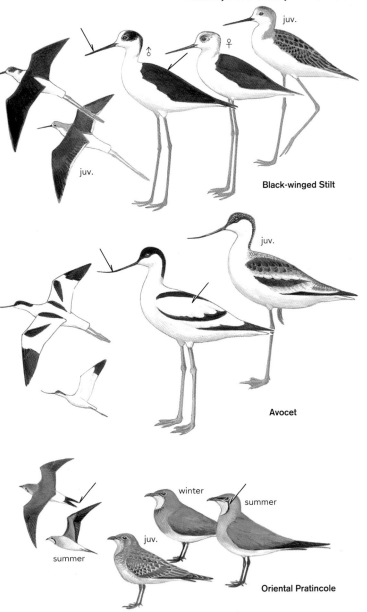

juv.

↑♂ ♀ juv.

Black-winged Stilt

juv.

Avocet

winter summer

juv.

summer

Oriental Pratincole

Skuas

Family Stercorariidae (World : 7 species, Korea : 1 species)
Large, mostly dark, piratical seabirds which often feed by chasing other seabirds until they release their catch. Plumage generally dark-greyish brown resembling immature gulls, but all show wing-flash of some white at base of primaries.

ARCTIC SKUA [Parasitic Jaeger] *Stercorarius parasiticus* <Bukgeukdodukgalmaegi> Vag L 46cm · W 105cm. Central tail feathers elongated and pointed. Dark morph uniformly blackish-brown; Light morph has a blackish cap, pale yellowish chin and hindneck, upperparts dark greyish-brown; underparts whitish usually with dark breast band. **Habitat:** coasts, open seas.

Gulls

Family Laridae (World : 91 species, Korea : 23 species)
Sexes are alike with adults usually having white bodies and grey wings with black tips; white spots in these tips are called 'mirrors' and may be important in identification. Larger species taking several years to reach adult plumage. Long wings, short tails, powerful bill and webbed feet. Gregarious.

BLACK-LEGGED KITTIWAKE *Rissa tridactyla* <Segarakgalmaegi> WV/uc L 42cm · W 91cm. Solidly black wing tips edged white; bill greenish-yellow, legs black. **Br:** white head. **Non-Br:** blackish ear spot extends round nape. **1stW:** distinct black bar on upperwings forms 'W'; black band across back of neck. **Habitat:** coasts, seas.

MEW GULL [Common Gull] *Larus canus* <Galmaegi> WV/c L 43cm • W 120cm. Rounded head, plain greenish-yellow bill and legs; in flight, shows narrow wings with white-tipped, black primaries and large mirrors. **Non-Br:** brown streaks on head and nape. **Juv/Imm:** brown and grey with dark wingtips, tail band and bill. **Habitat:** coasts, lakes, rivers.

BLACK-TAILED GULL *Larus crassirostris* <Gwaeng-igalmaegi> Res/ab L 47cm • W 120cm. Most ages show distinctive black tail band. **Ad:** yellow bill with red tip and black subterminal band, yellow legs. **Br:** upperwing dark grey; primaries black with no white mirrors. **Non-Br:** brown streaks on head and nape. **Imm:** lacks red bill tip until 2ndW, browner above. **Juv:** mostly dark brown with broad black tail bar; unscaled browny-grey plumage with black-tipped pinkish bill and pink legs until 2ndW. **Habitat:** coasts, estuaries, rivers. lakes.

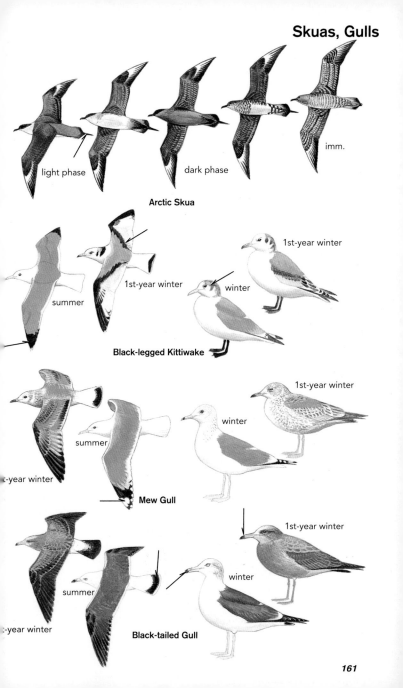

light phase · dark phase · imm.

Arctic Skua

summer · 1st-year winter · winter · 1st-year winter

Black-legged Kittiwake

-year winter · summer · winter · 1st-year winter

Mew Gull

-year winter · summer · winter · 1st-year winter

Black-tailed Gull

BLACK-HEADED GULL *Larus ridibundus* <Bulgeunburigalmaegi> WV/c L 40cm • W 92cm. Longish red bill, red legs and eye-ring; pale grey upperwing has white leading edge to outer wing and blackish tips to outer 6-8 primaries. **Br:** dark brown hood and white nape. **Non-Br:** white head with blackish ear spot; red bill has black tip. **1stW:** tertials and part of wing-coverts dark brown; bill and legs dull orange. **Habitat:** coasts, estuaries, lakes, rivers.

SAUNDERS' GULL *Larus saundersi* <Geomeunmeorigalmaegi> WV/uc • Res/sc L 32cm • W 85cm. Dark red legs and short, black bill. **Br:** black hood, white eyering; at rest, white tips on closed primaries make distinctive pattern; in flight, upperwing lacks black trailing edge to primaries. **Non-Br:** white head with dark ear spot. **1stW:** tertials and part of wing-coverts dark brown. **Voice:** shrill, tern-like 'keek-keek'. **Habitat:** mudflats, estuaries.

RELICT GULL *Larus relictus* <Godaegalmaegi> WV/r L 46cm. Deeper-bellied, and sloping forehead **Ad:** in flight, shows black tips to wings with conspicuous mirrors on outer 2 primaries. **Br:** has black hood with white crescents above and below eyes, with dark red bill and legs. **Non-Br:** whitish head usually with dusky ear-patch and streaking on nape. **1stW:** dark has brown streaks on hindneck, brown carpal bar on upperwing, and secondaries and inner primaries have dark subterminal spots; bill is grey-brown. **Habitat:** mudflats, estuaries.

SABINE'S GULL *Xema sabini* <Moktegalmaegi> Vag L 34cm • W 88cm. Striking tricoloured upperwing pattern; has long, narrow wings, shallowly forked tail, black legs and yellow-tipped, black bill. **Br:** dark-grey hood with black neck ring. **Non-Br:** white head with dark grey nape and hindneck. **1stW:** upperparts greyish-brown, scaly on wing-coverts, black bill. **Habitat:** seas.

ROSS'S GULL *Rhodostethia rosea* <Soemoktegalmaegi> Vag L 31cm. Pale grey upperparts and broad, white trailing-edge to wing, and very short, black bill, red legs and longish tail with pointed tip. **Br:** White or pinkish-white head and neck, underparts, rump, and tail; dark underwings. **Non-Br:** loses pink tinge and black collar. **1stW:** dark W-pattern on wings.

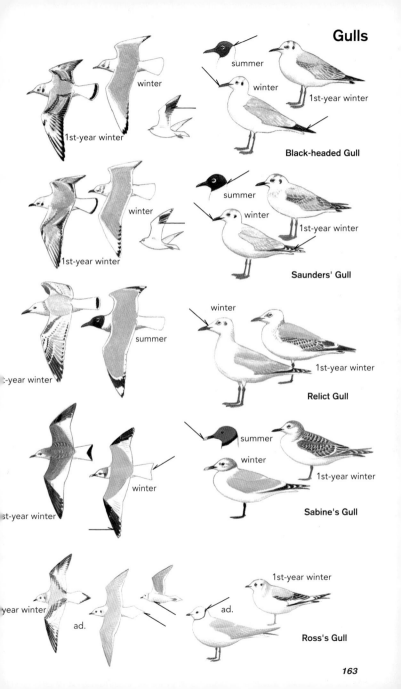

Gulls

1st-year winter

winter

Black-headed Gull

summer

winter

1st-year winter

1st-year winter

winter

Saunders' Gull

summer

winter

1st-year winter

-year winter

summer

Relict Gull

winter

1st-year winter

st-year winter

winter

Sabine's Gull

summer

winter

1st-year winter

year winter

ad.

1st-year winter

ad.

Ross's Gull

HERRING GULL *Larus argentatus* <Jaegalmaegi> WV/c L 62cm • W 139cm. Back and wings grey; outer primaries black with white tips, showing a medium-sized mirror on 10th and smaller one on 9th; legs always pink; iris usually pale yellow, but variable. **Non-Br:** much brown streaking on head and neck, mottled around breast; dark eye patch. **1stW** inner webs of inner primaries are pale. **2ndW:** pink bill with black tip; grey back and white rump. **Habitat:** coasts, coastal wetlands, estuaries.

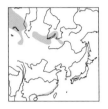

YELLOW-LEGGED GULL *Larus cachinans* <Norangbalgalmaegi> WV/uc L 62cm. Rounded head with smaller bill. **Ad:** white head, with little or no streaking on nape, even in winter; wings and mantle pale to medium grey, darker than Herring Gull, paler than Heuglin's Gull usually one largish mirror on outer primary; leg colour variable: often yellow, also orange or pink; iris pale yellow, usually darker than Herring Gull, but variable. **1stW:** paler inner primaries and underwing-coverts than Heuglin's. **Habitat:** coasts, rivers, estuaries, lakes.

HEUGLIN'S GULL *Larus heuglini* <Julmunui-norangbalgalmaegi> WV/uc L 62cm. darker grey wings and mantle than Yellow-legged and Herring Gulls, paler than Slaty-backed; with mirrors as Herring Gull; sloping forehead. **Br:** yellow legs; head and neck all-white. **Non-Br:** legs sometimes pinkish; rather light streaking on head, more on nape. **1stW:** darker greater upperwing-coverts and inner primaries than 1stW; broader dark tail band, darker underwing coverts and inner primaries than Yellow-legged. **Habitat:** coasts, rivers, estuaries, lakes.

SLATY-BACKED GULL *Larus schistisagus* <Keunjaegalmaegi> WV/c L 65cm • W 135cm. Upperparts much darker grey than Herring gull complex; legs dark pink. **Br:** plain white head. **Non-Br:** heavily streaked on head, neck and upper breast. **1stW:** dark tips to secondaries on upperwing; tail with broad dark terminal band and paler base; bill all dark; lores and forehead whitish. **2ndW:** pink bill with black tip; dark grey back and white rump; head whitish, dusky around eye. **Status:** commoner in eastern coasts.

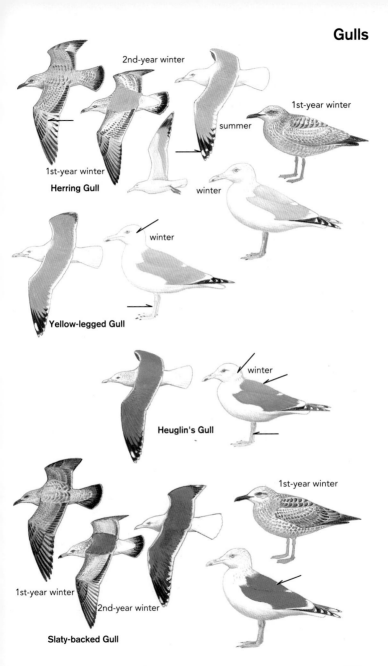

Gulls

2nd-year winter

1st-year winter

Herring Gull

summer

winter

1st-year winter

Yellow-legged Gull

winter

Heuglin's Gull

winter

1st-year winter

1st-year winter

2nd-year winter

Slaty-backed Gull

GLAUCOUS-WINGED GULL *Larus glaucescens* <Surigalmaegi> WV/r L 65cm • W 134cm. **Ad:** wings pale grey; wing-tips greyer with white tips. **Br:** white head and dark pink legs. **Non-Br:** brown streaks on crown and hindneck. **Juv/1stY:** grey-brown body and tail lacks much contrast; upper wing-coverts are finely speckled brown, primaries greyish; large black bill becomes pinkish at base. **2ndY:** wing-coverts and back greyish; bill has more black on tip than Glaucous Gull. **Similar species:** Juv. Slaty-backed Gull has dark-brown wing-tips and dark patch around the eye. Wing tips of Glaucous Gull are white, of other large white gulls are black. **Habitat:** coasts, harbours, open sea.

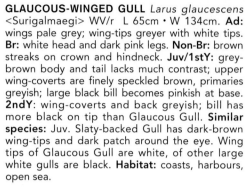

GLAUCOUS GULL *Larus hyperboreus* <Huin-galmaegi> WV/sc L 70cm • W 137cm. Large gull with small eye, large head on thick neck and very pale grey upper wings and mantle, all flight feathers tipped white. **Ad. Non-Br:** streaks on head and nape; bill yellow. **Juv:** even pale brown, scaled on back and upper wings. **1stW:** 2/3 of bill pinkish with clear-cut black tip. **2ndW:** more mottled with pale tip to pink and black bill. **Similar species:** like Iceland Gull but larger, bill and head appear heavier, proportionately shorter, blunt-tipped wings; beware leucistic gulls of other species which can look very similar. **Habitat:** coasts, estuaries, ocean.

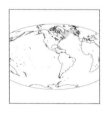

ICELAND GULL *Larus glaucoides* <Jageunhuin-galmaegi> Vag L 60cm • W 127cm. Very similar to larger Glaucous Gull but has smaller bill, more rounded head and shorter legs; projection of the primaries beyond the tail is obviously longer than its bill length; bill sometimes greenish yellow. **Juv:** similar to juv. Glaucous but smaller bill is smudged dark for half its length and fades into paler pinkish or darkish base. **Habitat:** ocean, coasts. **Status:** One record at Goseong, Gangwon-do on December 1997.

IVORY GULL *Pagophila eburnea* <Bukgeuk-huingalmaegi> Vag L 43cm • W 110cm. Unmistakable, very white, black-legged, arctic gull lacking marked seasonal variation. **Adult:** wholly white with yellowish bill. **1stW:** brownish bar across upper wing-coverts and blackish tips to flight feathers; black markings around lores and throat. **Habitat:** seas.

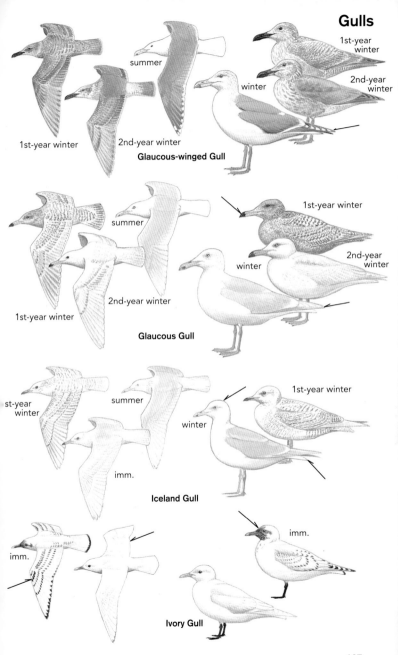

Gulls

Glaucous-winged Gull

1st-year winter

summer

2nd-year winter

winter

1st-year winter

2nd-year winter

Glaucous Gull

1st-year winter

summer

2nd-year winter

winter

1st-year winter

2nd-year winter

Iceland Gull

st-year winter

summer

imm.

winter

1st-year winter

Ivory Gull

imm.

imm.

WHISKERED TERN *Chlidonias hybridus* <Gure-narutjebigalmaegi> PM/r L 25cm · W 69cm. **Br:** black cap, white 'whiskers' across face and grey body; darker grey underparts from neck to belly; pale grey wing-coverts; dark red bill and legs. **Non-Br:** white forehead; solid black ear patch extends up and round rear of crown on to streaked hindneck; white underparts; pale grey back and mantle. **Juv:** scaly brownish-black back contrasts with pale grey rump and wings; tail often with dark terminal band; wing usually lacks dark carpal bar. **Similar species:** White-winged Black Tern has black face (Br.), or black crown extending to the face (Non-Br.). Juv. has dark back with white rump. **Habitat:** seashore, marshes, rivers, lakes. **Status:** Recorded at Yeongjongdo, Namyangman (Gyeonggi-do), and Songjiho (Gangwon-do).

WHITE-WINGED BLACK TERN *Chlidonias leucoptera* <Huinjukjigalmaegi> PM/r L 23cm · W 66cm. **Br:** black head, back, underwing-coverts and underparts contrast with whitish upper wings, white tail and tail coverts; shortish black bill, dark red legs. **Non-Br:** pale grey wings; mostly white body including rump; white crown streaked darker; separated dark ear-spot. **Juv:** dark back contrasts with white rump and pale wings, which have dark carpal bar along front edge; has more distinct white collar than Whiskered Tern; tail pale grey with white edges. **Habitat:** Seashore, marshes, rivers, lakes. **Status:** Recorded along most parts of the western seaboard, Nakdong-gang(Gyeongsangnam-do) and Sok cho(Gangwon-do); more often seen than Whiskered Tern.

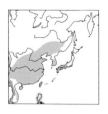

LITTLE TERN *Sterna albifrons* <Soejebigalmaegi> SV/c · PM/c L 24cm · W 53cm. Small tern with pale upperparts, and gently forked tail. **Br:** white forehead with black lores, crown and nape; legs yellow, and bill yellow with black tip. **Non-Br:** forecrown and lores become white, legs duller and bill black. **Juv:** crown and nape brown; back scaly. Hovers close to sea surface before diving. **Habitat:** coasts, estuaries, rivers, lakes.

Terns

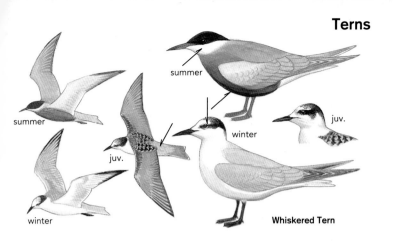

summer

summer

juv.

winter

summer

juv.

winter

Whiskered Tern

summer

summer

juv.

winter

juv.

winter

White-winged Black Tern

summer

summer

Little Tern

juv.

winter

GREATER CRESTED TERN [Crested Tern] *Thalasseus bergii* <Keunjebigalmaegi> Vag L 45cm • W 104cm. Large tern with dark-grey upperparts, large greenish-yellow bill and black legs. **Br:** white forehead with complete black cap and crest. **Non-Br:** forehead and crown mostly white, hindcrown and nape remain black, crest shorter. **Juv:** upperparts dark brown with pale fringes; in flight 3 dark bars along inner wing; bill dull yellow. **Habitat:** coasts, estuaries. **Status:** Single specimen record from an island near Incheon city, on 5 July 1917.

GULL-BILLED TERN *Gelochelidon nilotica* <Keunburijebigalmaegi> Vag L 38cm • W 94cm. Medium-sized tern with thick, black, rather short bill, very pale grey, broader wings, shortish, shallowly forked tail and black legs; in flight, shows noticeable dark trailing edge to outer primaries. **Br:** black cap. **Non-Br:** white head with black patch through eye to ear-coverts. **Juv:** pale brown wash from crown to hindneck; back and wings may show brown edges to feathers, but not as strongly as other terns. **Habitat:** coasts, estuaries, lakes. **Status:** two records; one at Jeju-do on 29 April 1993 and two at Asanman on 30 September 1993.

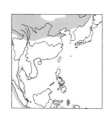

COMMON TERN *Sterna hirundo* <Jebigalmaegi> PM/c L 36cm • W 80cm. Medium-sized tern with deeply forked tail and pale grey wings, all ages showing broad black tips to outer primaries of underwings; at rest, wings reach tail tip. **Br:** black crown; race longipennis has black bill and black, sometimes dark-red, legs; race minussensis has red bill and legs. **Non-Br:** white forehead; black edges to outer tail. **Juv:** As non-Br, but dark brown crown and dark carpal bar; usually brownish wash and scaling on mantle; legs orange. **Habitat:** coasts, estuaries, lakes.

SOOTY TERN *Sterna fuscata* <Geomeundeungjebi-galmaegi> Vag L 44cm • W 90cm. Large, blackish-backed tern lacking much seasonal variation, with strongly forked tail, black bill and legs. **Ad:** white on forehead does not extend behind eyes. **Juv:** upperparts blackish brown tipped with buff-white; underparts mostly blackish-brown, with underwing-coverts and lower belly whitish-grey. **Habitat:** coasts, seas.

Terns

summer

summer

winter

juv.

Greater Crested Tern

winter

summer

winter

juv.

summer

Gull-billed Tern

summer

summer

winter

summer

Subsp. *minussensis*

imm.

Common Tern

juv.

Sooty Tern

Auks (Alcids)

Family Alcidae (World : 22 species, Korea : 8 species) Small to medium-sized seabirds of the northern oceans. This group includes guillemots, (or murres) murrelets, puffins, and auklets. Generally have large heads, short tails, plump bodies, and short legs. Plumage is usually black, and many are white below. Fly rapidly with fast wingbeats; propel themselves underwater with their wings. Predominantly pelagic; breed in colonies on rocky islands and cliffs. Sexes are similar.

COMMON GUILLEMOT [Thin-billed Murre] *Uria aalge* <Badaori> WV/r L 43cm. A large auk with a longish black bill. **Br:** Blackish-brown head, throat and upperparts; white underparts; narrow white line behind eye; in flight shows white edge to primaries from above; black underwings have white underwing-coverts; dark greyish legs. **Non-Br:** White extends to throat and face; black line from eye across ear-coverts. **Similar species:** Brunnich's Guillemot has thicker bill usually with white line along base of upper mandible (could occur as vagrant).

SPECTACLED GUILLEMOT *Cepphus carbo* <Huinnunsseopbadaori> WV/r L 37cm. Conspicuous white spectacles and bright red feet. **Br:** Black with large white spectacles that extend behind the eye, and white at base of black bill. **Non-Br:** Chin, throat, foreneck, and underparts white; small white spectacles and greyish sides to neck make distinctive pattern. **Similar species:** Pigeon Guillemot has conspicuous white wing-coverts in both Br. and Non-Br. plumages; head all-black in Br., light and mottled in Non-Br. (could occur as vagrant).

RHINOCEROS AUKLET [Horn-billed Puffin] *Cerorhinca monocerata* <Huinsuyeombadaori> Res/sc(n) • WV/sc L 37cm. Stocky, guillemot-sized auklet with thick, reddish bill, resembling slender-billed puffin; flies low, and sits low in water, sometimes with tail cocked showing whitish undertail coverts; upperparts blackish-brown; throat, flanks brownish grey; belly to rear dirty white; legs yellowish with grey webs to toes. **Br:** short yellowish horn projects from base of bill; two white facial plumes. **Non-Br:** head sooty, horn and plumes absent; belly darker. **Juv/1stW:** as non-br. but smaller, brownish bill. **Status:** Breeds on some North Korean islands.

Auks (Alcids)

Common Guillemot

summer

summer

winter

Spectacled Guillemot

summer

summer

winter

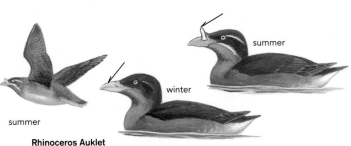

Rhinoceros Auklet

summer

winter

summer

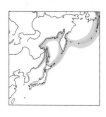

MARBLED MURRELET *Brachyramphus marmoratus* <Allaksoe-ori> WV/sc L 24.5cm. Smallish, with long, slender, black bill, sloping forehead and long, thin neck. **Br:** speckled brown, darker on upperparts and wings; white scapulars. **Non-Br:** blackish cap, hindneck and upperparts; white below; long white scapular lines, and white sides to rump noticeable at take-off. **Imm/Sub-Ad:** as Non-Br. for 1-2 years. **Similar species:** Non-Br. Ancient Murrelet. **Habitat:** seas.

ANCIENT MURRELET *Synthliboramphus antiquus* <Badasoe-ori> WV/c · Res/uc L 25.5cm. Commonest auklet in Korean waters. Dark above, white below; black cap and half collar, bluish-grey back; short bill; white side of neck; white underwing-coverts. **Br:** white stripe from above eye to nape; grey back outlined by black line along sides; bill pale. **Non-Br:** lacks head stripes; white sides of nape obvious; bill less pale. **Similar species:** Japanese Murrelet. **Habitat:** seas.

CRESTED MURRELET [Japanese Murrelet] *Synthliboramphus wumizusume* <Ppulsoe-ori> Res/r L 24cm. Resembles Ancient but has larger, pale bluish bill, black crest and broad white stripes from front of crown that meet on nape in Br., more white on chin and throat; center of crown, face and hindneck black, extending along flight feathers and outlining slaty blue upperparts; underparts white; underwing white, edged black. **Non-Br:** crest shorter. **Habitat:** seas.

WHISKERED AUKLET *Aethia pygmaea* <Huin-suyeomjageunbadaori> Vag L 17cm. Slightly larger than Least Auklet and darker below, with 3 white plumes on head; black crest curls forward from forehead; two white plumes extend from lores - one above eye, another below; third plume extends from behind eye; bright red bill with white tip. **Juv-1stW:** no crest, only traces of plumes; bill black. **Habitat:** seas.

LEAST AUKLET *Aethia pusilla* <Jageunbadaori> Vag L 15cm. Tiny, with stubby bill, and white scapular bar on black back **Br:** single white plume behind eye; red tip to stubby bill; throat white; breast, underparts, and sides white variably mottled with dark sooty-brown. **Non-Br:** more white on face; white scapular bar visible in flight; bill black; white underparts. **Habitat:** seas.

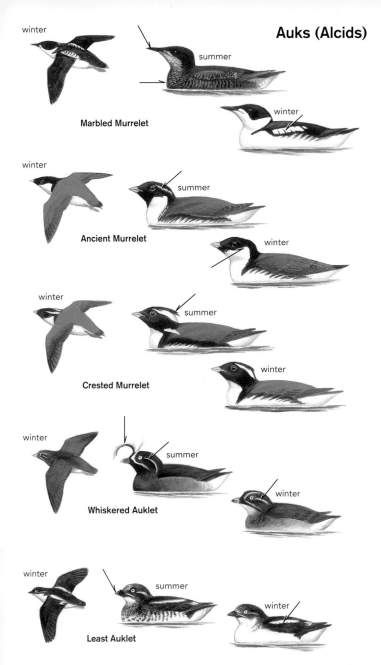

Auks (Alcids)

winter

summer

Marbled Murrelet

winter

winter

summer

Ancient Murrelet

winter

winter

summer

Crested Murrelet

winter

winter

summer

Whiskered Auklet

winter

winter

summer

Least Auklet

winter

Sandgrouses
Family Pteroclididae (World : 16 species, Korea : 1 species) Have short bills and pointed wings and tail. Short legs are feathered. Sexes different in plumage.

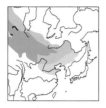

PALLAS' SANDGROUSE *Syrrhaptes paradoxus* <Samak-kkwong> Vag L 38cm. **Male:** needle-like central tail feathers; pale yellowish-brown upperparts speckled with black; mostly orange head with yellowish-grey cheeks, crown and nape; in flight shows contrasting black, central belly-patch, buffy underwing-coverts and whitish flight feathers. **Female:** darker scaling on body than male; sandy throat separated by narrow blackish line from breast. **Habitat:** grasslands, openfields.

Pigeons and Doves
Family Columbidae (World : 301 species, Korea : 7 species) A distinct group of plump, small-headed birds with pointed wings, short legs and crooning voices. Flight is strong and direct, Walk frequently, bobbing their heads. Feed on fruits, seeds, buds, etc. Lay one or two eggs. Sexes are similar in most species.

BLACK WOOD PIGEON *Columba janthina* <Heukbidulgi> Res/sc(l) L 40cm. Largest pigeon in Korea. Blackish, glossed with purple on head and shoulder, green on breast; legs red. **Voice:** long, wailing 'oot-oo, oot-oo' or 'krii-kru'. **Habitat:** broad-leaved evergreen woodlands on remote islands.

HILL PIGEON *Columba rupestris* <Yangbidulgi> Res/sc L 33cm. Similar to Domestic Pigeon but easily distinguished by white on tail, and paler belly. Grey rump contrasts with pale lower back and broad white subterminal tail band; tail tipped black; two black wing-bars on folded wing; has reddish legs and eyes, and black bill with pink cere. Gregarious. **Voice:** 'gut-gut-gut'. **Habitat** cliffs, bridges, and buildings mainly on islands or coastal areas.

STOCK DOVE *Columba oenas* <Bunhonggaseum-bidulgi> Vag L 33cm. Similar to Domestic Dove but more compact; plumage more blue-grey with grey underwings and rump, and wider black terminal bar on tail; folded wing shows 2 short black bars on secondaries; purplish gloss on breast and green and pink gloss on sides of neck; bill pink at base with yellowish tip; very dark eye. **Habitat:** cultivated fields, forest edges.

Sandgrouses, Pigeons, Doves

Pallas' Sandgrouse

Black Wood Pigeon

Hill Pigeon

Stock Dove

COLLARED DOVE *Streptopelia decaocto* <Yeomjubidulgi> Res/r L 33cm. Similar to female Red Turtle Dove, but much larger and longer tailed, with greyer breast; pale dusty brownish-grey plumage with black band on nape; distinct dark primaries in flight; red legs; bill black. **Juv:** duller, browner, lacks neck bar, buffish fringes above. **Voice:** deep 'coo-cooo, cuk'. **Habitat:** Open country, cultivation near coastal areas, islands.

RED-COLLARED DOVE *Streptopelia tranquebarica* <Hongbidulgi> Vag L 23cm. Small dove with black band on nape. **Male:** vinaceous pink with grey head; grey tail has black outer feathers tipped white forming white corners; white undertail coverts. **Female:** paler, more brownish plumage. Juv. buffish fringes above, sometimes lacks neck bar. **Voice:** urgent, rather rasping, 'kr-kru-kr-kr', repeated rapidly without a pause. **Habitat:** fields, forest edges. **Status:** three records; one record in South Korea at Chuja-do, Jeju-do on August 1993.

RUFOUS TURTLE DOVE *Streptopelia orientalis* <Metbidulgi> Res/c L 33cm. Common dove with greyish or pinkish brown underparts; black stripes with whitish edges on each side of the neck; back and scapulars blackish brown with rufous edges; rump and uppertail coverts grey; dark tail with pale grey tip. **Juv:** neck patch indistinct; pale fringes to plumage. **Voice:** deep, sleepy 'croo, croo, croo-croooo', 3rd and 4th notes higher and faster. **Habitat:** wooded areas, open fields, cultivated fields.

WHITE-BELLIED GREEN PIGEON *Treron sieboldii* <Nokseakbidulgi> Vag L 33cm. Yellowish-green plumage with darker, slaty flight feathers, paler underparts and greyish-white belly; undertail coverts greenish-white with dark green centres; bill blue, legs pink; wing-coverts chestnut in male, green in female. **Voice:** eerie, slow wailing 'ah-, oh-, ah-, oh-' **Habitat:** broad-leaved mountain forests along seacoast.

Doves, Pigeons

Collared Dove

Red-collared Dove ♂ ♀

Rufous Turtle Dove

White-bellied Green Pigeon ♂ ♀

Cuckoos

Family Cuculidae (World : 139 species, Korea : 6 species) Slender birds with long pointed wings and long graduated tails. Bills slightly decurved. All 6 species in Korea lay their eggs in other birds' nests. Usually heard calling from the tree tops, where they can be very difficult to see, their presence sometimes being indicated by the noisy mobbing of small birds. Two toes point forward and 2 backward. Some species have rufous and grey morphs. Best distinguished by calls in the field.

HODGSON'S HAWK CUCKOO *Cuculus fugax* <Maesachon> SV/uc • PM/uc L 32cm. Slate-coloured above and rufous below with whitish throat; distinct yellow eyering; greenish yellow at base of bill; may showwhite bands on nape and on back(inner tertial). **Juv:** browner with pale tips to coverts and brown streaks on underparts. **Voice:** Repeated 'ju-ichi' or 'gee--whiz', often at night. **Similar species:** like accipiters but flight weaker; tail broader and strongly rounded; bill longer. **Habitat:** forest; second growth. **Status:** considered as distinct species by some authors, *C. hyperythrus*.

INDIAN CUCKOO *Cuculus micropterus* <Geomeundeungppeo-kkugi> SV/uc L 33cm Grey head; dark, grey-brown upperparts, tail with broad subterminal black band and white tip; undertail coverts unbarred. **Similar species:** Common and Oriental Cuckoos, but overall colour and tail pattern differ. **Voice:** Loud 'ka-ka-ka-ko', 4th note lower. **Habitat:** forests.

COMMON CUCKOO *Cuculus canorus* <Ppeo-kkugi> SV/c L 35cm. **Ad:** grey or rufous-brown upperparts contrasting with darker tail; prominent yellow iris and eyering; barring on underparts narrower and duller than other cuckoos; undertail coverts bright white, with narrow, broken barring. **Female:** may have brown tinge on breast; rufous morphs also occur. **Imm:** white spot on nape. **Juv:** variable; throat and breast whitish; upperparts dark brown; with light brown and whitish bars above, dark bars below. **Voice:** loud, mellow 'cuc-coo', 2nd syllable lower; also various bubbling trills. **Habitat:** forest edges, open countries including wetlands, cultivatied fields.

Cuckoos

Hodgson's Hawk Cuckoo

juv.

Indian Cuckoo

red phase ♀

Common Cuckoo

♂ ♀

red phase ♀

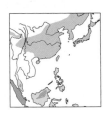

ORIENTAL CUCKOO *Cuculus saturatus* <Beong-eorippeo-kkugi> SV/uc L 33cm. Very similar to Common Cuckoo, often indistinguishable in the field unless calling, but blackish bars on underparts broader and stronger, and often washed rufous below, especially females; back and wings slightly darker, bluer grey; undertail coverts pale buff, unbarred to strongly barred and visible in flight; yellow to brown iris. **Female:** rufous morphs occur. **Juv:** variable; throat and breast whitish; upperparts dark brown; with fine whitish bars above, dark bars below; rufous morph juv. also has fine chestnut barring above. **Voice:** typically an even, monotonous 'po-pop,' (similar to call of hoopoe), usually preceded by loud, rapid 'po-po-po-pop' and often also some grating notes. **Habitat:** forests.

LITTLE CUCKOO *Cuculus poliocephalus* <Dugyeoni> SV/uc L 28cm. Often indistinguishable from Common and Oriental Cuckoo in field unless calling, but smaller and slimmer; black barring on underparts often bolder and more widely spaced than Oriental, undertail coverts off-white, with barring lacking or broken. **Female:** rufous morphs occur, sometimes being unmarked on crown, nape and rump. **Juv:** Similar to Juv. Oriental Cuckoo. **Voice:** loud, staccato whistle 'pot-pot chip-chip-to-you', 2nd pair of notes somewhat higher than the lst, the last note lower. **Habitat:** forests, open scrub, hills.

RED-WINGED CRESTED CUCKOO [Chestnut-winged Cuckoo] *Clamator coromandus* <Bamsaengnalgaeppeo-kkugi> Vag L 46cm. Large cuckoo, shaped like a magpie, with distinct crest and chestnut wings, black upperparts and whitish underparts with buffy rufous throat and upper breast. **Imm:** upperparts scaled with rufous; throat and upper breast whitish. **Voice:** loud and harsh 'creech-creech-creech'. **Habitat:** forests and second growth. Sometimes near habitation. **Status:** one record; one juvenile was observed with Black-billed Magpie at Jeju-do on April 1994.

Cuckoos

red phase

♀

juv.

♂

♀

Oriental Cuckoo

Little Cuckoo

red phase
♀

Red-winged Crested Cuckoo

OWLS
Family Strigidae (World : 160 species, Korea : 11 species)
Nocturnal birds of prey. Characterized by large forward-facing eyes, flat facial disks, short feathered legs, and hooked bills. Fly silently on broad rounded wing. All have distinctive calls usually made at night. Several have well-developed 'ear-tufts' which can be erected but often lie flat. A few species are moderately active by day. Normally sexes alike in colour, but females larger than males.

SNOWY OWL *Nyctea scandiaca* <Huinolppaemi> Vag L 60cm. Unmistakable, large, white owl of open country, occasionally active by day; yellow eyes. **Male:** nearly pure white. **Female:** finely barred with black. **Habitat:** open country, grasslands along seacoasts.

EURASIAN EAGLE OWL *Bubo bubo* <Suribu-eong-i> Res/sc L 66cm. Huge owl with large orange-yellow eyes and long ear tufts; facial disk outlined with black; upperwings are fairly uniform rusty brown, and underwings lack strong contrast; breast thickly spotted and streaked with dark brown, belly with fine vermiculations; legs and toes covered with tawny feathers. **Juv:** white 'lips' and inner eyebrows. **Voice:** booming 'ooo-hu' **Habitat:** forests, rocky mountains, often near cliffs.

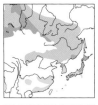

LONG-EARED OWL *Asio otus* <Chikbueong-i> WV/uc L 38cm. Longish, narrow wings and prominent, long ear tufts; streaked and narrowly vermiculated underparts, streaking continuing on to belly; variable ground colour from whitish to rich rufous-buff; orange eyes; tips of primaries with 4-5 narrow dark bars. Nocturnal. **Habitat:** prefers coniferous forests.

SHORT-EARED OWL *Asio flammeus* <Soebueong-i> WV/uc L 38.5cm. Open country owl typically roosting on ground. Has short ear tufts; ground colour variable, usually paler than Long-eared Owl, breast appearing darkest due to heavy streaking; unstreaked on belly and lacks any vermiculations on underparts; tail strongly barred dark brown; yellow eyes. In flight, shows white or pale trailing edge to wing and 2-3 black bands on tips of primaries, making wingtips appear dark. Nocturnal, but often hunts in daylight. **Habitat** open grasslands near rivers and marshes.

Owls

Snowy Owl ♂ ♀

Eurasian Eagle Owl

Long-eared Owl

Short-eared Owl

TAWNY OWL *Strix aluco* <Olppaemi> Res/uc L 38cm. Medium-sized, round-headed owl with broad, round wings; no ear tufts; narrowly vermiculated whitish underparts heavily streaked dark grey on breast; pale grey facial disk with dark brown eyes, pale bill, and white 'eyebrows' on forecrown. **Similar species:** Ural Owl is much larger, with longer, more evenly barred tail, and lacks vermiculations below. **Voice:** deep 'boo-', followed at an interval by a long tremulous 'oo-oo-ohoo-'. **Habitat:** woodlands, mountain forests.

URAL OWL *Strix uralensis* <Ginjeombagiolppaemi> Res/r(n) L 50cm. Large owl with round facial discs edged darker on brows; ground colour from white to grey-brown; bill pale yellowish; eyes dark; lacks vermiculated markings on underparts; boldly barred, broad wings and tail. **Voice:** loud gruff 'wo-ho', barking 'haf'. **Habitat:** mountain forests, usually coniferous or mixed woodlands.

NORTHERN HAWK OWL *Surnia ulula* <Ginkkori-olppaemi> Vag L 38cm. Medium-sized owl, with mottled brown upperparts and conspicuous white scapular lines; buff underparts with dark barring below breast; face whitish outlined on sides with black; two pale patches on nape create false face. In flight, has hawk-like appearance with relatively long tail and narrow, bluntly pointed wings, but head is much larger than a hawk. Active by day, flying with strong beats mixed with glides, and perching fearlessly in open. **Voice:** brief 'kirit, kirit' **Habitat:** mountain forest edge; mainly coniferous or mixed woodlands.

BROWN HAWK OWL *Ninox scutulata* <Solbueong-i> SV/uc L 29cm. Dark chocolate-brown upperparts, dark greyish-brown head and blackish bill; may show whitish patch between large, yellow eyes; head lacks prominent facial disks and ear tufts; creamy-white underparts marked with broad rich-brown streaks and spots; longish tail with black bars. **Juv:** underparts brownish-white, lacking clear pattern of adult. Nocturnal. **Voice:** mellow, repeated whistle 'hoo-ho', rising on '-ho' **Habitat:** woodlands, city parks in mountains and lowlands.

Owls

Tawny Owl

Ural Owl

Brown Hawk Owl

Northern Hawk Owl

187

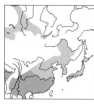

EURASIAN SCOPS OWL *Otus scops* <Sojjeoksae> Res/uc • PM/uc L 20cm. Very similar to Collared Scops Owl, but smaller in size, with yellow eyes, and lacking greyish collar on nape. Best distinguished by voice. **Voice:** repeated, high, 'choik, choi-choik'. **Habitat:** forests in low mountains and lowlands, city parks.

COLLARED SCOPS OWL *Otus lempiji* <Keun-sojjeoksae> Res/uc • PM/uc L 24cm. Similar to Eurasian Scops Owl, but slightly larger; with dark orange eyes; a greyish collar on nape. **Voice:** male: rising 'whoop'; female: soft, mellow, 'hoo-o', falling on second part of note. **Habitat:** forests in low mountains and lowlands.

LITTLE OWL *Athene noctua* <Geumnunsoe-olppaemi> Res/r(n) • WV/r L 23cm. Small, often diurnal, owl with broad rounded head and no ear tufts; crown with fine white spots; white brows slope in towards pale bill; dark-brown upperparts spotted with white; whitish underparts streaked with brown; yellow eyes. Nocturnal, but sometimes active by day, and often seen perched in open; bobs up and down on perch when excited. Undulating flight over longer distances. **Habitat:** open country, old walls, wooded areas.

Nightjars

Family Caprimulgidae (World : 83 species, Korea : 1 species) Nocturnal birds with marvellously soft owl-like plumage, intricately cryptic in pattern and coloration. Spend daylight hours on ground or perched lengthwise on horizontal branches. They are solitary birds with large eyes, huge gape and well-developed rictal bristles for funnelling insect prey on the wing.

JUNGLE NIGHTJAR [Grey Nightjar] *Caprimulgus indicus* <Ssokdoksae> SV/c L 29cm, Well camouflaged with heavily barred, spotted and speckled markings; white submoustachial streak and patches on sides of throat. Shows long, slender wings and tail in flight. **Male:** white patches near wingtip and on outer tail feathers, visible in flight. **Female:** white wing and tail patches of male replaced by buff, not distinct in flight. **Voice:** Sharp 'chuck' repeated rapidly, 6 per sec, usually at dusk and dawn. **Habitat:** open forests, scrubs, clearings.

Owls, Nightjars

rufous phase

Eurasian Scops Owl

Collared Scops Owl

Little Owl

Jungle Nightjar

Swifts

Family Apodidae (World : 92 species, Korea : 3 species) Small, agile fliers with long, slender, sickle-like wings, and short feet. Similar to swallows, but different wing-shape and wing-stroke. Seldom land. Gregarious. Catch aerial insects and nesting materials in wide mouth on the wing. Needletails are among the fastest flying birds. Sexes alike.

WHITE-THROATED NEEDLE-TAILED SWIFT *Hirundapus caudacutus* <Baneulkkorikalsae> PM/uc L 21cm • W 50cm. Largest swift in Korea with a short square, tail; pointed bare feather shafts at tip of tail rarely visible in the field; throat and undertail coverts contrastingly white, small, white patches on tertials; wings often show characteristic sickle shape, rather narrower near bend of wing, bulging out along trailing edge of primaries. **Juv:** often has dark markings on undertail coverts. Can fly very fast, making 'whooshing' noise. **Habitat:** open areas, forests, mountains.

HOUSE SWIFT *Apus affinis* <Soekalsae> Vag L 13cm • W 28cm. Small with shallowly forked short tail; fork disappears when tail is fanned; trailing edge of primaries straight or curving in. Plumage blackish with white rump and throat. More fluttery flight than White-rumped Swift. **Habitat:** shoreline cliffs, caves, rocky islets; also often near civilization. **Status:** recorded at Jeju-do and Hataedo, Jeollanam-do.

WHITE-RUMPED SWIFT *Apus pacificus* <Kalsae> SV/c L 20cm • W 43cm. Typical swift of coastal areas. Similar to House Swift, but larger and has longer, more deeply forked tail, the fork still visible when tail fanned; scaly bars on blackish underparts are only visible at close range; silhouette shows longer tail than other swifts; trailing edge of primaries usually straight or curving in (as shown, though wings usually appear narrower). **Habitat:** shoreline cliffs, islets, mountains. **Status:** common summer visitor in many islands. small numbers on coastal areas during migration season.

Swifts

White-throated Needle-tailed Swift

House Swift

White-rumped Swift

Kingfishers

Family Alcedinidae (World : 92 species, Korea : 4 species) Large-headed birds with long massive pointed bills, short legs, tails, and necks. Most live near water feeding mainly on fish, but several are forest birds, and catch amphibians, reptiles or insects. Flight rapid and direct; some can hover.

GREATER PIED KINGFISHER *Megaceryle lugubris* <Ppulhobansae> Vag L 38cm, Large kingfisher with shaggy double crest, barred black-and-white on crown back and wings; black bill with tiny pale tip. **Ad:** Wing lining and axillaries white in male, rufous in female. **Male:** rufous patch in streaked submoustachial, and rufous mixed in with black spots of the breastband. **Habitat:** streams, lakes, mountain rivers.

BLACK-CAPPED KINGFISHER *Halcyon pileata* <Cheonghobansae> SV/c L 30cm. Black cap, red bill, deep blue upperparts with white collar, throat and centre of breast, with rufous underparts; in flight shows obvious white patches at base of black-tipped primaries, and also black shoulders. **Imm:** rufous collar and scaly black mottling on upper breast. **Voice:** loud, shrill, cackling 'kahaha', or 'kyorr, kyorr' in alarm. **Habitat:** wooded streams, rice-fields, coastal areas.

RUDDY KINGFISHER *Halcyon coromanda* <Hobansae> SV/uc L 27cm. Secretive, forest kingfisher. Plumage rufous, darker above with purplish gloss, and paler chin and throat; narrow blue line on the rump; large bill and short legs red. **Juv:** paler; with scaly black mottling around neck and breast. **Voice:** loud, rolling, and descendants 'kirrrrrrr-.' **Habitat:** deciduous woods and forests near mountain streams.

COMMON KINGFISHER *Alcedo atthis* <Mulchongsae> SV/c • Res/r L 17cm. Smallest kingfisher. Bluish-green upperparts scaled with brighter spots contrast with orange underparts; white throat and neck patch, orange lores and ear-coverts; bright blue line down centre of back; bill black, but lower mandible reddish in female. **Juv:** duller, breast streaked brownish lores and ear-coverts orange-buff. **Voice:** high-pitched 'tuu', often trilling when chasing its mate or a rival 'ti-ti-ti-ti'. **Habitat:** streams, rivers, lakes in open country.

Kingfishers

Greater Pied Kingfisher

Black-capped Kingfisher

Ruddy Kingfisher

hovering

juv.

Common Kingfisher

193

Rollers
Family Coraciidae (World : 12 species, Korea : 1 species)
Stout birds with broad wings, hooked strong bills, and big heads. Often seen waiting on exposed perches such as electric poles or treetops to chase aerial insects. Their name comes from their acrobatic courtship flight.

BROAD-BILLED ROLLER [Dollarbird] *Eurystomus orientalis* <Parangsae> SV/c L 29.5cm. Large-headed, dark bird with distinct white patches at base of primaries in flight. Body blue-green, bluer on throat and wings, with brown head, and prominent red bill and feet; often appears blackish in bright light. **Juv:** bill appears blackish. **Voice:** repeated, grating 'ket-ket-ket'. **Habitat:** forests, forest edges.

Hoopoes
Family Upupidae (World : 1 species, Korea : 1 species)
Medium-sized birds with long, full, erectile crests and long, slender, slightly decurved bills. Wing broad and rounded. Sexes alike. Flight undulating.

HOOPOE *Upupa epops* <Hututi> SV/c L 28cm. Unmistakable. Light pinkish-brown plumage with boldly barred black-and-white wings and tail; black-tipped crest usually carried flat on head. **Voice** low, soft 'hoop- hoop-hoop', call rather similar to Oriental Cuckoo. **Habitat:** open woodlands, open country, cultivated fields, lawns.

Pittas
Family Pittidae (World : 29 species, Korea : 1 species) Large-headed, plump birds with short necks and tails. Many are colourful, but usually secretive and difficult to observe. Terrestrial, but sometimes call from branches. Usually stay in undergrowth and feed on earthworms and insects.

FAIRY PITTA *Pitta brachyura* <Palsaekjo> SV/r • PM/r L 18cm. Unmistakable. Brilliantly coloured with distinct, broad, black mask through eye to nape, and red patch on buffy lower belly; white patch on wing when flushed from undergrowth is diagnostic. **Voice:** loud, mellow whistle 'wee-weep, wee-weep'. **Habitat:** mainly broad-leaved forests, often close to streams. **Status:** breeding in Jeju-do and islands of south coast. A few records in Gwangneung, Gyeonggi-do.

Rollers, Hoopoes, Pittas

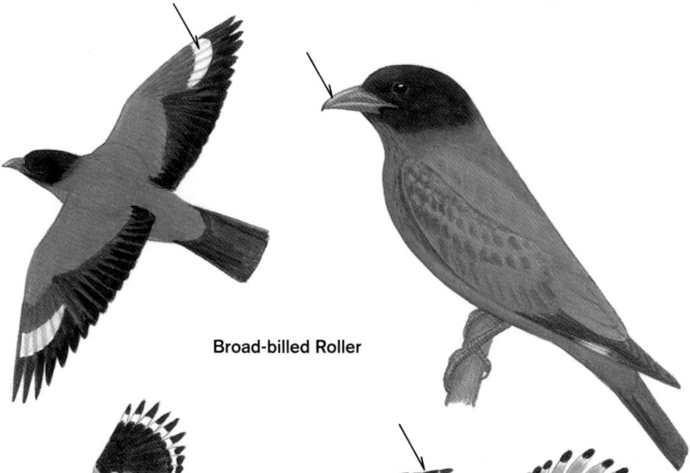

Broad-billed Roller

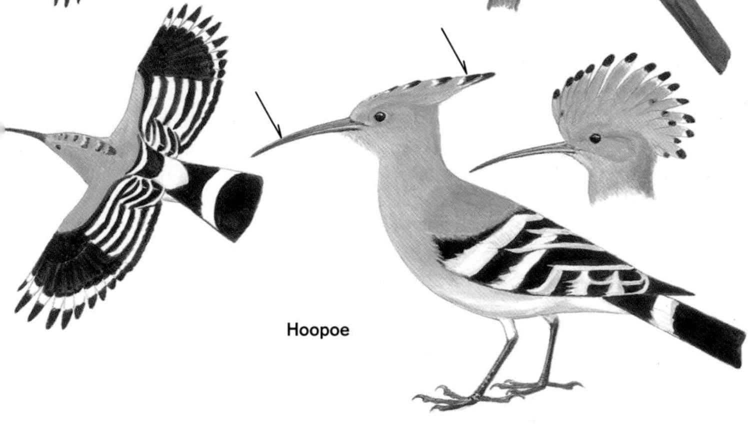

Hoopoe

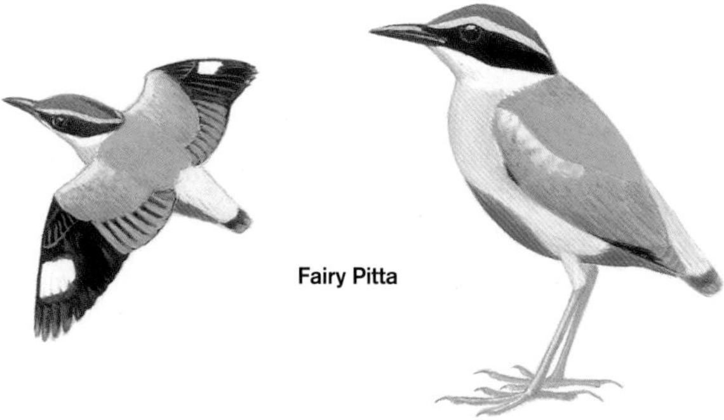

Fairy Pitta

Woodpeckers

Family Picidae (World : 200 species, Korea : 11 species) Unmistakable tree-climbing birds with straight chisel bills, long barbed tongue and stiff pointed tail feathers. Feed mostly on wood- and bark-boring insects, although some feed on ants on the ground. Nest in tree holes. Undulating flight. Woodpeckers are sexually dimorphic in head colour or pattern. Many 'drum' on trees.

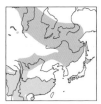

WRYNECK *Jynx torquilla* <Gaemijabi> WV/r • Res/r(n) L 18cm. Cryptic nightjar-like pattern distinctive. Mottled above and barred below, with broad dark stripe down nape and back; looks all grey-brown at a distance. Clings to tree-trunks but, unlike woodpeckers, often perches across branches with the pointed bill angled upward; often feeds on ground. **Voice:** constantly repeated 'kwee-kwee-'. **Habitat:** forest edges, sparse woods, cultivation.

GREY-CAPPED WOODPECKER *Dendrocopos canicapillus* <Amulsoettakttaguri> Res/sc L 20cm. Brownish line from eye to ear-coverts and black line down side of neck gives distinctive head pattern; no red on streaked white underparts; squared white patch in center of blackish back and white patches on wing-coverts are diagnostic, in flight and when perched. **Male:** red streak behind and above eye. **Habitat:** wooded areas.

JAPANESE PYGMY WOODPECKER *Dendrocopos kizuki* <Soettakttaguri> Res/c L 15cm. Smallest woodpecker. Brownish-grey head with white supercilium, moustachial stripe, throat and neck patch; darker grey-brown upperparts with white barring; brownish-white underparts with brown streaks; no red on vent. **Male:** small red spot behind eye. Associates with mixed species flocks in winter. **Voice:** distinctive, grating 'gweeek'; 'zi-zi-zi'. **Habitat:** wooded areas.

LESSER SPOTTED WOODPECKER *Dendrocopos minor* <Soe-osaekttakttaguri> Res/r(n) L 16cm. Black moustache not joined to flat-looking crown; extensive white on forehead; no red on vent; underparts very faintly streaked. **Male:** red crown. **Female:** black crown. Associates with mixed species flocks in winter. **Voice:** high-pitched 'ki-ki-ki'. Drumming like a rattle, c.1.5secs. **Habitat:** wooded areas.

Woodpeckers

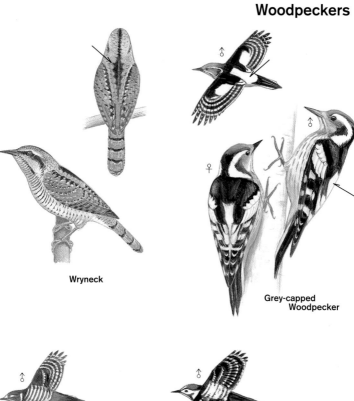

Wryneck

Grey-capped
Woodpecker

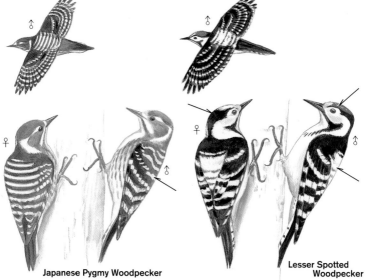

Japanese Pygmy Woodpecker

Lesser Spotted
Woodpecker

197

GREAT SPOTTED WOODPECKER *Dendrocopos major* <Osaekttakttaguri> Res/c L 24cm. Pied plumage with white barring on flight feathers of black wings, two large white patches on scapulars and black rump; no streaks on white underparts; contrasting red lower belly and undertail coverts; black moustachial line joins or nearly joins nape. **Male:** red nape. **Female:** black crown. **Juv:** red crown with black lateral stripe. **Voice:** sharp 'kik' often repeated once per second, sharper and higher pitched than White-backed Woodpecker. **Similar Species:** Lesser Spotted Woodpecker is much smaller and shorter-billed with no red on underparts; different face. **Habitat:** forests and wooded areas.

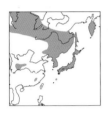

WHITE-BACKED WOODPECKER *Dendrocopos leucotos* <Keunosaekttakttaguri> Res/uc L 28cm. Resembles Great Spotted Woodpecker but larger, with coarse, black streaks on flanks, pinkish underparts; black upperparts with more barred, particularly on scapulars and centre of back. **Male/Juv:** crown red. **Female:** crown black. **Voice:** short, harsh 'kuok'; 'kyo, kyo, kyo'; drums c.2secs, accelerating to end. **Habitat:** mountain forests.

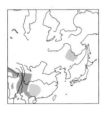

RUFOUS-BELLIED WOODPECKER *Dendrocopos hyperythrus* <Bulgeunbae-osaekttakttaguri> Res/r(n) L 24cm. Rufous underparts and sides of neck are diagnostic; dark brown upperparts with white barring with pale face, and red undertail coverts. **Male:** crown and nape red. **Female:** crown black with white spots. **Juv:** throat streaked brown on white; underparts barred; dark-brown wings spotted more than barred. **Voice:** calls with 'chi-i-i-i-i-i-i-i'. **Habitat:** forests.

THREE-TOED WOODPECKER *Picoides tridactylus* <Segarakttakttaguri> Res/r(n) L 22cm. Dark-looking, rather black-headed woodpecker having distinctive striped face with white line from eye to nape, and white moustachial stripe; broad white stripe down center of back; both sexes lack any red marking; 3 toes. **Male:** crown yellow. **Female:** crown black streaked with white. **Voice:** seldom vocal; call: 'kik' similar to Great-spotted Woodpecker but softer. **Habitat:** coniferous forests.

Woodpeckers

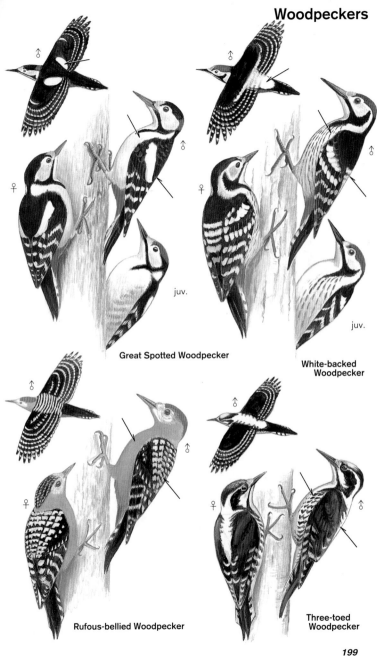

Great Spotted Woodpecker

White-backed
Woodpecker

Rufous-bellied Woodpecker

Three-toed
Woodpecker

juv.

juv.

♂

♀

♂

♀

♂

♀

♂

GREY-HEADED WOODPECKER *Picus canus* <Cheongttakttaguri> Res/c L 30cm. The only green woodpecker in Korea. Green wings and back with brighter rump, and grey head with thin black moustachial. Dark primaries with white spots. **Male:** red forehead. **Female:** slightly less distinct moustachial stripe than male. **Voice:** Descending 'pyo, pyo, pyo, pyo' 6-9 times, slowing after fast beginning. Loud drumming of c.1.5 secs. **Similar Species:** dark bill and plainer head separates from Black-Naped Oriole. **Habitat:** deciduous forests on low mountains and lowlands.

BLACK WOODPECKER *Dryocopus martius* <Kkamakttakttaguri> Res/sc L 45cm. Very large, with black plumage recalling crow, and pale, ivory-coloured bill. **Male:** red crown with slight crest. **Female:** red patch only on back of crown. **Juv:** duller and sootier, paler on throat. **Voice:** loud, grating 'kleea' or high, 'krii-, krii-, krii-, krii-'; loud drumming in spring, 2-3 secs. **Similar species:** see White-bellied Woodpecker. **Habitat:** Mixed woodlands, coniferous forests. **Status:** considered as a rare resident. But, after 1990, many new breeding areas (mainly mountain forest) are found in Gyeonggi-do and Gangwon-do, including Gwangneung, Gyeonggi-do.

WHITE-BELLIED WOODPECKER *Dryocopus javensis* <Keunaksae> Res/r L 46cm. Very large, distinctive, black woodpecker with black bill, white belly and rump. **Male:** red crown with slight crest and moustachial stripe. **Female:** head entirely black (unique to this highly endangered, endemic Korean subspecies). **Juv:** brownish. **Voice:** loud, sharp 'kiyow, kiyow' or 'kleea, kleea'. **Habitat:** mixed woodlands. **Status:** Gwangneung, Gyeonggi-do, and Seoraksan, Gangwon-do were known as a breeding areas, but no confirmed record after 1990 in South Korea. A few breeding areas are known in North Korea.

Woodpeckers

♂

♀

Grey-headed
Woodpecker

♂

♀

Black Woodpecker

♂

♂

White-bellied
Woodpecker

♀

Larks Family Alaudidae (World : 85 species, Korea : 4 species)

Brown streaked songbirds. Feed on the ground, walking, not hopping. Hind claw usually elongated. Varied musical song. Sexes alike.

GREATER SHORT-TOED LARK *Calandrella brachydactyla* <Soejongdari> Vag L 14cm. Compact, pale lark with short, pointed bill; sandy- or greyish-brown upperparts with strong dark streaks on back and crown; tertials almost completely cover primaries; distinct whitish supercilium, broken at forehead; ear-coverts unstreaked; buffy tinge on pale underparts; variable darker patches on neck and breast may be difficult to see, but are good field marks when present. Breast may have some fine streaks. **Voice:** call 'prripp'. **Habitat:** usually in open, dry habitats.

ASIAN SHORT-TOED LARK *Calandrella cheleensis* <Bukbangsoejongdari> PM/uc L 14cm. Rather nondescript, greyish lark, very similar to Greater Short-toed Lark, but 3-4, dark primary tips show clearly beyond tertials. Fine but strong streaking on crown, back and across breast, sometimes extends to flanks; indistinctly streaked on ear-coverts, supercilium less distinct; thicker bill; may show a crest. **Voice:** call: 'chidirr', 'chidiri', 'chilidi' 'chirididi'.

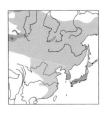

EURASIAN SKYLARK *Alauda arvensis* <Jongdari> Res/ab • WV/ab L 18cm. Noticeably crested; white outer tail feathers and white trailing edge to secondaries visible in flight. Rather undulating, erratic flight over long distances; soars and hovers during song flight. **Juv:** no crest, spotted. **Voice:** call: short 'byur-rup'. The only bird in Korea which sings continuously from high in the sky, though sometimes it will sing from a song post. **Status:** subspecies *A.a. arvensis* parachutes while singing; *A.a. japonica* does not, and also has a slightly different song and may prove to be a distinct species.

CRESTED LARK *Galerida cristata* <Ppuljongdari> Res/sc L 17cm. Large lark with very distinct spiky crest over rear of head; overall greyish sandy-brown, streaked above and on breast; long bill; tail with distinctive pattern; underwing tinged rufous-buff. **Voice:** melodious 'du-dooee' on take-off. **Status:** breeding population is decreasing.

Larks

Greater Short-toed Lark

Asian Short-toed Lark

Eurasian Skylark

Crested Lark

Swallows

Family Hirundinidae (World : 81 species, Korea : 4 species) Graceful flyers which spend almost as much time in flight as swifts, but wingbeat is different and wings are broader and shorter. Gregarious. Sexes alike.

SAND MARTIN *Riparia riparia* <Galsaekjebi> PM/uc L 12.5cm. Brown upperparts; white underparts with narrow, brown breast-band. Breeds colonially; excavating nest holes in sand banks. **Similar species:** House Swift has brown underparts. **Voice:** rassping call. **Status:** In flocks, often near wetlands. Seldom seen at higher elevations.

BARN SWALLOW [House Swallow] *Hirundo rustica* <Jebi> SV/ab L 18cm. Very familiar. Glossy blue-black upperparts; deeply forked tail with long outer feathers, and subterminal band of white spots; dark orange forehead and throat bordered with black across the breast; white underparts including wing linings and undertail coverts. **Juv:** lacks long outer tail feathers; throat is duller orange with indistinct black breast band. Nest is an open mud cup. **Status:** during migration roosts in large flocks in marshes and along coasts.

RED-RUMPED SWALLOW *Hirundo daurica* <Gwijebi> SV/c L 19cm. Glossy blue-black upperparts; very deeply forked tail with black undertail coverts; dull orange rump and sides of neck; buffy-white underparts finely streaked with black; mud nest is gourd-shaped, with long entrance tube. **Similar species:** Barn Swallow is smaller with rufous throat, dark rump, and white band in tail, white undertail coverts. **Voice:** call, a distinctive 'twi' followed by a rattling chuckle.

ASIAN HOUSE MARTIN *Delichon urbica* <Huinteolbaljebi> SV/r(n) • PM/r L 14.5cm. Glossy bluish-black upperparts and underwings; conspicuous white rump has front edge in line with trailing edge of wings; white underparts often indistinctly mottled with brown on breast and belly. Makes almost-closed mud nests colonially under eaves and bridges from seacoast to mountains. **Voice:** call a hard unmusical 'tchin', 'trit-it'. **Similar species:** Sand Martin has obvious brown breast band and rump; House Swift is brown below.

Swallows

Sand Martin

Barn Swallow

juv.

Red-rumped Swallow

nest of
Barn Swallow

nest of Red-rumped
Swallow

and Martin   Asian House   Barn   Red-rumped
              Martin   Swallow   Swallow

Asian House Martin

Wagtails and Pipits

Family Motacillidae (World : 59 species, Korea : 14 species) Wagtails and pipits are slender, mostly terrestrial birds with long legs. Most wag their tails up and down. Some have a strongly undulating flight. Many give distinctive calls during flight. Wagtails have longer tails and unstreaked plumage. Pipits are brownish with streaked plumage.

YELLOW WAGTAIL *Motacilla flava* <Ginbaltophalmisae> PM/c L 17cm. Several subspecies occur in Korea. **Ad-Br:** mostly have olive-green backs, olive-yellow rumps, yellow underparts, pale edges to wing feathers, and black legs. Intergrades occur. **Non-Br:** the subspecies are very similar with brownish-grey upperparts, whitish submoustachials and supercilia that do not extend around ear-coverts, and whitish underparts. Subspecies *M.f. taivana* Br. has olive-green mask and yellow throat and supercilium. *M.f. simillima* Br. has bluish-grey crown and nape with darker mask, white supercilium and moustachial. *M.f. macronyx* has dark-grey crown with white chin and lacks the white supercilium and moustachial. *M.f. plexa* has dark blue-grey crown and nape, white supercilium and throat. **Voice:** variably shrill 'shreep'. **Habitat:** prefers wet grasslands and riverbanks.

CITRINE WAGTAIL *Motacilla citreola* <Norangmeorihalmisae> Vag L 18cm. Black wings with two broad white wing bars, grey back and rump, dark legs and white vent. **Male:** underparts and head yellow with black half-collar. **Female:** grey crown and nape, whitish below; yellow face and throat with darker ear-coverts; breast yellowish. **Juv:** lacks yellow; buffy supercilium; spotted breastband. **1stW:** lacks yellow until early winter, then as female, but paler yellowish around face and breast. **Voice:** distinctive 'zzrrut.'

GREY WAGTAIL *Motacilla cinerea* <Noranghalmisae> SV/c L 20cm. Grey crown, sides of head, nape and back; yellow rump and underparts; white supercilium; pale legs. In flight, shows whitish bar along base of flight feathers. **Male Br:** black throat and white submoustachial stripe. **Female:** throat with less or no black. **Juv:** whitish throat. **Voice:** A sharp 'ztit' 'stit-tit'. **Habitat:** found mostly near water.

Wagtails

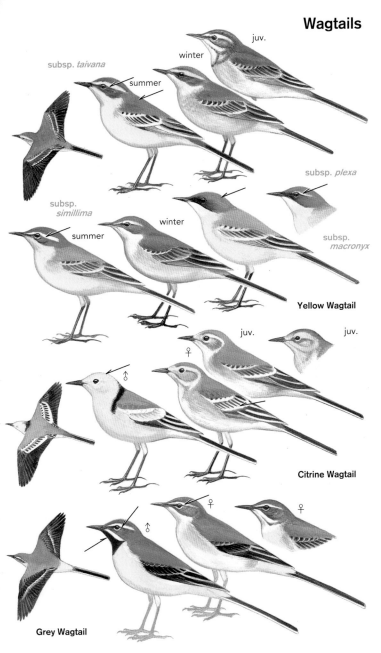

juv.

winter

subsp. *taivana*

summer

subsp. *plexa*

subsp. *simillima*

summer

winter

subsp. *macronyx*

Yellow Wagtail

juv.

juv.

♀

♂

Citrine Wagtail

♀

♀

♂

Grey Wagtail

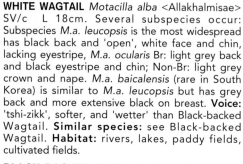

WHITE WAGTAIL *Motacilla alba* <Allakhalmisae> SV/c L 18cm. Several subspecies occur: Subspecies *M.a. leucopsis* is the most widespread has black back and 'open', white face and chin, lacking eyestripe, *M.a. ocularis* Br: light grey back and black eyestripe and chin; Non-Br: light grey crown and nape. *M.a. baicalensis* (rare in South Korea) is similar to *M.a. leucopsis* but has grey back and more extensive black on breast. **Voice:** 'tshi-zikk', softer, and 'wetter' than Black-backed Wagtail. **Similar species:** see Black-backed Wagtail. **Habitat:** rivers, lakes, paddy fields, cultivated fields.

BLACK-BACKED WAGTAIL *Motacilla lugens* <Baekhalmisae> WV/c L 21cm. **Ad:** wings almost all-white in flight; black crown, nape and tail with black throat, eyestripe and breast patch. **Male Br:** black back, usually white chin. **Non-Br:** similar to female but may retain some black on back. **Female:** darkish grey back. **1stW: male:** yellowish face and throat, broken breast patch; female as male but whitish face and throat. **Juv:** greyish head, breast and back with pale supercilium and submoustachial. **Voice:** call, a hard 'tizz-it'.

JAPANESE WAGTAIL *Motacilla grandis* <Geomeundeunghalmisae> Res/sc L 21cm. Typically larger than other wagtails. Black head, breast and back with white supercilium and forehead; underparts white; wings white with black tips to primaries. **1stW:** some black at base of primaries. **Juv:** grey hood and back, often lacking supercilium, and always with plain grey ear-coverts. **Voice:** twangy 'jujun jujun'. **Similar species:** smaller Black-backed and White Wagtails have white face with black patch on throat; show less black on wing tips in flight. **Habitat:** prefers water's edge of gravelly rivers, ponds.

FOREST WAGTAIL *Dendronanthus indicus* <Mullesae> SV/uc L 16cm. Olive-brown upperparts; whitish underparts with double blackish breastband; whitish supercilium; contrasting black and white wing bars are distinctive, especially in flight. Sways rear end from side to side in characteristic manner. Feeds on ground in forest and often found walking cautiously down forest paths; often lands close-by after flushing, sometimes in trees. **Voice:** tit-like 'ee-dzit-ee-dzit-ee-dzit'. **Habitat:** forests.

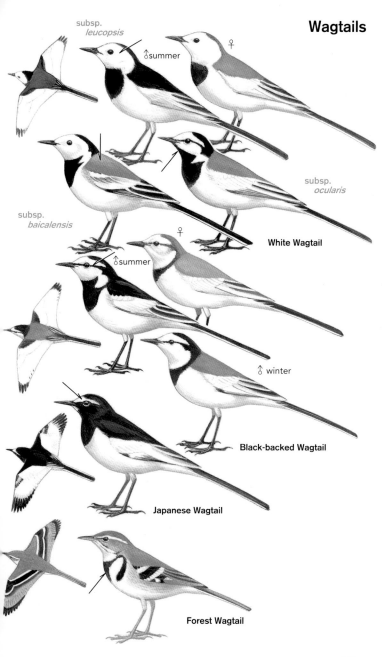

Wagtails

subsp.
leucopsis

♂summer

♀

subsp.
oculars

subsp.
baicalensis

♂summer

White Wagtail

♀

♂ winter

Black-backed Wagtail

Japanese Wagtail

Forest Wagtail

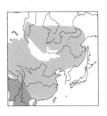

RICHARD'S PIPIT *Anthus richardi* <Keunbatjongdari> PM/sc L 18cm. Largest pipit in Korea with long legs and tail; rather deep-chested, with upright posture; walks swiftly; wags tail up and down. Long hind claw; median coverts fringed buff, not white (except narrowly in 1stW); pale lores; distinct blackish malar joins breast streaking. **Voice:** harsh, abrupt 'shree-eep', 'skeeut', or softer 'skeer', or chanting 'tyee-tyee-tyee-tyee'. **Habitat:** grasslands, cultivated fields.

BLYTH'S PIPIT *Anthus godlewskii* <Soebatjongdari> PM/r L 17cm. Very similar to Richard's Pipit in plumage; has proportionally shorter tail and legs, shorter more pointed bill, and much shorter hind claw; less erect posture. **Juv(1stW):** distinguished by distinctive square, dark centres to juvenile median coverts. **Voice:** softer, short 'chewp' or 'chuup'.

PECHORA PIPIT *Anthus gustavi* <Huindeungbatjongdari> PM/sc L 14cm. Usually seen as it flushes silently out of grass, showing white wingbars and striped upperparts. Resembles Red-throated Pipit with pale cream or whitish lines down back, but upperparts somewhat darker; facial pattern only slightly more distinct; has pale rufous-brown ear-coverts and sides of neck, and narrow dark line joins eye to base of thickish, pinkish bill; indistinct, pale supercilium extends from just behind eye to bill; has long, pale creamy or whitish submoustachial and narrow malar often ending in dark patch; whitish or yellowish underparts heavily streaked black; tertials do not fully cover primaries; legs pink. **Voice:** rather similar to Grey Wagtail, 'tit', occasionally 'tut', 'pit', 'pipit', or 'pwit', usually repeated three times.

RED-THROATED PIPIT *Anthus cervinus* <Bulgeun-gaseumbatjongdari> PM/sc L 15cm. Resembles Buff-bellied Pipit but has paler, sandier upperparts with more distinct black streaks, including on rump, and two paler lines down centre of back. **Br:** orange or pinkish-red face, supercilium, throat and upper breast, often brownish on ear-coverts; Extent and strength of red vary greatly with season and individual. Bill with greenish-yellow base. **Non-Br:** Red of face less marked. **1stW:** more boldly streaked above and below, especially on flanks; black malar line and patch. **Voice:** drawn out, high-pitched 'speeeii'.

Pipits

summer

1st-year winter

Richard's Pipit

summer

1st-year winter

Blyth's Pipit

Pechora Pipit

1st-year winter

♂ summer

♂ winter
♀ summer

Red-throated Pipit

OLIVE-BACKED PIPIT *Anthus hodgsoni*
<Hingdungsae> SV/r(n) • PM/c • WV/uc(s) L
16cm. Very widespread pipit of forests and dry
scrub areas. Greenish-olive upperparts with
indistinct black streaks; white underparts with
distinct black streaks on breast, sides and flanks;
supercilium creamy, deeper buff in front of eye;
often shows dark spot behind ear with creamy
spot above it. **Voice:** Call, drawn out 'zheeep',
sometimes shorter harder 'tsep,' 'tsui'. **Similar
species:** Buff-bellied Pipit has greyish-brownish
back; lacks white spot behind ear. Red-throated
Pipit has distinct black streaks on back, and
different call habitat, prefers different habitat.
Habitat: forests, shrubs, and forest edges. Winter:
pine woods or forest edges on lowland.

BUFF-BELLIED PIPIT *Anthus rubescens*
<Baljongdari> PM/c • WV/c L 16cm. The
widespread pipit of open, damp areas. Grey-
brown back; pale eye-ring; face not strongly
marked. **Br:** back with indistinct short black
streaks; buffy underparts with faint (to strong)
spots and streaks on breast, sides and flanks; pale
brow behind eye, and across forehead. **Non-Br:**
more strongly streaked on back and on whitish or
buffy underparts with narrow black malar joining
spotting on lower throat and breast. **Voice:**
'chichichit' or 'pipipit'. **Similar species:** see Olive-
backed and Red-throated Pipits. **Habitat:** rice
stubble fields, riverbanks, wetlands, and coasts.
Status: common migrant throughout and
common winter visitor in more southern areas.

ROSY PIPIT *Anthus roseatus* <Hangukbat-
jongdari> Vag L 15 cm. Olive upperparts strongly
streaked with black; broad supercilium and dark
eyeline and lores; underparts whitish, mostly
unstreaked; olive-green edges to greater coverts,
tertials and secondaries; broad white wing bars.
Br: greyish head, pinky purplish wash on
supercilium, throat and breast; some dark streaks
on sides and flanks. **Non-Br:** underparts white,
washed buffy on sides; thin dark malar joins heavy
dark streaking on breast, sides and flanks. **Similar
species:** see other pipits. **Voice:** thin 'seep-seep'.
Habitat: mainly grsssland of wetland.

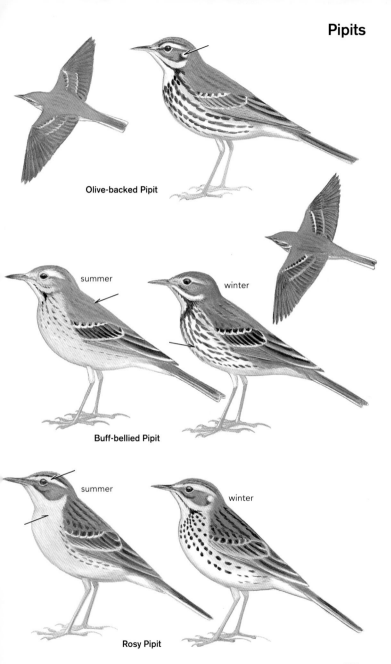

Pipits

Olive-backed Pipit

summer

winter

Buff-bellied Pipit

summer

winter

Rosy Pipit

213

Minivets

Family Campephagidae (World : 78 species, Korea : 2 species) Arboreal birds of various sizes and colors. Sexes mostly differ. Short, thickish bills and longish wedge-shaped tails. Most species form loose flocks after Br. season.

ASHY MINIVET *Pericrocotus divaricatus* <Halmisaesachon> SV/sc · PM/uc L 20cm. Grey above, white below; white wing bars are conspicuous during undulating flight. **Male:** white forecrown, black hindcrown, nape, eye-line and bar extending towards ear coverts. **Female:** short, black eye-line from bill to eye; grey crown, streaked whitish on forecrown, ear coverts and nape. **Juv:** overall pale brownish-grey, showing two whitish wing bars on darker brown wings. **Voice:** 'hee-ree-reen', usually in flight. **Similar species:** Grey Wagtail has yellow underparts, more bouncing flight, distinct voice. **Habitat:** forests.

BLACK-WINGED CUCKOO SHRIKE *Coracina melaschistos* <Geomeunhalmisaesachon> Vag L 23.5cm. **Male:** dark slaty grey with black wings and tail; underparts paler towards belly with greyish-white undertail coverts; graduated tail has white tipped outer feathers, seen from below. **Female:** paler grey with barring on underparts, pale edging to flight feathers, and blackish scaling on whitish undertail coverts. **Juv:** browner, with more heavily barred underparts. **Imm:** as female but more distinct barring on underparts, also on rump. **Voice:** song is a series of slow, descending whistles. **Habitat:** forests and forest edges. **Status:** 1 record of a male in Jodo, Jindo-gun, Jeollanam-do in August 1998.

Bulbuls

Family Pycnonotidae (World : 122 species, Korea : 1 species) Medium-sized arboreal birds with short round wings and longish tails. Usually vocal Sexes alike.

BROWN-EARED BULBUL *Hypsipetes amaurotis* <Jikbakguri> Res/c L 28cm. Overall greyish, more rusty brown on wings and belly, with large tail. head, mantle and back heavily washed with silvery-grey, with whitish spotting on underparts; earcoverts chestnut; long brown undertail coverts have conspicuous white tips. **Juv:** browner, lacking silvery wash. Undulating flight. **Voice:** typical song; 'peet peet, pii yieyo'. **Habitat:** low mountian forests, city parks and gardens. **Status:** many move southward in winter.

Minivets, Bulbuls

♂

♀

♂

Ashy Minivet

♀

♂

Black-winged Cuckoo Shrike

♀

Brown-eared Bulbul

Shrikes

Family Laniidae. (World : 81 species, Korea : 6 species) Small to medium-sized birds with large heads and long tails. Bills are short, stout and hooked, and feet strong with sharp-claws. Prey on insects and amphibians, sometimes on birds, by pouncing from an exposed perch, often impaling them on thorns as a food store.

GREAT GREY SHRIKE [Northern Shrike] *Lanius excubitor* <Keunjaegaegumari> WV/r L 24cm. Large shrike with pale grey upperparts, and usually paler rump, whitish underparts and black wings and tail; white patch in wing at base of primaries, and white scapulars are conspicuous in flight; may show paler grey or whitish rump in flight; black mask may have narrow white supercilium. **Juv:** tinged brownish. **Similar Species:** Chinese Grey Shrike. **Habitat:** open country and cultivated fields.

CHINESE GREAT GREY SHRIKE *Lanius sphenocercus* <Multtaekkachi> WV/r L 31cm. A very large, long-tailed shrike typically found near water; larger and longer-tailed than similar Great Grey, with more white on wing; black wings have larger white patch at base of primaries and small white bar at base of secondaries, as well as white scapular patches; may also have narrow, white supercilium; uppertail coverts and rump same tone as back and tail. **Juv:** tinged brownish and vermiculated below. **Voice:** call; a very harsh 'chaek', song; long and rambling, with some musical note. **Habitat:** open wetlands including rice-fields and wetland edge.

LONG-TAILED SHRIKE *Lanius schach* <Ginkkorittaekkachi> Vag L 25cm. Characteristic long, blackish tail and broad black mask; crown, nape and mantle grey, merging into variable amount of rufous on the back and rump; underparts white at throat becoming deep rufous at vent, and on under and upper tail coverts; wings black with small white patch at base of primaries. **Voice:** call; typical rasping screech. **Similar species:** Bull-headed, thick-billed shrikes. **Habitat:** open country, cultivated fields, and forests edge. **Status:** 2 records of single individuals, near Daeho, Chungcheongnam-do in December 1994 and on the Mangyeonggang in Jeollabuk-do, on October 1999.

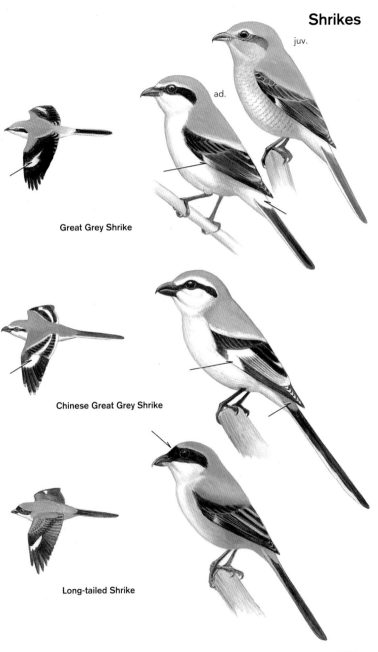

Shrikes

juv.

ad.

Great Grey Shrike

Chinese Great Grey Shrike

Long-tailed Shrike

THICK-BILLED SHRIKE [Tiger Shrike] *Lanius tigrinus* <Chikttaekkachi> SV/uc L 18cm. Prefers to sit in bushes rather than conspicuously in the open; appears large-headed and thick billed. **Male:** crown and nape clean slaty-blue, with broad black mask and no white supercilium or wingspot; chestnut back and tail, back variably scaled with black; clean white underparts, though there may be some black scaling on flanks. **Female:** as male, but whitish lores break up the mask and give a different facial pattern; black scaling from sides of neck to flanks. **Similar species:** female Bull-headed is scaled below but has 'thicker neck', browner underparts and crown. 1stW Brown Shrike may have grey crown and scaling below, but is never chestnut on the back. **Habitat:** lowland forests, forest edges, and open country.

BULL-HEADED SHRIKE *Lanius bucephalus* <Ttaekkachi> Res/c L 20cm. **Male:** rufous-brown crown, grey back; distinct white patch at base of primaries, conspicuous in flight. **Female:** lacks white wing patch and black mask, having only a dark brown bar behind the eye; underparts with fine brown vermiculations; grey back and tail washed with variable amount of rufous-brown. **Similar species:** Brown Shrike. **Voice:** harsh and rapid 'kikikikiki-'. **Habitat:** open country, cultivated fields, and forests edges.

BROWN SHRIKE *Lanius cristatus* <Norang-ttaekkachi> SV/uc L 20cm. Similar to Bull-headed, but dull grey or brown on crown and back. **Male:** underparts richly washed with buff below with clear white throat; black mask may have a white supercilium but this is a very variable character; tail dull, dark brown; lacks white patch in wing. **Female:** not always distinguishable from male but often has less distinct mask, and fine vermiculations on breast and flanks. **Juv:** pale lore breaks dark mask; dark scaling on throat, sides and flanks. Subspecies *L c. cristatus* is a rare migrant with rich reddish-brown upperparts, and conspicuous white supercilium and forehead. **Habitat:** open country, cultivated fields, and forests edges. **Status:** *L. c. lucionensis* is a summer visitor, but decreased in these days.

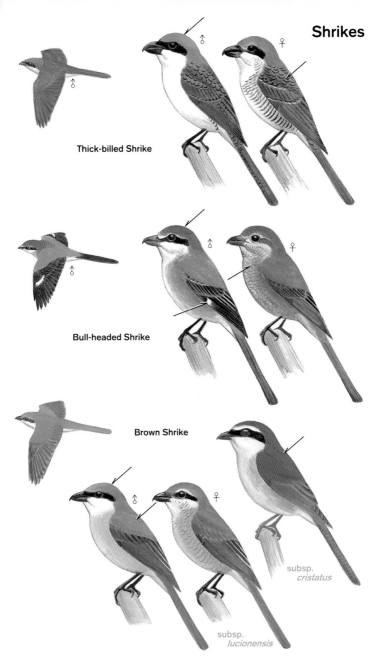

Shrikes

Thick-billed Shrike ♂ ♂ ♀

Bull-headed Shrike ♂ ♂ ♀

Brown Shrike ♂ ♂ ♀

subsp. *cristatus*

subsp. *lucionensis*

Waxwings

Family Bombycillidae (World : 8 species, Korea : 2 species) Sleek birds with prominent crests. Silky plumage predominantly greyish-brown. Have characteristic waxy appendages on tips of secondaries; sexes very similar.

WAXWING [Bohemian Waxwing] *Bombycilla garrulus* <Hwang-yeosae> WV/c L 20cm. **Male:** black eyeline extends to nape, not into crest; undertail coverts chestnut not red; outer edge of primaries tipped yellow, inner edge white. white wing bars at base of primaries and near tips of secondaries. **Female:** as male but yellow tail tip is narrower, black throat less distinct; fewer red. **Voice:** weak repeated trill, 'zhrie rie rie rie'. **Habitat:** forests edges, city parks, gardens and coniferous forests.

JAPANESE WAXWING *Bombycilla japonica* <Hong-yeosae> WV/uc L 18cm. Pale greyish-brown body is richer brown on head and greyer on wings, rump and tail; black throat and eyeline which extends into rear of long swept-back crest; grey tail has black subterminal band and diagnostic, dark pink tip; undertail coverts are reddish, centre of belly yellowish **Juv:** greyer below, mottled with white; lacks black behind eye. **Habitat:** forests edges, city parks, gardens and coniferous forests.

Dippers

Family Cinclidae (World : 5 species, Korea : 1 species) Medium-sized bird. Dives for aquatic invertebrates, swims underwater using wings. Sexes alike.

BROWN DIPPER *Cinclus pallasii* <Mulkkamagwi> Res/c L 22cm. Chubby, rich chocolate-brown bird with short wings and shortish, often cocked, tail, confined to rocky stretches of usually fast-flowing streams. **Voice:** short, strong clicking 'tzikk'. **Similar species:** Winter Wren. **Habitat:** waterside and on stones in forest streams especially in mountains.

Wrens

Family Troglodytidae (World : 69 species, Korea : 1 species) Small birds with loud, elaborate song. Sexes alike.

WINTER WREN *Troglodytes troglodytes* <Gulttuksae> Res/c L 10cm. Tiny, dark, woodland bird often seen with tail cocked. Rich brown plumage finely-barred on back, wings, underparts and tail, with indistinct, narrow, whitish supercilium. **Voice:** harsh churring 'tchek' call and explosive song with trills, loud for its size. **Habitat:** open forests and ravines, rocky areas in forests.

Waxwings, Dippers, Wrens

Waxwing

Japanese Waxwing

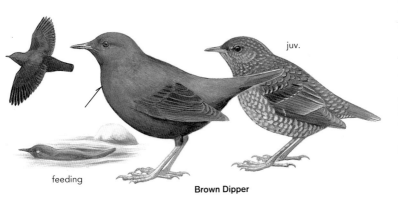

juv.

feeding

Brown Dipper

Winter Wren

Accentors

Family Prunellidae (World : 12 species, Korea : 2 species) Small, brownish, usually solitary birds with thin pointed bills. Feed on ground. Sexes alike. Dish shaped nest on ground or trees.

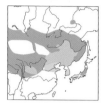

ALPINE ACCENTOR *Prunella collaris* <Bawi-jongdari> SV/uc(n) • WV/sc L 18cm. Very tame, brownish bird of mountain tops, and rocky areas in winter. Grey head and breast, with throat finely scaled whitish; eye with broken white eye-ring; sides, flanks and uppertail coverts rufous-chestnut; whitish tips to outer tail feathers; bill base and lower mandible yellow. **Juv:** pink bill. Flies quickly with shallow dipping like small thrush. **Habitat:** high mountains.

SIBERIAN ACCENTOR *Prunella montanella* <Metjongdari> WV/c L 15cm. Brown upperparts, sides and flanks, streaked darker; head with broad black mask, dull yellow supercilium and ear-covert spot; brown central crown stripe edged black; throat and underparts dull yellowish; sides of neck bluish-grey, and rump brownish-grey. **Voice:** 'zi-ii-ee'. **Habitat:** open forests, forest edge and bushy grasslands.

Thrushes

Family Turdidae (World : 322 species, Korea : 24 species) A group of small to medium sized, mainly terrestrial birds including robins, redstarts, wheatears and thrushes. Compact with long legs and slender bills; many have habit of cocking or twitching tail when perched. Sexes usually differ; Juveniles like female but spotted or speckled.

JAPANESE ROBIN *Erithacus akahige* <Bulgeun-gaseumulsae> Vag L 14cm. Skulking. **Male:** upperparts dark reddish olive-brown, more rufous on tail; face, throat, upper breast, and neck bright orange merging to rufous-brown on crown and nape; lower breast and belly with whitish centre. **Female:** duller, lacking dark breast band, and with more mottled underparts. **Juv:** as female but very scaled. **Habitat:** forests.

RUFOUS-TAILED ROBIN [Swinhoe's Robin] *Luscinia sibilans* <Ulsae> PM/c L 14cm. Brown with chestnut tinge to tail; whitish underparts scaled with greyish-brown, mottled on sides sometimes forming an indistinct breast band; distinct pale eyering, forehead and supercilium in front of eye. **Similar species:** female Siberian Rubythroat has distinct whitish supercilium, lacks scaling and is slightly bigger. **Voice:** rapidly descending trill 'diririririririrrirrrr'. **Habitat:** forests, parks and gardens.

Accentors, Small Thrushes

Alpine Accentor

Siberian Accentor

Japanese Robin ♂ ♀

Rufous-tailed Robin

SIBERIAN RUBYTHROAT *Luscinia calliope* <Jinhonggaseum> PM/sc L 15.5cm. **Male:** upperparts plain olive brown; supercilium and moustachial stripe bright white, lores black; bright red throat with distinct border; breast and flanks greyish-brown; belly dirty white. **Female:** like male but facial colours are duller, and has whitish throat; some females may show some pink on the throat. **Voice:** song; melodius, slightly scratchy, call; whistled 'seelewee', with nasal 'nguk'. **Habitat:** bushy grassland and wetland edge.

BLUETHROAT *Luscinia svecica* <Huinnunsseob-ulsae> PM/r • WV/r L 15cm. Droops wings and cocks tail. Upperparts olive-brown, including central tail feathers; tail tipped black, with rufous base to outer feathers; conspicuous whitish supercilium. **Male:** blue throat and upper breast with orange spot in center; black and orange breast bands. **Female:** creamy-white supercilium, submoustachial and throat; black malar stripe and streaky broken breast band. **Similar species:** see Rosy Pipit: tail pattern is different and pipits never cock tail; female Daurian Redstart. **Habitat:** scrubs and grasslands near wetland.

SIBERIAN BLUE ROBIN *Lucinia cyane* <Soe-yurisae> SV/c L 14cm. **Male:** upperparts blue, underparts pure white; black from lores to side of neck. **Female:** upperparts and flanks olive brown, wings browner; pale eye-ring; olive-brown wash on breast and flanks; bill pale pinkish. **Voice:** call; a slow, clucked 'tuc...tuc', song; series of 15-20 thin high-pitched 'tsit' followed by a short trill of notes e.g. 'tree-tri-tri-tri-tri-tri' or 'siritsiritsrit'. **Habitat:** mountain forests, ravines and alpine zones.

RED-FLANKED BLUETAIL [Orange-flanked Blue Robin] *Tarsiger cyanurus* <Yurittaksae> PM/c • WV/uc L 14cm. **Male:** rich blue upperparts and tail with orange flanks; clear white throat, whitish underparts and often a short white supercilium. **Female:** olive brown above, paler below with triangular white throat patch; blue on tail only; pale eye-ring and pale orange wash on sides. **Voice:** call; 'cheet cheet cheet'. **Similar species:** female Daurian Redstart has distinctive tail and white wing spot, Siberian Blue Robin. **Habitat:** forests and parks.

Small Thrushes

♂

♀

Siberian Rubythroat

imm.
♂

♂

♀

Bluethroat

♂ imm.

♂

♀

Siberian Blue Robin

♂ imm.

♀

♂

Red-flanked Bluetail

225

BLACK REDSTART *Phoenicurus ochruros*
<Geomeunmeorittaksae> Vag L 14cm Rufous-orange tail with black centre. **Male:** head, upper breast, wings are black or blackish; underparts, outer tail feathers rufous orange. **Female:** brown above, pale brown below. Eye-ring indistinct. **Habitat:** open country preferring rocky, open areas.

DAURIAN REDSTART *Phoenicurus auroreus*
<Ttaksae> Res/c L 14cm. **Male:** black face, back and wings, orange underparts, silvery-grey crown and nape with lighter brown markings; black tail with rufous outer tail feathers, lower mantle and rump; white wing patch. **Female:** rump and tail as male; body rather uniform brown with plain face, paler below; pale buff eye-ring. **Voice:** a thin 'ziit' followed by a tutting... 'chak-chak'. Song repeated endlessly, a thin rambling with melodious notes, often from tree top or high point 'chi-chi-wirrr'. **Habitat:** hillsides, open cultivated fields, parks, and gardens.

COMMON STONECHAT *Saxicola torquata*
<Geomeunttaksae> SV/c L 13cm. **Male:** black head and upperparts, with white neck, shoulders, rump, and underparts; orange patch on breast. **Non-Br:** black parts become pale brown streaked darker, underparts washed with rufous-buff below; face blackish. **Female:** dark brown head and upperparts finely streaked paler; pale supercilium; white wing patch smaller than male; pale buff rump contrasts with black tail; unstreaked buffy underparts with paler throat and vent. **Juv:** as female but spotty and scaly. **Voice:** call; loud grating 'tsch-tsch', sometimes with whistling note, song; short squeaking warble. **Habitat:** bushy grasslands, paddy fields.

GREY BUSHCHAT *Saxicola ferrea* <Geomeun-ppyamttaksae> Vag L 15cm. Lacks paler rump of Common Stonechat. **Male:** upperparts slaty grey streaked with black; black mask with white supercilium and throat; wings dark with white covert patch; tail black with white outer feathers; underparts whitish. **Female:** brown upperparts streaked darker and with greyish wash; rump and outer tail feathers noticeably reddish-brown; dark brown mask with pale supercilium and throat; supercilium whitish. **Habitat:** cultivated fields near the seashore and grasslands.

Small Thrushes

Black Redstart

♂ ♂ ♀

Daurian Redstart

♂ ♂ imm. ♀

Common Stonechat

♂ ♂ summer

winter ♀

Grey Bushchat

♂ ♀

PIED WHEATEAR *Oenanthe pleschanka* <Geomeundeungsamakttaksae> Vag L 14.5cm. Tail pattern distinctive; rump and tail white, always showing black edge to outer tail feathers. **Male:** white head and nape; black on face and throat joined to black of mantle and wings. **Female:** pale grey-brown upperparts, greyish to blackish throat. **Similar species:** back of Black-eared wheatear is white. **Habitat:** sandy areas, cultivated fields and seashores. **Status:** one record of a female in Yeochari, Ganghwado in May 1988.

BLACK-EARED WHEATEAR *Oenanthe hispanica* <Huinmeorittaksae> Vag L 14.5 cm. **Male:** similar to Pied Wheatear but crown, mantle and breast white washed with yellowish-brown, whiter in summer; black of head does not meet black of wings; white throated morphs also occur. **Female:** perhaps more yellowish-brown on breast and back but may not be safely separable. **Habitat:** open fields, having bussy, grassland. **Status:** recently considered conspecific with Pied Wheathear owing to extensive hybridisation where ranges meet.

BLUE ROCK THRUSH *Monticola solitarius* <Badajikbakguri> Res/c L 23 cm. Shortish tail and flattish crown are distinctive. **Male:** head, breast, back, wing-coverts, flanks and rump slate blue; underparts rufous; wings and tail dark blackish brown. **Female:** looks grey-brown, but is dusted with slaty-blue on head back and wing-coverts; underparts are creamy, heavily scaled with dark brown. **Voice:** call a hard 'tseeet',song a melodius, slow-panced, short warble, variably repeated. **Habitat:** islands, rocky seashores and harbour areas.

WHITE-THROATED ROCKTHRUSH *Monticola gularis* <Kkokkajikbakguri> PM/r L 18cm. **Male:** crown, nape, and lesser wing-coverts bright cobalt-blue; back and wings black with white wing patch, tail dark grey; narrow white throat, be difficult to see in the field; rest of underparts, cheeks, and rump rufous-orange. **Female:** upperparts pale brown barred with black; underparts white barred with black; white or buffish line on throat. **Voice:** fluty 'we-tee-tee-wee-tee-tee-chirchir' rising and falling in pitch and volume. **Habitat:** forests including many rocky area.

Wheatears, Rockthrushes

Pied Wheatear

Black-eared Wheatear

Blue Rock Thrush

White-throated Rock Thrush

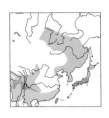

WHITE'S THRUSH [Scaly Thrush] *Zoothera dauma* <Horangjippagwi> SV/c • Res/sc(s) L 29.5cm. Large, rather pale thrush of forest floor, showing white tail corners when flushed. Sexes similar. Upperparts golden-brown, underparts paler, heavily scaled above and below with crescent-shaped black marks; pale eye-ring; facial markings variable; thin dark malar, ear-covert bar, and sometimes cheek bar; underwings black with white bar; bill dark horn; legs pinkish or yellowish. **Voice:** song is a high, thin whistle and an even higher whistle given as duet at very slow pace. Often sings at night. **Habitat:** forests, parks and inhabited regions.

PALE THRUSH *Turdus pallidus* <Huinbaejippagwi> SV/c • Res/uc(s) L 23cm. **Male:** upperparts olive brown; head and throat bluish-grey, browner around the neck; underparts paler brown, darker brown on flanks, white belly and undertail coverts; flight feathers and tail grey, tail showing conspicuous white tips in flight. **Female:** duller with pale throat. **Voice:** 'gyoro, gyoro, gyororo-', call 'tschuck-tschuik, bock bock bock.' curious harsh bubbling alarm note. **Similar species:** Brown Thrush has rufous flanks, lacks white tips to tail. **Habitat:** forests and parks.

DUSKY THRUSH *Turdus naumann* <Gaettongjippagwi> WV/c L 23cm. The only thrush likely to be found in flocks in winter both in forested areas and more open rice-fields. Two forms occur with a continuous range of intermediates so plumage is variable. In both, bill is yellowish with dark tip and legs pale. Subspecies *T. n. naumanni* (commoner in north): brown upperparts with rufous outer tail and markings on wings; rufous breast, throat, neck and face, with brown ear coverts; whitish underparts also spotted with rufous. Subspecies *T. n. eunomus* (commoner in the south) has creamy-white supercilium, submoustachials and throat, with narrow dark-brown malar stripes, and dark-brown lores and ear coverts. **Male:** white underparts with black breast band, and heavily blotched with black below; large chestnut panel on wing. **Female:** weaker back markings below, wing panel less chestnut. **Habitat:** forests, cultivated fields, gardens and fields. **Status:** observation from the southern district in winter, the middle as for *T. n. eunomus*. Intermediates widely occur.

Thrushes

White's Thrush

Pale Thrush ♂ ♀

subsp. *eunomus*

subsp. *naumanni*

Dusky Thrush

SIBERIAN THRUSH *Zoothera sibiricus* <Huin-nunsseopjippagwi> PM/sc L 23cm. In flight, show bold black and white underwing bars. **Male:** black with broad white supercilium and white tips to undertail coverts white. **Female:** upperparts dark brown with buffy or whitish supercilium, eye-ring, submoustachial and throat; underparts yellowish-brown, heavily marked with brown crescents; legs pink or yellowish. **Voice:** song 'chooeloot...chewee' followed by trill; call a hard 'zic' similar to Hawfinch. **Habitat:** forests and parks.

GREY THRUSH *Turdus cardis* <Geomeunjippagwi> Vag L 21.5cm. Small, forest thrush. **Male:** black upperparts, head and upper breast; rest of underparts white spotted black on upper belly, sides and flanks; bill and eye-ring bright yellow. **Female:** olive-brown above, greyer on rump; underparts white with orange sides, flanks, and underwing-coverts; throat streaked and breast and belly spotted with black; bill dark. **Voice:** song rich in quality, long and warbling; usually given from tops of high trees. **Habitat:** forests.

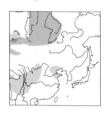

BLACK-THROATED THRUSH *Turdus ruficollis* <Geomeunmokjippagwi> Vag L 23.5cm. Subspecies *T. r. ruficollis*. **Male:** rufous face, throat, and breast and outer tail feathers; white belly. **Female: :** as male but whitish below with black streaks for malars and on breast; rufous parts paler; supercilium distinct. Subspecies *T. r. atrogularis*. **Male:** black face, throat, and breast. **Female:** throat white, black mottling on breast and streaky malars. **Similar species:** male Grey Thrush has black upperparts, black spots on underparts, and yellow legs. Dusky Thrush *T. n. naumanni* has mottled red area extending down to belly, brown on upperparts. **Habitat:** forests.

BLACKBIRD *Turdus merula* <Daeryukgeomeunjippagwi> Vag L 24cm. Very dark thrush preferring open pine forest. **Male Br:** Body all black; bill, legs, *and* eye-ring yellow. **Female:** brown, much paler on throat, streaked darker on throat and breast; bill and legs dark; no eye-ring. **Voice:** call a very harsh chacking 'teck tek tek'; song, loud with phrases repeated three or four times, 'swoot-swee-hirhu'...'chit-chit-chit'. **Similar species:** male Grey Thrush is smaller with white belly. Siberian thrush male has white supercilium with black bill. **Habitat:** forests and parks.

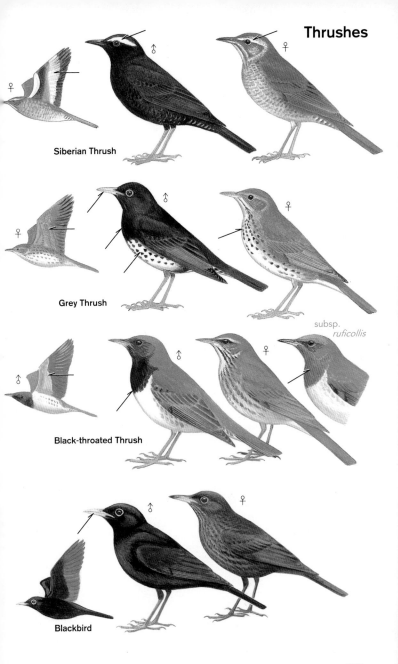

Thrushes

♀

♂

♀

Siberian Thrush

♀

♂

♀

Grey Thrush

subsp.
ruficollis

♂

♂

♀

♀

Black-throated Thrush

♂

♀

Blackbird

GREY-BACKED THRUSH *Turdus hortulorum*
<Doejippagwi> SV/uc L 23cm. Pale but bright-coloured thrush of open forests. **Male:** head, back, rump and tail bluish-grey, darker on wings and tail (throat whitish in some birds); flanks orange; rest of underparts white; wing linings orange. **Female:** upperparts pale brown washed with grey; underparts whitish, throat streaked with black, breast with black spots; sides and flanks rufous-orange. Bill all yellow. **Similar species:** Eye-browed Thrush has distinct white supercilium. **Habitat:** forests and parks.

BROWN THRUSH *Turdus chrysolaus* <Bulgeun-baejippagwi> Vag L 24cm. **Male:** upperparts olive brown, chin and throat darker; thin yellowish eye-ring; underparts rufous-orange; center of lower breast, belly and undertail coverts white; wing linings pale greyish. **Female:** duller; whitish chin and throat often with brown malar; may have indistinct supercilium stripe. **Habitat:** broad-leaved forests. **Status:** 6 records in May and September during passage.

EYE-BROWED THRUSH *Turdus obscurus*
<Huinnunsseopbulgeunbaejippagwi> PM/sc L 21.5cm. Brownish thrush with distinctive supercilum and white line from bill to below eye. **Male Br:** head and nape grey, or greyish-brown, with white supercilium, chin and lower lore; short black eyeline to bill; back olive-brown; rufous-brown breast merges into rufous sides; belly white greyish brown head; throat and breast dark brown merging into russet brown of upper belly and flanks; belly white. **Female:** as male but head brown, eyeline dark brown, white streaking on throat, narrow greyish band across upper breast. **Voice:** song; rather grating 'chirri-to-choy' 'chi-row' 'chiroro' 'chi-roro', call; typical thrush-like: 'chock chock'; thin 'zee'. **Similar species:** female Brown Thrush has richer rufous sides, supercilium if present always less distinct; Pale Thrush lacks supercilium, sides not noticeably rufous. **Habitat:** forests and parks. **Status:** appearing as early as September; rare in spring.

Thrushes

Grey-backed Thrush

Brown Thrush

Eye-browed Thrush

Thrushes

Robins

Starlings

Larks

Pipits

Silhouettes of terrestrial birds

Babblers

Family Timaliidae (World : 225 species, Korea : 1 species) Generally gregarious and noisy. Most species have rather harsh, chattering calls. All are rather weak fliers with short rounded wings. Many species tend to be active or close to the ground. In most species, sexes are alike.

CHINESE BABBLER *Rhopophilus pekinensis* <Kkorichire> Res/r(n) L 18cm. Upperparts brown streaked black, crown often tinged with chestnut; underparts buffy white streaked with rufous on sides of belly and breast; long, graduated tail tipped white; supercilium greyish; throat white, with black moustachial streaks and lores; bill yellowish brown. **Habitat:** forests.

Warblers

Family Sylviidae (World : 264 species, Korea : 23 species) Small, dull coloured birds with slender, straight and pointed bill rather weak legs and feet. Songs are distinctive, often differing widely between closely related species. Insectivorous. In most species, sexs are alike.

SPOTTED BUSH WARBLER *Bradypterus thoracicus* <Jeommunuigaseumjwibalgwi> SV/r(n) L 13cm Olive-brown above, buffy-tinged supercilium with brownish ear-coverts and sides of neck; breast sparsely spotted (less spotting in females and juveniles) with brownish (not greyish) wash. **Habitat:** forest glades, damp and open grassy areas on scrubby hillsides.

FAN-TAILED WARBLER [Zitting Cisticola] *Cisticola juncidis* <Gaegaebisachon> SV/uc • Res/sc(s) L 12.5cm. **Br:** brown upperparts streaked black on wings and mantle, rufous tinged unmarked back and rump; graduated tail with subterminal black band, tipped white; crown darker. **Voice:** in song flight, a series of whistling 'hit-hit-hit' as the bird ascends, 'chat-chat-chat' as it descends, call; sharp 'plit'. **Habitat:** coastal and riverside reedbeds and grasslands.

JAPANESE MARSH WARBLER *Locustella pryeri* <Keungaegaebi> Vag L 13cm. Brown upperparts tinged rufous, broadly streaked with black on back and tertials, narrowly streaked on crown; whitish below washed with rufous-buff; pale whitish or buff supercilium and lores; indistinct eyeline behind eye only; rather short-billed; crown often appears rather flat, sloping on to bill; rounded tail. **Voice:** monotonous 'chi-chi-chi-chi-chi' given from the top of a reed, followed by a song flight. **Similar species:** Fan-tailed Warbler. **Habitat:** reedbeds in wetland and coastal grasslands.

Babblers, Warblers

Chinese Babbler

Spotted Bush Warbler

Fan-tailed Warbler

summer

winter

Japanese Marsh Warbler

SHORT-TAILED BUSH WARBLER [Asian Stubtail]
Urosphena squameiceps <Supsae> SV/c L
10.5cm. Small and very short-tailed bird of forest
floor. Dark brown above with pronounced pale
creamy buff supercilium; distinct black eyeline,
which contrasts with brown ear-coverts, pale
pinkish legs; whitish washed with pale brown
below. **Voice:** song; high-pitched, insect-like 'see-
see-see-see...' increasing in volume. **Habitat:**
forests and bushy grasslands. **Status:** widespread
summer visitor to densely wooded lowland hills;
skulks close to ground.

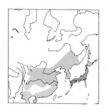

JAPANESE BUSH WARBLER *Cettia diphone*
<Hwiparamsae> SV/c • Res/uc(s) L 14~16cm.
Polygynous, males larger than females. Rufescent
brown upperparts, whitest underparts, clearest
supercilium, usually greyish tinged around face,
rufous-tinged forecrown and dull, thickish bill. *C.
d. borealis* is less strongly marked, and *C. d.
cantans* has least distinct face pattern and greyish
underparts. **Voice:** fastly 'hoho-o, ho-o ho-ot ket-
kyot'; call a harsh 'chek'. **Habitat:** forests, parks,
bushy grasslands and shrubbery zones. **Status:**
Korean Bush Warbler *C. d. borealis* largely a
summer visitor, *C. d. cantans* is possibly locally
resident and summer visitor in the south-west.

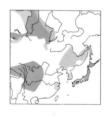

GOLDCREST *Regulus regulus* <Sangmosolsae>
WV/c L 9cm. Tiny warbler of conifers; dark olive
green above, paler below; crown stripe bright
yellow with blackish border, and with orange-red
centre (often concealed) in male; white eye-ring,
but lacks supercilium; black and white bars across
base of flight feathers. **Juv:** lacks crown stripes,
duller. **Voice:** call; 'tsi-tsi-tsi', higher-pitched than
Long-tailed Tit. **Habitat:** coriferous forests, hills to
sub alpine zones in summer, low hills in winter.

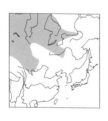

LESSER WHITETHROAT *Sylvia curruca* <Soe-
huinteokttaksae> Vag L 13cm Rare vagrant found
in bushy areas. Greyish-brown above with whitish
underparts; grey crown, blackish lores and ear-
coverts; tail square-ended with white outer
feathers. **1stW:** brownish-grey crown, grey-black
eyeline, pale supercilium. **Voice:** 'tek' rather
similar to Dusky Warbler. **Habitat:** cultivated
fields, forests and bushy grasslands. **Status:** 1
record of collection near Geumgangwon(Zoo) in
Busan.

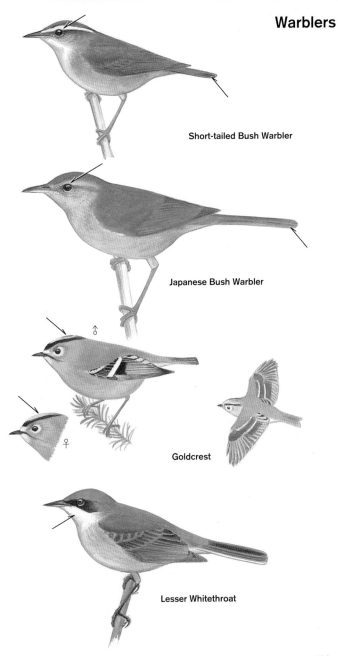

Warblers

Short-tailed Bush Warbler

Japanese Bush Warbler

♂

♀

Goldcrest

Lesser Whitethroat

GRAY'S GRASSHOPPER WARBLER *Locustella fasciolata* <Bulgeunheorigaegaebi> PM/uc L 18cm. Slightly greyish brown above; distinct whitish supercilium to rear of crown; eye-stripe brown; broader behind eye; throat and cheeks whitish, rusty buff on belly and on very long undertail coverts; tail wedge-shaped. **Voice:** loud, explosive, distinctive 'top-pee, top-ping, kaketaka', given from hidden perch both day and night. **Similar species:** Japanese Bush Warbler. **Habitat:** around forests and rivers near flatland.

PALLAS' GRASSHOPPER WARBLER *Locustella certhiola* <Bukbanggaegaebi> PM/r L 13 cm. From other small brown skulkers by combination of heavily streaked, brown upperparts (including uppertail coverts) with richer brown or rusty rump, darker crown and tail. Distinct broad, whitish supercilium. **Voice:** call 'rit-tic-tic'. **Habitat:** ditches with plentiful vegetation, reedbeds.

LANCEOLATED GRASSHOPPER WARBLER *Locustella lanceolata* <Jwibalgwigaegaebi> PM/uc L 12cm. Brown upperparts heavily streaked on back and crown, with lighter streaking on throat, breast and flanks; whitish underparts washed rich brown on sides and flanks. Tail lacks white tips. **Voice:** very thin 'tick'. **Habitat:** reedbeds in wetland, grasslands and grassy plains.

MIDDENDORFF'S GRASSHOPPER WARBLER *Locustella ochotensis* <Allak-kkorijwibalgwi> PM/uc L 15.5cm. Crown, nape, lores, eye-stripe greyish brown; mantle browner and more olive; supercilium pale creamy extending to ear coverts; rump and uppertail coverts more yellowish or rufous brown; graduated, white-tipped tail may appear rounded. **Voice:** song;high-pitched, spaced 'chit, chit', precede trilled 'trrrrrrrr-schoy-schoy-schoy', call;'tluk, tluk,...' also a short song flight. **Habitat:** forests near water and scrubwoods.

STYAN'S GRASSHOPPER WARBLER *Locustella pleskei* <Seomgaegaebi> SV/sc(I) • PM/sc L 16.5cm. Supercilium pale greyish-brown, not extending behind the eye so far; lores darker than crown; eye-stripe behind eye very thin or absent; mantle, back, rump and uppertail coverts uniform greyish-brown, not rich brown and not showing contrast. **Voice:** very similar to Middendorff's Grasshopper Warbler. **Habitat:** seashores, grassy zones on islands and shrubbery zones.

Warblers

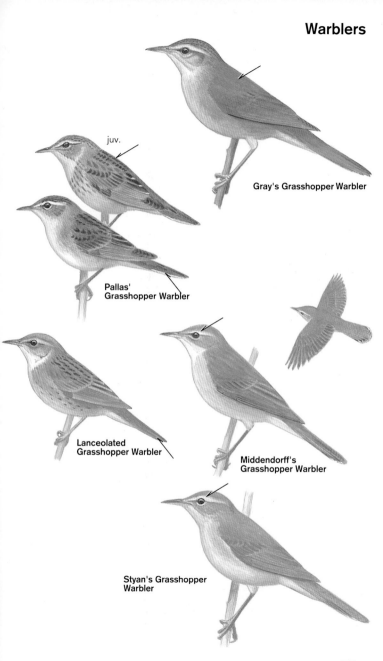

Gray's Grasshopper Warbler

juv.

Pallas' Grasshopper Warbler

Lanceolated Grasshopper Warbler

Middendorff's Grasshopper Warbler

Styan's Grasshopper Warbler

BLACK-BROWED REED WARBLER *Acrocephalus bistrigiceps* <Soegaegaebi> PM/uc • SV/r L 13.5cm. Noisy brownish bird of reedbeds with distinct head pattern. Similar to Oriental Reed Warbler and occurs in similar habitat but is smaller, and has browner upperparts; broad whitish (to pale brownish) supercilium is bordered by black lateral crown stripe; short blackish eyeline; peaked crown; underparts white, washed brown on sides and flanks, white of throat contrasting with pale brown face. **Voice:** disapproving tutting, 'tsut, tsut-tsut-tsut'; song, a complex warbling including harsh notes and trills. **Habitat:** reedbeds and grassy forests near water.

ORIENTAL GREAT REED WARBLER *Acrocephalus orientalis* <Gaegaebi> SV/c L 18.5cm. Greyish-olive brown above; paler below with whitish throat and belly; distinct whitish supercilium; dark eyeline; greyish streaks on breast in worn plumage; tail often looks square-ended and may show white tips; rump often contrastingly pale in flight; long bill shows bright orange gape when singing. **Voice:** loud, grating 'gork-gork-gork-kechi-kechi-eek-eek-eek'. **Similar species:** Thick-billed Warbler. **Habitat:** coastal and island reedbeds and marshes.

THICK-BILLED WARBLER *Acrocephalus aedon* <Keunburigaegaebi> PM/r L 20cm. Resembles Oriental Great Reed Warbler, but the face is very plain with paler lores and no distinct eyeline or supercilium; crown is rounded rather than peaked, and bill is slightly shorter and stouter, lacking dark tip to lower mandible. **Habitat:** dry, scrubby areas and forest edge (not reedbeds). **Status:** records of collection in western district, Korea.

Oriental Great Reed Warbler

Warblers

Black-browed Reed Warbler

Oriertal Great Reed Warbler

Thick-billed Warbler

DUSKY WARBLER *Phylloscopus fuscatus*
<Solsaesachon> PM/sc • SV/sc(n) L 12cm Very small, dull-brown bird, usually keep near ground, often flicking wings and tail. Overall brownish, lacking any olive or yellow in plumage; supercilium usually white in front of eye, becoming buffy behind eye, and contrasting with dark eyeline; bill usually dark-tipped with pale base to lower mandible; legs often dull pink. **Voice:** hard 'tec' or 'di! di!', song a trill of 'tiriririr' followed by 'tschwee-tschwee-tschwee...' etc. **Habitat:** scrubby grassland and forest edge.

RADDE'S WARBLER *Phylloscopus schwarzi*
<Gindarisolsaesachon> PM/sc • SV/sc(n) L 13cm Thicker-billed and with stronger legs; supercilium is also usually longer, more defined, and often buffy in front of eye, becoming white behind eye. Often cocks tail. **Voice:** call; soft 'tec' or 'tyeuk' song; 'tyuk tyuk weekweekweekweekweek' etc. **Habitat:** grassland and forests. **Status:** breeds in Backdusan and Myohyangsan in North Korea.

YELLOW-BROWED WARBLER [Inornate Warbler]
Phylloscopus inornatus <Norangnunsseopsolsae>
PM/c • SV/sc(n) L 10.5cm. Olive-green above, whitish below; lacks rump-patch, yellow on vent, white in tail and central crown stripe; has pale yellow(ish) supercilium; whitish wing bars and edges to tertials. **Voice:** call, repeated, loud, high-pitched and rising 'wee-eet' 'ooeet' 'sooweet'. **Habitat:** breeds in forests, also in parks and gardens on passage.

PALLAS' LEAF WARBLER *Phylloscopus proregulus*
<Norangheorisolsae> PM/r • SV/sc(n) L 10cm. Very small. Green above; yellow crown stripe, supercilium, wing bars, and rump; pale spot on ear-coverts; tertials edged white; short tail. In worn plumage, much duller with narrow wing bars. Short, thin bill with dark tip to lower mandible. **Voice:** song; rambling set of repeated phrases 'tuee-tuee-tueesi-si-si-si-chi-chi-chi-chewee-chewee-chewee-chewee...' each repeated 2-4 or more times, call; loud 'tueet'. **Similar species:** Yellow-browed Warbler lacks yellow rump. **Habitat:** forests, especially coriferous.

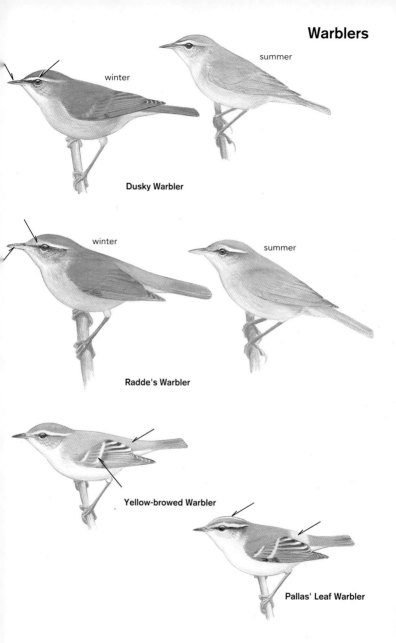

Warblers

winter

summer

Dusky Warbler

winter

summer

Radde's Warbler

Yellow-browed Warbler

Pallas' Leaf Warbler

ARCTIC WARBLER *Phylloscopus borealis* <Soesolsae> PM/c • SV/uc L 13cm. Dark olive green above with long, narrow, whitish supercilium which does not reach to forecrown; underparts greyish, tinged yellow; long primary projection gives short-tailed appearance; may show 1(-2) narrow wing bars. Subspecies *P. b. borealis* which is less yellowish below. **Br:** lower mandible orange. **Voice:** song, repeated 'chirree-chirree-chirree-'. **Similar species:** Pala-legged Willow Warbler is pale. **Habitat:** forests, gardens and parks.

PALE-LEGGED WILLOW WARBLER *Phylloscopus tenellipes* <Doesolsae> PM/uc • SV/uc L 12cm. Brownish upperparts with contrasting greyish-brown crown and nape; whitish supercilium contrasts strongly, not reaching forehead but extending well behind eye; eyeline dark brown, wider behind eye; cheeks mottled pale brown, throat whitish; white undertail coverts contrast with paler olive-brown rump and uppertail coverts, lacks greenish tinge; breast and belly whitish, washed pale brown. **Voice:** song, 'tiririririririririri' recalling Short-tailed Bush-warbler, call; rising 'tsik!'. **Habitat:** usually in lower canopy of trees and bushes.

EASTERN CROWNED WILLOW WARBLER *Phylloscopus coronatus* <Sansolsae> SV/c L 12.5cm. Olive green upperparts, washed greener on wings, mantle, and tail, and with indistinct white wing bar; (greyish-)white below with contrasting yellowish undertail coverts; yellowish-white supercilium reaches forehead and is outlined by dark grey-brown lateral crown stripe and eyestripe; centre of crown often distinctly paler olive or dull yellow; lower mandible orange-yellow; legs darkish pink. **Voice:** call high-pitched 'hweet', song; rambling combination of 'chiyawee-chiyawee-chiyawee', 'see'. **Habitat:** forests, gardens and parks.

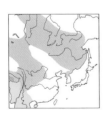

GREENISH WARBLER *Phylloscopus trochiloides* <Beodeulsolsae> PM/r L 11cm. Long yellowish-white supercilium extends from nape to bill base; dark eyestripe is less distinct in front of eye; ear-coverts are paler and plainer; usually has two wing bars, lower broad, white, upper narrower in worn plumage; legs and feet are duller and darker. **Voice:** call high-pitched 'chireeree'. **Similar species:** Yellow-browed Warbler is small and thin with dark bill. **Habitat:** forests, gardens and parks.

Warblers

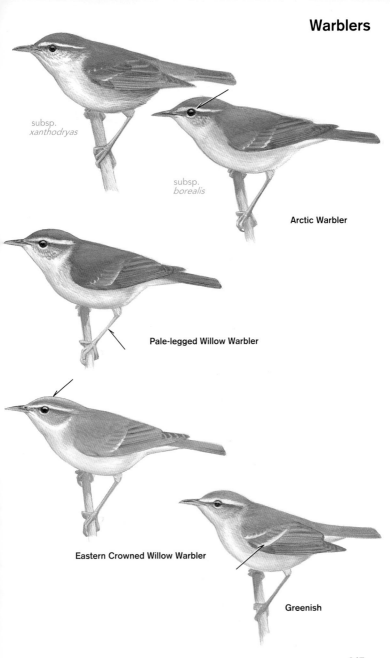

subsp.
xanthodryas

subsp.
borealis

Arctic Warbler

Pale-legged Willow Warbler

Eastern Crowned Willow Warbler

Greenish

Flycatcher Family Muscicapidae. (World : 108 species, Korea : 8 species) Small migratory birds with long wings and thin, broad-based bills, adapted for catching insects on wing. Eyes are proportionally large. Sexes differ, except *Muscicapa*.

TRICOLOR FLYCATCHER [Yellow-rumped Flycatcher] *Ficedula zanthopygia* <Huinnunsseophwang-geumsae> SV/uc L 13cm. **Male:** black upperparts with white supercilium and wingpatch, rich yellow underparts and rump. **Female:** greyish or olive-green above, paler below, with white wingbar and yellow rump; may show yellow on throat. **Voice:** contact call 'ttuu', song; melodious but slightly grating, thrush-like. **Habitat:** forests, gardens and parks.

NARCISSUS FLYCATCHER *Ficedula narcissina* <Hwanggeumsae> PM/sc(s) L 13.5cm. **Male:** black upperparts with rich yellow supercilium; rump, throat, breast and sides; conspicuous white patch on wing; deep orange on throat; white undertail coverts. **Female:** very plain olive brown above, olive rump contrasting with richer brown on tail, ear-coverts and forehead; flight feathers edged more olive; underparts whitish, undertail coverts long and white; narrow, pale creamy eye-ring; pale tips to tertials and greater coverts above. **Juv:** brownish above, feathers scaled with pale fringes. **Similar species:** Blue-and-white Flycatcher. **Habitat:** deciduous and mixed hill forests.

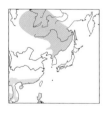

MUGIMAKI FLYCATCHER *Ficedula mugimaki* <Norangttaksae> PM/c L 13cm. **Male:** black above with white spot above and behind eye; broad white patch on wing-coverts and tertial edges; base of outer tail feathers white; throat and breast deep orange; belly white. **Female:** brown above, no white on tail; deep orange on throat, and breast; white belly. **Voice:** 'ttyu' contact; also metallic rattle call. **Habitat:** open woodlands with big trees, gardens and parks.

RED-THROATED FLYCATCHER *Ficedula parva* <Huinkkori-ttaksae> PM/r L 12cm. Black tail, often cocked, with white sides near base and long white undertail coverts striking; distinct whitish eye-ring. **Male:** upperparts greyish brown with blue-grey on face extending across upper breast; throat orange. **Female:** upperparts plain greyish brown; underparts white with creamy wash on throat and breast. **Habitat:** open woodlands, gardens and parks.

Flycatchers

Tricolor Flycatcher

Narcissus Flycatcher

Mugimaki Flycatcher

Red-throated Flycatcher

Tricolor
Flycatcher

Narcissus
Flycatcher

Mugimaki
Flycatcher

249

BLUE-AND-WHITE FLYCATCHER *Cyanoptila cyanomelana* <Keunnyurisae> SV/c L 16.5cm. **Male:** rich glossy blue upperparts; black or blue-black face and breast; white underparts. **Juv:** males are brown spotted with buff, blue appearing on wings and tail first. **Female:** very plain brown with pale eye-ring; often has white throat and center of belly; tail and flight feathers often richer brown. **Voice:** call is harsh 'tac', song a melodious warble with distinctive, final 'jit-fit'. **Habitat:** deciduous and mixed hillforests near streams.

SOOTY FLYCATCHER [Dark-sided Flycatcher] *Muscicapa sibirica* <Solttaksae> PM/uc • SV/r(n) L 13.5cm. Upperparts dark greyish brown; pale tertial edges form distinct pale wing panel; dark on sides and flanks heavily washed with brown, streaked in centre with white; white throat outlined by brown malar stripes; often has whitish submoustachials and pale line across side of neck; distinct buffy eye-ring, slightly broader behind eye; short black bill. **Similar species:** female Narcissus has olive-brown upperparts; female Blue-and-white is larger. **Habitat:** open woodlands, forests and gardens. Breeds at higher elevation than Brown.

GREY-SPOTTED FLYCATCHER [Grey-streaked Flycatcher] *Muscicapa griseisticta* <Jebi-ttaksae> PM/c L 14.5cm. Resembles smaller Sooty, but rather paler, breast, sides and flanks whitish, heavily streaked with dark greyish brown; whitish spots on tips of greater coverts, secondaries and tertials form narrow wing bars; base of upper tail may show a few whitish spots; bill black. **Voice:** thin 'seet' contact call. **Habitat:** woodlands and edges of forests in plains and low hills.

ASIAN BROWN FLYCATCHER *Muscicapa dauurica* <Soesolttaksae> PM/c • SV/r L 13cm. Plain greyish brown above, usually with pale lores and distinct whitish eye-ring slightly broader behind eye; blackish bill has pale base to lower mandible; underparts variable, whitish to pale greyish-brown with indistinct mottling. **Juv:** spotted paler. **Voice:** a soft rattle; song a very quiet and insignificant, scratchy and rambling. **Similar species:** Sooty, Grey-spotted Flycatchers. **Habitat:** open woodlands, forests, gardens. **Status:** breeds in open wooded hills up to about 1,500m.

Flycatchers

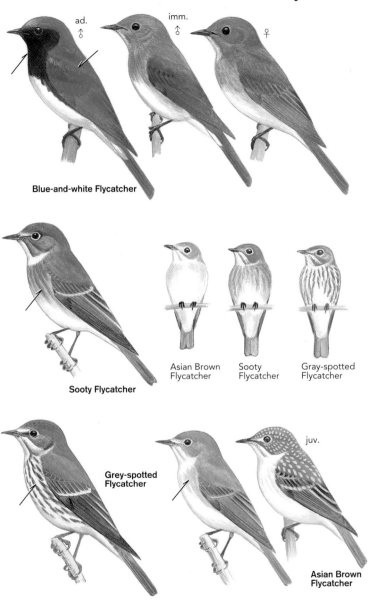

Blue-and-white Flycatcher

ad. ♂ imm. ♂ ♀

Sooty Flycatcher

Asian Brown Flycatcher

Sooty Flycatcher

Gray-spotted Flycatcher

Grey-spotted Flycatcher

juv.

Asian Brown Flycatcher

Paradise Flycatcher

Family Monarchidae (World : 132 species, Korea : 2 species) Bills are flat, wide base and sharp tip; extremely long tails of male; inhabit tops of trees and mainly eat insects.

ASIAN PARADISE FLYCATCHER *Terpsiphone paradisi* <Byeolsamgwangjo> Vag L ♂ 48cm/♀ 21cm. Bill and eye-ring blue. **Male:** rufous-chestnut back, wings and tail; crested head is black glossed (greenish-)blue and, contrasting with greyer breast. **Female:** as rufous-winged male but crest and tail are shorter, head glossy but plumage rather duller. **Habitat:** forests.

BLACK PARADISE FLYCATCHER *Terpsiphone atrocaudata* <Samgwangjo> SV/uc L ♂ 45cm/♀ 18cm. Younger males have shorter tails. Black head slightly glossed with purplish-blue on hind crown has shaggy crest; bright blue eye-ring and bill. **Male:** extremely long, blackish tail; purplish back and mantle becoming purplish-brown on wings. **Female:** duller, chestnut-brown wings and tail. **Voice:** three syllable chitter followed by fast, whistled 'heeyoy hoy-hoy-hoy'. **Habitat:** forests, and woods of lowerhills; prefers canopy.

Bearded Tits and Parrotbills

Family Panuridae (World : 19 species, Korea : 2 species) A group close to babblers (Timalidae) with main population in southeast Asia. Small to medium long-tailed birds with characteristic strong parrot-like bills.

BEARDED TIT *Panurus biarmicus* <Suyeomomongnuni> Vag L 16.5cm. Short, thin, yellowy-orange bill. pale rufous-brown upperparts, flanks and tail; whitish outer edge to upper wing, and black and white bar along inner wing. **Male:** blue-grey head with drooping black moustache; black undertail coverts. **Juv:** black back and sides of tail. **Female:** brownish head, lacking black moustache and undertail coverts. **Habitat:** reedbeds, climbing easily through red stems.

VINOUS-THROATED PARROTBILL *Paradoxornis webbianus* <Bulgeunmeoriomongnuni> Res/ab L 13 cm. Very common, tiny brown bird often occurring in large, noisy, unseen flocks moving through the undergrowth. Has brown upperparts and long tail, chestnut-brown cap and wings and pale buffish underparts; bill is short, grey, tipped paler. **Voice:** high pitched, 'siu-sii-siiiuuu' and churring contact calls. **Habitat:** scrubby areas, bamboo, and reedbelts.

Paradise Flycatchers, Parrotbills

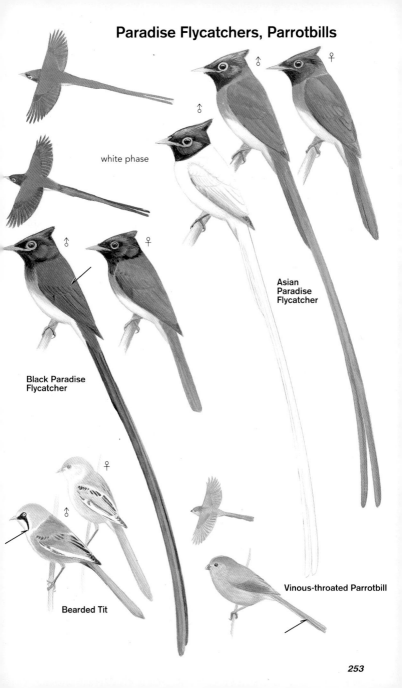

♂

♀

♂

♂

white phase

Asian
Paradise
Flycatcher

♂

♀

Black Paradise
Flycatcher

♀

♂

Bearded Tit

Vinous-throated Parrotbill

Long-tailed Tits
Family Aegithalidae (World : 8 species, Korea : 1 species) Small with long tails. Behave like true tits, being active and restless, and often moving around in mixed parties. Sexes alike.

LONG-TAILED TIT *Aegithalos caudatus* <Omongnuni> Res/c L 14cm. Tiny, long-tailed bird of wooded areas, often in mid- or upper canopy. Upper mantle black, lower mantle and rump dull pink; primaries black with white edged tertials; tail long, black with white outer feathers; *A. c. caudatus:* (northern North Korea) head and underparts entirely white; *A. c. magnus:* (South Korea) blackish lateral crown stripes and line of blackish spots across breast; some pink on flanks. **Juv:** head white with broad sooty brown mask. **Voice:** thin tzee(rr)-tzee(rr). and distinctive soft 'tssirr'. **Habitat:** wooded lowland hills.

Penduline Tits
Family Remizidae (World : 10 species, Korea : 1 species) Similar to birds true tits, but make characteristic penduline nests. Inhabit in openfield and around wetland. Sharp bill tips. Sexes alike.

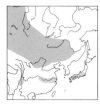

CHINESE PENDULINE TIT *Remiz consobrinus* <Swinhoomongnuni> WV/uc L 11cm. Small, pale bird of reedbeds with fine-pointed bill, often in flocks of 10-20+. **Male:** greyish crown and nape; black mask from forehead edged white; chestnut mantle, half-collar and wing-coverts contrast with dark wings and black tail in flight; whitish underparts are marked with buff. **Female:** mask brown; upperparts browner lacking chestnut. **Voice:** very thin drawn out 'tseeoo', 'sseeoo'. **Habitat:** coastal reedbeds and marshes.

Tits
Family Paridae (World : 54 species, Korea : 5 species) Small active birds with short bills, and strong legs and feet; often feed by hanging acrobatically from twigs. Often in mixed parties. Sexes similar.

VARIED TIT *Parus varius* <Gonjulbagi> Res/c L 14cm. Black crown and throat with whitish cheeks, forehead, rear crown stripe and upper breast, variably washed with buff; back and wings blue-grey; rear collar and underparts rufous. **Juv:** upperparts browner, black of head and throat much paler; later, as adult, but rufous parts are grey, rufous appearing on sides. **Voice:** song is slow, repeated 'tsu-tsuwheee', with accent on the last nasal whistle. **Habitat:** forests, woodlands, gardens and parks with mature trees.

Long-tailed Tits, Penduline Tits, Tits

juv.

subsp. *caudatus*

Long-tailed Tit

Chinese Penduline Tit

♂   ♀

Varied Tit

MARSH TIT *Parus palustris* <Soebaksae> Res/c   L 11cm. Crown, nape, and bib black, crown of adult glossy. Cheeks and underparts white or whitish; back, wings, and tail dull greyish brown. **Voice:** song resembles combined songs of Great and Coal Tits with some jarring notes; call, harsh and scolding. **Similar species:** Willow Tit best distinguished by voice. **Habitat:** forests, woodlands, gardens and parks. **Status:** resident in highlands south to Gyeonggi-do

WILLOW TIT *Parus montanus* Willow Tit <Bukbangsoebaksae> Res/r L 12.5cm. Very similar to Marsh Tit but crown is duller sooty black, lacking gloss, sometimes brownish; pale edges to secondaries usually show as a pale panel. **Voice:** song, fluty 'chee-hoo-chee'; call, soft and nasal 'eez-eez-eez'. **Habitat:** forests, woodlands, gardens and parks. **Status:** breeds locally in northern North Korea in Yangganagdo and Hamgyeong-do; rare winter visitor to South Korea sometimes reaching Gyeongsangnam-do.

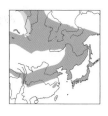

COAL TIT *Parus ater* <Jinbaksae> Res/c L 11cm. Very small, short-tailed tit with white nape and cheeks; crown black, slightly crested; throat extensively black; upperparts dark bluish-grey; tail blackish; white spots on wing-coverts make two narrow wing bars; underparts offwhite or buff. **Voice:** resembles Great Tit's, but much faster and higher in pitch, 'ssitsibbing'. **Habitat:** coniferous forests, forests, gardens and parks. **Status:** breeding troughout including Jeju-do.

GREAT TIT *Parus major* <Baksae> Res/ab L 14cm. Crown, throat and sides of neck black, encircling white cheek; hind crown white; nape yellowish merging to olive green mantle; wings bluish-grey, with white wing bar; tail dark grey. **Male:** has broad black line from throat to belly. **Female:** has narrower, less distinct line. **Juv:** dark brown crown and mantle. **Voice:** wide range including repeated 'chuppi chuppi' notes. **Habitat:** forests, woodlands and gardens.

Tits

Marsh Tit

Willow Tit

Coal Tit

Great Tit

♂ ♀

Nuthatches

Family Sittidae (World : 25 species, Korea : 2 species) Small, mostly grey-backed birds with pointed bills, and short tails. Move up and down vertical tree trunks without using tail. Sexes similar.

EURASIAN NUTHATCH *Sitta europaea* <Donggobi> Res/c L 14cm. Bluish-grey crown and upperparts; black eyestripe sometimes with narrow, white supercilium; face and underparts white with pale rufous flanks and lower belly; under-tail coverts white, tipped darker rufous. **Voice:** call 'chwit-chwit'; also a rattling 'chiriririri'. **Habitat:** woodlands, preferring deciduous forests.

CHINESE NUTHATCH *Sitta villosa* <Soedonggobi> Res/uc(n) • WV/r L 12cm Bluish-grey upperparts and buffy to orange-cinnamon underparts; bill appears uptilted. **Male:** black cap and eyestripe with white supercilium; cheeks and throat whitish. **Female:** grey crown, with narrower supercilium; duller and browner above and below than male. **Habitat:** mature coniferous forests or groves of trees.

Tree Creepers

Family Certhiidae (World : 7 species, Korea : 1 species) Small brown birds with thin decurved bills. Creep up or along tree trunks using stiff pointed tail to help grip. Sexes alike.

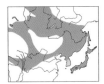

COMMON TREECREEPER [Eurasian Treecreeper] *Certhia familiaris* <Namubalbari> Res/uc(n) • WV/uc L 13cm. Upperparts dark brown streaked white and buff, barred on wings; tail plain brown; underparts white (though often difficult to see); supercilium whitish. **Habitat:** coniferous and mixed forests.

White-eyes

Family Zosteropidae (World : 85 species, Korea : 2 species) Small, greenish arboreal birds with thin bills. Sexes alike. Eats insects, fruits, beazies and dectars.

CHESTNUT-FLANKED WHITE-EYE *Zosterops erythropleurus* <Han-gukdongbaksae> PM/r L 10.5cm. Distinct chestnut patch on flanks; bill base and lower mandible may be pinkish; underparts whiter. **Similar species:** Japanese White-eye is pale brown on flanks. **Habitat:** forests prefer rather deep mixed and coniferous.

JAPANESE WHITE-EYE *Zosterops japonicus* <Dongbaksae> Res/c(s) L 11.5cm. Small, green upperparts, yellow throat, white belly; pale brown breast and flanks, distinct white eye-ring. **Habitat:** wooded lowland hills, also parks and gardens in winter. Chiefly prefer evergreen forests.

Nuthatches, Creepers, White-eyes

Eurasian Nuthatch

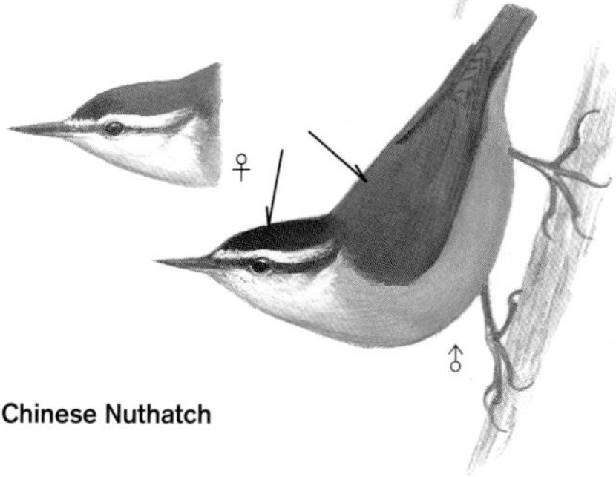

Chinese Nuthatch

♀
♂

Common Treecreeper

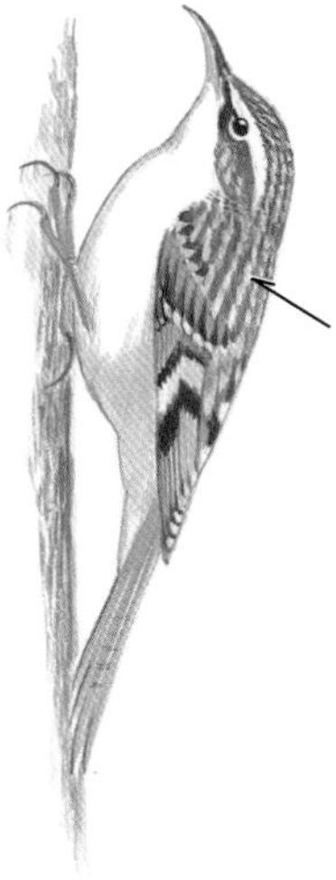

Chestnut-flanked
White-eye

Japanese
White-eye

Buntings

Family Emberizidae (World : 583 species, Korea : 20 species) A large family of seed eaters, often feeding on ground or in low bushes. Plumage of breeding males distinctive but females and non-breeders typically duller and can be hard to distinguish.

PINE BUNTING *Emberiza leucocephala* <Huin-meorimetsae> WV/r L 17cm. Large, rather rufous bunting with longish notched tail. **Male Br:** chestnut face and throat with white stripe below eye to ear-coverts; white crown stripe edged with black; broken white neck collar, and breast patch. **Male Non-Br:** grey streaks on crown, and in chestnut of face, make head pattern much less distinct. **Female Br:** greyish-brown head with pale supercilium and brownish-grey ear-coverts; **Voice:** reluctant 'dtlut'. **Habitat:** open woodlands, cultivated fields and often near arivulet.

MEADOW BUNTING *Emberiza cioides* <Metsae> Res/c L 16cm. Rufous crown; white supercilium and throat join greyish neck; chestnut ear-coverts, white submoustachial and black malar stripe; unstreaked reddish-brown underparts. **Juv:** head, breast and back brownish with dark streaks gradually becoming rufous. **Voice:** call is a clear, metallic note given 1-3 times, 'chi chi chi'. **Habitat:** open woodlands, cultivated fields.

JANKOWSKI'S BUNTING [Rufous-backed Bunting] *Emberiza jankowskii* <Jeombagimetsae> Vag L 16cm. Ear-coverts grey, lacks rufous underparts; narrow white edges to wing-coverts form narrow wingbars. **Male Br:** rufous crown, back and tail, with streaking on back. **Female Br:** duller, often with streaks on upper breast, centre of breast greyish. **Habitat:** dry overgrown sand dunes, with low bushes or trees and open grassy areas.

RUSTIC BUNTING *Emberiza rustica* <Ssuksae> WV/ab L 15cm. Short crest and noticeable white underparts. **Male Br:** black head with white supercilium, moustachial, rear crown stripe and throat; chestnut nape, sides, flanks and broken breastband. **Male Non-Br:** whitish submoustachial, supercilium and central crown stripe; dark brown ear-coverts, moustachial and malar stripes. **Female Br:** similar to male Br. but centre of crown white, with less striking head pattern, ear-coverts brown with pale spot at rear. **Voice:** single 'tclip' or 'tzit' often repeated. **Habitat:** open lowland woods, paddyfields, and riverbanks.

Buntings

Pine Bunting

summer ♂ winter ♂ ♀

Meadow Bunting

♂ ♀

Meadow Bunting Rustic Bunting Yellow-throated Bunting

Jankowski's Bunting

♂ ♀

Rustic Bunting

summer ♂ winter ♂ ♀

TRISTRAM'S BUNTING *Emberiza tristrami* <Huinbaemetsae> PM/c L 14cm. **Male:** head and throat black with narrow, white central crown stripe, supercilium, submoustachial stripe, and usually small earspot; back rufous-brown, streaked with black; rump and tail rufous; breast, sides and flanks rufous-brown streaked darker; rest of underparts white. **Female:** as male, but black parts are browner, ear-coverts and lores pale brown; throat streaked; blackish malar contrasts with rufous breast. **Voice:** high 'cheet'. **Similar species:** female Yellow-browed Bunting. **Habitat:** prefers open areas among cypress trees.

YELLOW-BROWED BUNTING *Emberiza chrysophrys* <Norangnunsseopmetsae> PM/sc L 14cm. **Male:** black head with white crown stripe, submoustachial, ear spot and throat; supercilium yellow above eye, becoming white on nape; upperparts greyish brown, streaked blackish; underparts white washed pale brown on sides of breast and flanks; throat, upper breast, and flanks streaked blackish brown. **Female:** like male but lores and cheeks pale brown; black parts are browner. **Voice:** 'tzit'. **Similar species:** Tristram's Bunting is darker. **Habitat:** forests, cultivated fields.

YELLOW-THROATED BUNTING *Emberiza elegans* <Norangteongmetsae> Res/c L 16cm. Distinctive crest and greyish rump. **Male:** black mask, crest; and breast patch; throat and hindcrown yellow; upperparts greyish-brown streaked with dark chestnut on back; underparts white with chestnut streaks on sides of breast and flanks. **Female:** lacks black on head and breast; brown crest and ear-coverts, pale yellowish-brown supercilium and throat. **Voice:** 'tzi tzit tzitzit' or 'choo-ee choo-ee'. **Habitat:** open woods and forest edges; usually stays in cover.

RED-HEADED BUNTING *Emberiza bruniceps* <Bulgeunmeorimetsae> Vag L 16cm. Very bulky. **Male:** chestnut head and breast (crown sometimes yellow); yellow underparts and rump; mantle greeny-yellow streaked blackish. **Female:** overall sandy-brown with some streaking on crown, nape and scapulars; wing-coverts and flight feathers with pale fringes. **Similar species:** extremely similar female Black-headed Bunting. **Habitat:** cultivated fields and open fields. **Status:** one male captured in Deokso, Namyangju, Gyeonggi-do in October 1982.

Buntings

Tristram's Bunting

Yellow-browed Bunting

Yellow-throated Bunting

Red-headed Bunting

YELLOW-BREASTED BUNTING *Emberiza aureola* <Geomeunmeorichoksae> PM/uc L 15cm. **Male:** black face and throat, chestnut crown, nape, back, rump, and breast band; white shoulder patch and wing bar; yellow underparts. **Female:** well-marked head pattern with broad creamy-white supercilium and pale crown stripe; clear wingbars; almost unmarked pale yellow underparts. **Habitat:** usually near wetlands, reedbeds and grasslands.

CHESTNUT BUNTING *Emberiza rutila* <Kkokka-chamsae> PM/c L 14cm. Smallish. **Male:** chestnut hood, back, rump and wing-coverts; yellow underparts with dark streaks on flanks. **Female:** non-descript; upperparts olive brown streaked black, rump dull chestnut; head greyish-buff with slightly paler supercilium; throat buffy, never yellow; rest of underparts including undertail coverts pale yellow with brownish streaks on sides and flanks. **Habitat:** cultivated fields with bushes and trees.

YELLOW BUNTING *Emberiza sulphurata* <Mudang-sae> PM/sc(s) L 14cm. **Male:** upperparts dark greenish-grey, streaked blackish on back; split white eye-ring, black lores and narrow black chin; two wing bars; underparts dull yellowish-green, brighter yellow on throat; some streaking on flanks. **Female:** as male but paler, especially on upperparts; lacks dark lores and chin; bill all bluish-grey. **Habitat:** cultivated fields with bushes and trees.

GREY-HEADED BUNTING [Chestnut-eared Bunting] *Emberiza fucata* <Bulgeunppyammetsae> SV/uc L 16cm. **Male:** grey head and nape grey streaked with black; chestnut ear-coverts, shoulder patch and lower breastband; back greyish-brown streaked black; throat and breast white; upper breast band streaked black. **Female:** duller with less prominent breastbands. **Voice:** Resembles Rustic Bunting's but usually quieter. **Habitat:** grassland and near wetlands, open fields and cultivated fields.

LITTLE BUNTING *Emberiza pusilla* <Soebulgeun-ppyammetsae> PM/uc • WV/sc L 13cm. Head and upper throat chestnut; distinct lateral crown stripes; pale eye-ring; lacks moustache; upperparts greyish brown streaked black; small thin bill whitish underparts streaked black on breast and sides. **Voice:** Similar to Rustic's but thinner. **Habitat:** open fields and open cultivated fields with grasses and trees especially near reedbeds.

Buntings

↑ imm.

♂

♀

Yellow-breasted Bunting

♂

♀

Chestnut Bunting

♂

♀

Yellow Bunting

♂

♀

Grey-headed Bunting

♂

♀

Little Bunting

BLACK-FACED BUNTING *Emberiza spodocephala* <Choksae> PM/c • WV/uc L 16cm. Bunting with peaked crown and most obvious white in tail; lower mandible pink. **Male:** head and breast grey with extensive black around lores and chin; back is dark chestnut brown streaked with black; rump is grey-brown, tail dark brown, edged white; underparts are yellowish, streaked brown on flanks. **Female:** head pattern variable but often dark brown with greyish supercilium and partial neck collar; paler malar stripe; underparts yellowish-buff to greyish white, streaked dark brown on breast and sides. **Voice:** single hard, metallic 'tzit' or 'tzee'. **Habitat:** forests and cultivated fields.

GREY BUNTING *Emberiza variabilis* <Geom-eunmetsae> WV/r(s) L 17cm. Lacks white in tail. **Male:** dark slaty-grey, streaked darker on back; white under tail coverts, pinkish lower mandible and legs. **Female:** Upperparts brown, streaked black and buff; richer brown on ear-coverts, crown, rump and uppertail coverts; pale throat and submoustachial stripes; pale, streaked underparts. **Habitat:** feeds on ground amongst trees in areas of dapplled sunlight.

LAPLAND LONGSPUR *Calcarius lapponicus* <Ginbaltopmetsae> WV/uc L 16cm. Long hind toe (longspur) of dark legs visible only at close range; bill yellowish or horn-colored. **Male:** black on crown, face, throat, and upper breast; white supercilium joins white on neck; hindneck chestnut; back brown, streaked with black; belly white, flanks streaked black. **Female:** upperparts light brown, streaked darker, chestnut greater wing-coverts and nape; pale supercilium and submoustachial; underparts white, streaked black on sides of breast and flanks. **Similar species:** Rustic Bunting has crest, different call. **Voice:** short trill, interspersed with a hard 'tuu'. **Habitat:** open fields as dry cultivated fields.

SNOW BUNTING *Plectrophenax nivalis* <Huin-metsae> Vag L 16cm. Long wings. **Male Br:** mostly white with black-patterned upperparts, notably wingtips. **Male Non-Br:** black on back becomes mottled with white and brown; crown, nape and breast suffused with orange-brown. **Female:** as non-Br. male but rather browner overall; with less white in wing. **Habitat:** forests, open fields and cultivated fields.

Buntings

subsp. *spodocephala* ♂ ♀

Black-faced Bunting

subsp. *personata* ♂ ♀

Grey Bunting ♂ imm. ♀

♂ summer ♂ winter ♀

Lapland Longspur

♂ winter ♀

♂ summer ♂ ♀

Snow Bunting

JAPANESE REED BUNTING *Emberiza yessoensis* <Soegeomeunmeorissuksae> WV/uc L 15cm. Typically, the richest-coloured of the reed buntings, with the pinkest legs and bill in winter. **Male:** dark back; upperparts chestnut, striped black and buff; off-white, unstreaked underparts washed with buff on breast and sides; nape brown but sides of neck whitish. **Female:** buffy submoustachial and throat, and black malar stripes, crown dark brown streaked pale. **Juv:** pale greyish brown central crown stripe; rump yellowish brown. **Voice:** call 'sur-swee-ik' or 'tik'. **Similar species:** male Stonechat, other Reed Buntings. **Habitat:** open fields near water.

PALLAS' REED BUNTING *Emberiza pallasi* <Bukbanggeomeunmeorissuksae> WV/c L 14cm. **Male:** black hood; white submoustachial stripe, collar, and underparts; pale buff rump, ash-grey lesser wing-coverts, and pale streaking on underparts sparse, often restricted to flanks; back and mantle pale brown streaked black; bill black. **Female:** throat whitish, wing patch is grey brown not ash-grey, rump indistinctly streaked rufous. **Similar species:** Reed Buntings. **Voice:** often a bored-sounding 'tirrink' or 'tirrip'. **Habitat:** marsh wetlands, reedbeds, grassland near water.

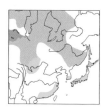

REED BUNTING *Emberiza schoeniclus* <Geomeunmeorissuksae> WV/uc L 16cm. More streaked on underparts than other reed buntings. **Male:** Similar to Pallas's but larger, back usually browner; rump greyish; closed wings rufous-brown with black streaks. **Female:** head brown with contrasting whitish supercilium and malar stripe; nape pale greyish-brown; back brown streaked whitish and black; rump greyish; underparts whitish with some brown streaking mainly on flanks. **Similar species:** other Reed Buntings. **Voice:** call, falling 'jirr', then rising 'chween'. **Habitat:** reedbeds, grasslands near water.

Pallas' Reed Bunting

Reed Bunting

Buntings

♂ summer ♂ winter ♀

Japanese Reed Bunting

♂ summer ♂ winter ♀

Pallas' Reed Bunting

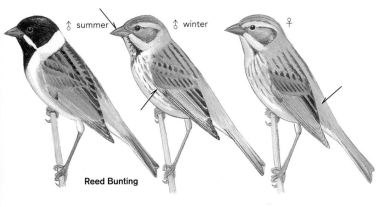

♂ summer ♂ winter ♀

Reed Bunting

Finches
Family Fringillidae (World : 124 species, Korea : 16 species)
Typical seed-eaters with thick bills.

ORIENTAL GREENFINCH *Carduelis sinica* <Bang-ulsae> Res/c L 14cm. Greenish finch with pale pink bill and yellow flashes on wings and tail in flight. **Male:** overall greenish brown, with grey crown and nape, and face washed greenish with dark lores; undertail and outer uppertail coverts. **Female:** more brown than green. **Juv:** like female with fine black streaks above and below, paler yellow on wing and tail. **Voice:** 'du-wee' contact call, and short trilling flight call. **Similar species:** Siskin is smaller, paler and yellower, with black streaks. **Habitat:** forests, open cultivated fields and gardens.

SISKIN *Carduelis spinus* <Geomeunmeoribang-ulsae> WV/c L 12.5cm. Streaky yellow-green finch with patterned head and longish, pointed, pink bill. **Male:** black crown and bib, yellow breast and face; yellow-green back and ear-coverts, with black streaks; blackish wings with two yellow wing bars. **Female:** yellow on head and wings much duller, crown and back brown streaked darker, underparts finely streaked. **Voice:** harsh twittering and 'tziilu'. **Habitat:** forests, coniferous forests, gardens.

COMMON REDPOLL *Carduelis flammea* <Hong-bang-ulsae> WV/uc L 13.5cm. A small brownish-grey finch, with short yellowish bill, and usually red forehead. **Male:** forehead and breast bright pink with dark bib and lores; face, flanks and rump often pinkish too; streaked grey brown back; whitish underparts with conspicuous dark streaks on sides, flanks and rump; two white wing-bars in blackish wings. **Female:** lacks pink on breast and flanks. **Similar species:** white flanks in Hoary Redpoll. **Voice:** much-repeated 'tyek-tyek-tyek'. **Habitat:** forests, coniferous forests, gardens. **Status:** varying greatly from year to year.

HOARY REDPOLL *Carduelis hornemanni* <Soe-hongbang-ulsae> WV/r(n) L 13cm. Fewer dark streaks on flanks; back appears whiter with more contrasting streaks; unstreaked white rump, may be tinged with pink in male. **Male:** red patch on forehead smaller. **Female:** darker than male. **Voice:** similar to Common Redpoll. **Habitat:** forests, coniferous forests and gardens. **Status:** captured(3 times) in Hamgyeongbuk-do and Pyeongannam-do.

Finches

♀

♂

Oriental Greenfinch

juv.

Siskin

♂

♀

Common Redpoll

♂

♀

Hoary Redpoll

♂

♀

271

BRAMBLING *Fringilla montifringilla* <Doesae> WV/c L 16cm. Usually a brown and orange finch, dark at a distance, with a striking white rump. **Male Br:** upperparts black with some pale scaling; black bill and tail; rufous breast, shoulders and wingbar. **Non-Br:** head and back scaled with rufous-buff and grey, grey sides to neck; yellowish bill tipped black. **Female:** two blackish lateral crown stripes. **Juv:** head washed brownish. **Similar species:** Bullfinch has white rump. **Habitat:** woodlands, cultivated fields and gardens. **Status:** hundred thounsands wintering at Hadong-gun Gyeongsangnam-do on middle 1990's.

COMMON ROSEFINCH [Scarlet Rosefinch] *Carpodacus erythrinus* <Jeogwonja> SV/sc(n) • PM/r L 14cm. **Male:** head, throat, breast and rump red, varying in extent individually; belly and flanks white. **Female:** upperparts dark brown, streaked black; underparts paler. **Similar species:** Red Crossbill has larger head, shorter tail, larger crossed bill. Pallas's Rose Finch is bigger. **Habitat:** forests prefering bushy areas and woodland edges. **Status:** breeding in northeast in North Korea, but rare South Korea.

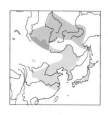

PALLAS'S ROSEFINCH *Carpodacus roseus* <Yangjini> WV/c L 15cm. A bulky forest finch, with medium-length tail lacking white edges. Bill pale grey or horn. **Male:** dark pink above and below with white lower belly, older birds lacking streaks on rump and underparts; forehead and throat scaled with silvery tips; back streaked black; pale pink edges to wing-coverts. **Female:** pale brown streaked black except on dark pink rump; head, throat and back tinged with variable amount of dark pink. **Voice:** 'Zeet'. **Habitat:** forests, cultivated fields with trees.

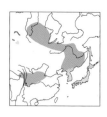

LONG-TAILED ROSEFINCH *Uragus sibiricus* <Ginkkorihong-yangjini> WV/c L 18cm. Pink or orange-brown finch with longish, white-edged black tail. **Male:** mostly pink; head heavily washed with silvery-white with dark pink lores; back streaked blackish; black wings have two white wing bars, and a white panel on the tertials. **Female:** pale brown above and below with some darker streaking, richer brown on uppertail coverts. **Similar species:** Rose Finch. **Habitat:** cultivated fields with bushes, forests, wetlands and forest edges.

Finches

↑ winter

↑ summer

♀

Brambling

↑

♀

↑ imm.

Common Rosefinch

♀

↑ imm.

↑

Pallas's Rosefinch

↑ summer

↑ winter

♀

Long-tailed Rosefinch

ROSY FINCH *Leucosticte arctoa* <Galsaeg-yangjini> WV/r L 16cm. A dark, rather long-winged finch of open country, with contrasting pale brown nape and yellowish bill. **Male:** forehead, face, and throat blackish, and contrasting with pale brown nape; back brown streaked with black; wing-coverts washed with pink, underparts brown, belly and rump spotted with pink. **Female:** generally duller with paler, less extensive pink on underparts. **Similar species:** Alpine Accentor has rufous belly and rump, grey head, and pinky-brown legs. **Habitat:** mountain forest, cultivated and open fields.

PINE GROSBEAK *Pinicola enucleator* <Sor-yangjini> Vag L 20cm. Large, rounded finch with grey rear underparts and large dark bill. **Male:** Pink head, breast and upper belly, streaked darker on back; black wings with white edges to wing-coverts and tertials. **Female:** as male but head, breast and upper belly yellow brown. **Voice:** 'pee pee pyui'. **Similar species:** Crossbills; Rosefinches. **Habitat:** forests, forests edge with bushes. **Status:** one captured in Hamgyeounbuk-do to November, 1959.

COMMON CROSSBILL [Red Crossbill] *Loxia curvirostra* <Soljatsae> WV/uc L 16.5cm. **Male:** red head and body, often mottled brown around face; blackish wings and tail. **Female:** brownish grey, unstreaked and washed with yellow on underparts, crown and back; yellow rump. **Juv:** as female but has conspicuous dark brown streaks on the underparts. **Voice:** hard 'jip-jip', 'tjupi-tjupi'. **Similar species:** female White-winged Crossbill is streaked. White-winged Crossbill. **Habitat:** coniferous forests.

WHITE-WINGED CROSSBILL *Loxia leucoptera* <Huinjukjisoljatsae> Vag L 15cm. Crossed black bill, and blackish wings with two broad white wing bars and white tertial tips diagnostic. **Male:** red head and body, often mottled brown around face, and black tail. **Female:** greyish-brown streaked brown and washed with olive yellow on crown, back and underparts, and greenish yellow rump. **Juv:** as female but more streaked, wingbars yellowish. **Voice:** short nasal 'zher-zher-zher' 'giyo giyo giyo'; also redpoll-like 'jet-jet-jet'. **Similar species:** see Common Crossbill. **Habitat:** coniferous forests. **Status:** one pair captured to Yangsan Gyeongsangnam-do, 1969.

Finches

Rosy Finch

Pine Grosbeak

♂ ♀ ♂ imm.

Common Crossbill

♂ ♀ juv.

White-winged Crossbill

♂ ♀

BULLFINCH *Pyrrhula pyrrhula* <Meotjaeng-i>
WV/uc L 15cm. Short-necked finch, with
diagnostic black cap and bib, and white rump.
Male: red face and pinky-brown breast; pale grey
body with black wings and tail, showing
conspicuous white wing bar and rump in flight.
Female: as male but back brown with grey nape,
cheeks and underparts pale pinky-brown. **Juv:**
head grey-brown, lacking black cap; cheeks buffy.
Subspecies *cassinii* male has red cheeks, breast
and upper belly; female is orange below and has
small white wingbar. **Voice:** soft, far-carrying,
whistled 'hsuu'. **Habitat:** forests, gardens and
open fields.

CHINESE GROSBEAK *Eophona migratoria*
<Milhwaburi> SV/uc L 19cm. **Male:** distinctive
glossy black head and throat, and blue black
wings; nape and back brown, with greyer rump
contrasting with black tail in flight; underparts
greyer, with rufous flanks. **Female:** head grey
brown; tips of primaries black edged white. **Juv:**
as female but has buff wing bar. **Similar species:**
Japanese Grosbeak is larger, greyer, with black on
head not extending to cheeks, and different wing
pattern. **Habitat:** forests, woodlands, gardens and
open fields.

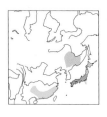

JAPANESE GROSBEAK *Eophona personata*
<Keunburimilhwaburi> WV/sc • SV/r(n) L 21cm.
Glossy black crown and face and wings; back and
underparts pale grey tinged brownish towards
tertials; white patch in primaries. **Juv:** greyish-
brown head, black around bill base only; black
wings and tail; bill duller. **Similar species:** see
Hawfinch, Chinese Grosbeak. **Habitat:** woodlands,
gardens. **Status:** Scarcely wintering Jeju-do, rare
breeding in North Korea. Wintering recorded in
Gwangneung.

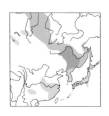

HAWFINCH *Coccothraustes coccothraustes*
<Kongsae> WV/c L 18cm. Compact-looking, with
massive bill and short tail tipped white; conspicuous
white wing bars in flight. **Male:** yellowish-brown head
with black bib and lores; grey nape; back and wings
dark brown with glossy blue secondaries; rump and
tail yellowish-brown tipped white; underparts pale
pinkish-brown; white wing bars and tail tip are
conspicuous in flight. **Female:** duller; lores dark
brown; head and underparts greyer; secondaries
pale blue. **Similar species:** Chinese Grosbeaks.
Habitat: forests, gardens and open fields.

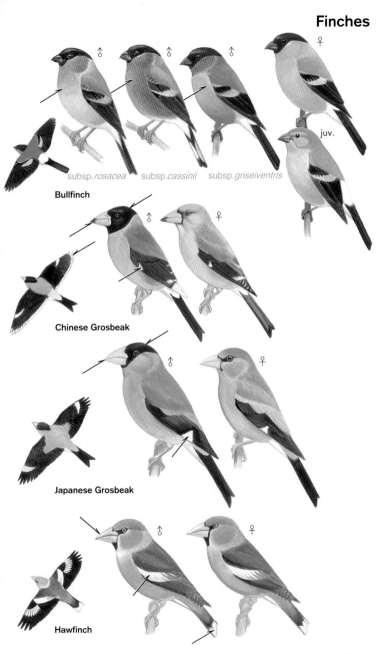

Finches

♀

subsp. *rosacea*   subsp. *cassinii*   subsp. *griseiventris*

♂   ♂   ♂

juv.

Bullfinch

Chinese Grosbeak
♂   ♀

Japanese Grosbeak
♂   ♀

Hawfinch
♂   ♀

Weaver Finches

Family Ploceidae (World : 161 species, Korea : 2 species) The genus Passer are small-sized members of this family.

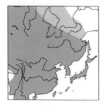

TREE SPARROW *Passer montanus* <Chamsae> Res/ab L 14.5cm. Sexes alike. Crown plain chestnut, white collar and cheeks with black cheek spot; black bib and lores; back rich brown streaked black; white line on nape; two narrow white wing bars. **Juv:** duller, cheekspot much paler. **Similar species:** Russet Sparrow lacks cheekspot. **Voice:** 'tjack, tjack'. **Habitat:** cultivated fields, village and near urban.

RUSSET SPARROW *Passer rutilans* <Seomchamsae> Res/c(l) • WV/c(l) L 13cm. Very limited range in South Korea. Looks shorter-tailed and paler than Tree Sparrow, with clear white on median coverts forming wing-bar on closed wing. **Male:** rufous-brown head and back with black streaks on back; whitish cheeks and greyish underparts. **Female:** upperparts, including eyestripe and crown, grey-brown; whitish supercilium; white wingbar. **Voice:** 'tsyo tsyo, tsick tsick'. **Similar species:** see Tree Sparrow.

Starlings

Family Sturnidae (World : 108 species, Korea : 5 species) Medium-sized birds with short tails. Often in large flocks.

GREY STARLING [White-cheeked Starling] *Sturnus cineraceus* <Jjireuregi> SV/c • WV/uc(s) L 24cm. The only widespread starling in Korea. Bulky, with white tip to tail, across face and as narrow band on rump; orange bill and legs. **Male:** glossy black head; upperparts grey-brown; underparts paler with blackish breastband. **Female:** duller. **Juv:** generally browner. **Voice:** variety of loud, deep chattering notes. 'tchirr tchirr'. **Similar species:** Violet-backed Starling. **Habitat:** gardens, suburb and near village.

VIOLET-BACKED STARLING [Chestnut-cheeked Starling] *Sturnus philippensis* <Soejjireuregi> SV/r L 19cm. **Male:** creamy-white head with chestnut cheeks and sides of neck; small white wing bar; black back glossed purple. Black wings and tail glossed green; underparts grey with buff vent; bill and legs black. **Female:** head and underparts pale greyish-brown, back brown with paler rump, tail blackish. **Similar species:** Daurian Starling is grey on head, blackspot on backhead. **Voice:** 'shaairr'. 'pbu-i, kue, kue, pbu-i'. **Habitat:** near village, gardens.

Weaver Finches, Starlings

summer   winter   juv.

Tree Sparrow

♂ summer   ♂ winter   ♀

Russet Sparrow

juv.

Grey Starling

♂   ♀

Violet-backed Starting

DAURIAN STARLING *Sturnus sturninus*
<Bukbangsoejjireuregi> SV/r(s) • SV/c(n) L 18cm.
Combination of dark nape-patch, whitish scapulars
and small tertial spots diagnostic. Black bill. **Male:**
grey head and underparts, black spot on nape,
black back glossed purple; wings black glossed
green, with white wingbar. **Female:** dull dark
brown on back, wings and nape. Fainter scapular
and tertial markings. **Voice:** soft 'prrup', 'tzir-rk
tzirr-rk'. **Similar species:** Violet-backed Starling.
Habitat: gardens, cultivated fields and near
building.

GREY-BACKED STARLING [White-shouldered
Starling] *Sturnus sinensis* <Jaetbitsoejjireuregi>
Vag L 18cm. **Male:** conspicuous white shoulder-
patch; upperparts and breast grey, paler on head
and rump, belly white; black tail edged white;
blue-grey bill and legs. **Female:** upperparts darker
grey than in male, with smaller white shoulder-
patch. **Juv:** lacks white shoulder-patch. **Habitat:**
woodlands, gardens. **Status:** recorded on Busan,
October 1959, to Dochodo Jeollanam do, July
1998.

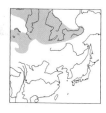

COMMON STARLING *Sturnus vulgaris* <Huin-
jeomjjireuregi> Vag L 21cm. A dark starling. **Non-
Br:** new feathers are tipped with arrow-shaped
white or buff marks giving very speckled
appearance; bill brownish. **Br:** plumage black with
greenish or violet gloss, and only light speckling.
Bill yellow. Legs are dark orange. **Similar species:**
Grey Starling is white on chick, flanks. **Voice:**
'gyyairr'. **Habitat:** parks, rural areas. **Status:**
recorded to Cheonsuman Choongcheongnam-do,
Haenam Jeollanam-do and Jeju-do.

Orioles Family Oriolidae (World : 26 species, Korea : 1 species)
Medium-sized birds with colourful male plumage though female is usually
duller.

BLACK-NAPED ORIOLE *Oriolus chinensis*
<Kkoekkori> SV/c L 26cm. **Male:** golden yellow
body and wing-coverts with black eyestripes meeting
on hindcrown and nape, black tail edged
with yellow; bill fleshy pink. **Female:** black
eyestripe is narrower and back and wings are
greenish yellow. **Juv:** more greenish-yellow above,
no napeband, creamy below with blackish streaks,
yellowish flanks and vent, dark bill. **Voice:** mewing
'meee-aooww' and 'too-ee-oo'. **Habitat:**

Starlings, Orioles

Daurian Starling

♂ ♀

Grey-backed Starling

♂ ♀

Common Starling

winter summer

Black-naped Oriole

♂ ♀ juv.

Drongos

Family Dicruridae (World : 22 species, Korea : 3 species) Arboreal birds usually with glossy black plumage, and tails of varied shape and length.

BLACK DRONGO *Dicrurus macrocercus* <Geomeunbaramkkamagwi> Vag L 29cm. Slightly glossed blue on nape, back, and breast. Tail long and deeply forked, flat or only slightly upcurved. Undulating flight. **Habitat:** open areas; likes to perch on wires or bushes and watch for prey. **Status:** one individual captured near Manripo, Chungcheongnam-do in May 1988. One photographed Kagodo, Jeollanam-do, May 2000.

HAIR-CRESTED DRONGO [Spangled Drongo] *Dicrurus hottentottus* <Baramkkamagwi> Vag L 32cm. Glossy black with waxy greenish gloss to back and tail; some long, glossy blue feathers on crown, throat and breast form 'spangles'; long tail with tips of tail feathers strongly curved upward and inward. **Juv:** sooty-brown, lacking gloss; tail curls not developed. **Habitat:** forests, marsh land of tropical seashore and evergreen forests. **Status:** one captured in Koseong Gyeongsang-nam-do in November 1959.

ASHY DRONGO *Dicrurus leucophaeus leucogenis* <Hoesaekbaramkkamagwi> Vag L 29cm. Upperparts mid-grey with black forehead, chin, and primaries, and dark-grey tail; patch surrounding the eye is very pale grey; underparts pale grey becoming whitish on vent and undertail coverts; tail long, feathers curving out. **Similar species:** Ashy Minivet. **Habitat:** forests, bushes and urban parks, prefers forest edges. **Status:** One captured in Yongcheon Pyeonganbuk-do in January 1961.

Wood Swallow

Family Artamidae (World : 10 species, Korea : 1 species) Catch insects in flight; make cup-shaped nests on branches or in holes in trees. Often gregarious.

WHITE-BREASTED WOOD SWALLOW *Artamus leucorhynchus* <Huingaseumsupjebi> Vag L 17.5cm. Chunky birds with rather straight-edged, triangular wings. Black upperparts, throat, and tail; white underparts and rump; strong, grey-blue bill and black legs. **Juv:** back scaled buff, bill brownish. **Habitat:** grasslands, cultivated fields, open areas. **Status:** single record on Jeju-do.

**Drongos,
Wood Swallows**

Black Drongo

Hair-crested Drongo

Ashy Drongo

White-breasted Wood Swallow

Crows Family Corvidae (World : 112 species, Korea : 9 species)
Medium to large birds with harsh voices. Sexes alike.

JAY *Garrulus glandarius* <Eochi> Res/c L 33cm. Rusty-brown head, breast and nape, black moustachial stripe and brown eye; pale greyish brown back; diagnostic blue on wing-coverts. White wing patch, and strongly contrasting white rump and black tail, are conspicuous in flight. **Voice:** loud harsh 'Khyaaah-Khyaaah' in alarm. **Habitat:** forests. especially coniferous.

AZURE-WINGED MAGPIE *Cyanopica cyana* <Mulkkachi> Res/c L 37cm. Black cap and bill, with whitish throat and collar, grey mantle and belly, and light blue wings and tail; tail is tipped white. Legs black. **Juv:** back mottled with brown; crown speckled with white. **Voice:** groups are very vocal, calling with coarse, rasping 'ghee jik'; also rising 'gil'. **Habitat:** forests of near water, hill and near orchards.

BLACK-BILLED MAGPIE *Pica pica* <Kkachi> Res/ab L 46cm. Makes domed nests in the branches of tall trees or bushes, or on poles. Unmistakable; black head and bill, breast, back, tail, wings and undertail coverts; tail is long and wedge-shaped, and, like wings, glossed with blue, green or purple; shoulders and belly are white; white primaries edged with black are conspicuous only in flight. **Voice:** 'chakak', 'kschak'. **Habitat:** cultivated and open fields of rural and urban areas.

SPOTTED NUTCRACKER *Nucifraga caryocatactes* <Jatkkamagwi> Res/r • WV/sc L 35cm. Short-tailed and broad-winged; dark brown body is heavily spotted with white, more streaked on face; crown is darker brown, and unspotted; wings are black; most of tail below and under-tail coverts are white; bill black. **Voice:** rasping 'kra'; also even pitched 'kraa'. **Habitat:** coniferous forests of high mountains. Often moving lower in winter.

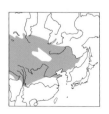

RED-BILLED CHOUGH *Pyrrhocorax pyrrhocorax* <Bulgeunburi-kkamagwi> Vag L 40cm. All black with distinctive, slender, curved, red bill and red legs. **Juv:** orange color bill. **Voice:** 'kiyaw', 'chaw'. **Habitat:** rocky forests. **Status:** one record in Saha Busan in January 1981, mixed in with a flock of Black-billed Magpies.

Jays, Magpies, Nutcrackers, Choughs

Jay

Azure-winged Magpie

Black-billed Magpie

Spotted Nutcracker

Red-billed Chough

juv.

DAURIAN JACKDAW *Corvus dauuricus* <Gal-kkamagwi> WV/uc L 33cm. Small black or pied crows the size of doves, with small bills. Dark phase is entirely black except for slightly grey nape; light phase has black face, back, wings and tail, with white nape, breast and belly. **Voice:** short 'chok', 'chayk' and 'chaa'. **Similar species:** Rook bill is straight, sharp. **Habitat:** open rice-fields; often sits on telephone wires or in trees. **Status:** usually in small flocks in with Rooks.

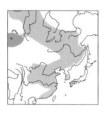

ROOK *Corvus frugilegus* <Tte-kkamagwi> WV/uc L 47cm. All black plumage, with slim, greyish-black bill, and black legs with loosely feathered thighs. Often perches on overhead cables. Whitish area of bare skin at base of bill; steep forehead and rather square-headed profile. **Voice:** 'kaa'. **Similar species:** Daurian Jackdaw, Carrion Crow. **Habitat:** cultivated and open fields. **Status:** winter and on migration forms large flocks, sometimes hundreds strong (e.g. near Jeonju).

CARRION CROW *Corvus corone* <Kkamagwi> Res/c L 50cm. Black plumage with indistinct purplish gloss; bill is thinner than that of Large-billed Crow or Rook; posture when calling is also different. Bill, crown, nape and shoulders usually appear smoothly rounded in profile. **Voice:** harsh, grating 'khaaw'. **Similar species:** Jungle Crow. **Habitat:** mainly mountains areas and forests near village. **Status:** widespread in mountains in summer; moves to more lowland areas in winter.

JUNGLE CROW *Corvus macrorhynchos* <Keunburi-kkamagwi> Res/c L 57cm. All black with variable degree of faint purplish or bluish gloss, particularly on wings; bill is very deep, with upper mandible very curved from centre to tip; feathers on forehead, and sometimes on chin, often erected to give diagnostic steep angle. Often in family groups. **Voice:** much less rasping than Carrion Crow; 'Kaw, kaw'. **Similar species:** Carrion Crow, Rook. **Habitat:** mostly woodlands, breeding to forest of near village, lower woodlands, cultivated and open fields in winter.

Crows

Daurian Jackdaw

juv.

imm.

Rook

juv.

Carrion Crow

Jungle Crow

Reference

<Korean>

Cultural Properties Administration. 1998. *A white book of Natural Monuments.* Cultural Properties Administration.

Kim, Jeong-Rak, Jin-Jo Gang, Don Lee, Hyeon-Sam Kim, Seok-Hyeon Gang, Shin-Won Choi, Heung-Dam Eo, Dong-Su Kim, Myeong-Chul Kim, Uk-Geun Hong and Gwan-Pil Lee. 1993. *Natural history of Mt. Baekdu (Animals).* Science & Technology Press. Pyoungyang.

Kim, Jin-Han, Jin-Young Park and Jeong-Yeon Yi. 1997. Spring and autumn avifauna of western coastal mudflats in Korea. *J. Kor. Biota.* 2:183-205.

Kim, Jin-Han, Jin-Young Park, Jeong-Yeon Yi, Byung-Ho Yoo and Kil-Cheol Lee. 1999. The migration routes and monitoring of the migratory birds in Korea. *NIER* No. 99-02-540.

Kim, Jin-Han, Sang-Wook Kim, Jin-Young Park and Jeong-Yeon Yi. 1996. Wintering status of waterbirds in major wetlands in Korea. *J. Kor. Biota.* 1:127-168.

Kim, Jung-Soo and Tae-Hoe Koo. 1999. *First record of Citrine Wagtail* Motacilla citreola in Korea. 1999 Annual meeting of Ornithological Society of Korea.

Lee, Do-Han. 2000. *A first record of Long-billed Dowitcher* Limnodromus scolopaceus *in Korea.* 2000. Annual meeting of Ornithological Society of Korea.

Lee, Geum-Cheol and Seong-Dae Lee. 1996. *A handbook of Natural Monuments in Korea.* Agriculture Press. D.P.R. Korea.

Lee, Han-Soo, Woon Ki Baek and Sung-Man Kim. 1999. First record of the Bonin Petrel *Pterodroma hypoleuca* in Korea. *Kor. J. Orni.* 6:133-134.

Lee, Han-Soo and Doo-Pyo Lee. 1999. A first record of the Black-winged Cuckooshrike, *Coracina melashistos*, in Korea. *Bull. Kor. Inst. Orni.* 7:53.

Lee, Jong-Nam and Yong-Tae Woo. 2000. *Ross's Gull* Rhodostethia rosea; a *new record for Korea.* 2000 Annual meeting of Ornithological Society of Korea.

Lee, Woo-Shin and Su-Man Kim. 1994. *One hundred species of bird in Korea.*

Hyunam Publ. Co. Seoul.

Ministry of Environment. 1997. *Annual censuses of wintering birds in Korea.*
Ministry of Environment.

Park, Haeng-Shin and Wan-Byung Kim. 1995. First records of Chestnut-winged
Cuckoo, European Starling and Black Bittern. *Kor. J. Orni.* 2:75-76.

Park, Haeng-Shin. 1998. *The birds of Cheju island.* Cheju National University
Press. Seoul.

Park, Jin-Young and Jeong-Yeon Yi. 1999. First records of the Ivory, Iceland
and Yellow-legged Gull in Korea. *Bull. Kor. Inst. Orni.* 7:55-57.

Park, Jin-Young and Ok-Sik Jeong. 1999. A first record of the Little Stint
(*Calidris minuta*) in Korea. *Bull. Kor. Inst. Orni.* 7:59-60.

Park, Jin-Young and Pyong-Oh Won. 1993. Wintering ecology of Bean Geese
Anser fabalis and White-fronted Geese *A. albifrons* in Junam Reservoirs,
Korea. *Bull. Kor. Inst. Orni.* 4:1-24.

Park, Jin-Young and Sang-Wook Kim. 1994. First records of Asiatic Dowitcher,
Greater Yellowlegs and Gull-billed Tern in Korea. *Kor. J. Orni.* 1:127-
128.

Park, Jin-Young, Jeong-Yeon Yi and Jin-Han Kim. 1998. *A report on four
newly recorded species and some recent noteworthy records in Korea.*
1998. Annual meeting of Ornithological Society of Korea.

Park, Jin-Young, Ok-Sik Jung and Jin-Won Lee. 1995. First records of
Pheasant-tailed Jacana (*Hydrophasianus chirurgus*) and Long-tailed
Shrike (*Lanius schach*) in Korea. *Kor. J. Orni.* 2:77-79.

Seo, Il-Seong. 1993. *Wild birds of Korea.* Pyonghwa Pub. Co. Seoul.

Won, Hong-Gu. 1963. *Birds of Korea 1, 2, 3.* Academy of Science Press. D.P.R.
Korea. Pyoungyang.

Won, Pyong-Oh and M. E. J. Gore. 1971. *The birds of Korea.* Royal Asiatic
Society, Korea Branch. Seoul.

Won, Pyong-Oh. 1969. *An annotated checklist of the birds of Korea.* Forest
Research Insititute.

Won, Pyong-Oh. 1981. *Illustrated flora and fauna of Korea Vol. 25;* Avifauna.

Ministry of Education. Seoul.

Won, Pyong-Oh. 1992. *Animal Treasures (Natural Monuments) in Korea.* Daewon Publ. Co. Seoul.

Won, Pyong-Oh. 1996. *A field guide to the birds of Korea.* Kyohak Publ. Co. Seoul.

Won, Pyong-Oh. 1996. Checklist of the birds of Korea. *Bull. Kor. Inst. Orni.* 5:39-58.

Woo, Yong-Tae and Jong-Nam Lee. 1996. Newly recorded birds of 6 species and subspecies in Korea. *Kor. J. Orni.* 3:59-61.

Yoon, Moo-Boo. 1992. *Wild birds of Korea in color.* Kyohak Publ. Co. Seoul.

<English>

Austin, O. L. 1948. *The birds of Korea*. Bulletin of the Museum of Comparative Zoology at Harvard College Vol. 101 No. 1.

Baker, K. 1993. *Identification Guide to European Non-Passerines*. BTO Guide 24. British Trust for Ornithology.

Baker, K. 1997. *Warblers of Europe, Asia and North Africa*. Christopher Helm, London.

Beaman, M. and Madge, S. 1999. *The Handbook of Bird Identification for Europe and the Western Palearctic*. London: Christopher Helm.

Bharat, B., Graham, F., Akira, H., Taeji, M., Dewi, M. P., Koichiro, S., Shunji, U. 1993. *A Field guide to the waterbirds of Asia*. Wild Bird Society of Japan, Tokyo.

Brazil, M. A. 1991. *The Birds of Japan*. London: Christopher Helm.

Brown, L. and Amadon, D. 1968. *Eagles, Hawks and Falcons of the World*. Feltham, Middlesex: Country Life Books.

Byers. C., U. Olsson and J. Curson. 1995. *Buntings and sparrows: A guide to the buntings and North American sparrows*. Pica Press, Sussex.

Carey, G. J. 1992. *The status and field identification of Snipe in Hong Kong*. Hong Kong Bird Report 1992:139-152.

Chantler, P & Driessens, G. 2000. Swifts: *A Guide to the Swift and Treeswifts of the World*. 2nd edn. Pica Press, Mountfield, U.K.

Cheng Tso-hsin 1987. *A Synopsis of the Avifauna of China*. Beijing: Science Press, and Hamburg: Paul Parey.

Clark, W.S. 1999. *A Field Guide to the Raptors of Europe*, The Middle East and North Africa. Oxford University Press, Oxford.

Clement, P., A. Harris and J. Davis. 1993. *Finches and sparrows: An identification guide*. Christopher Helm, London.

Clements, J. F. 1991. *Birds of the World: A Check List*. Ibis Publishing Company.

Collar, N J., Crosby. M. J. & Stattersfield, A. J. 1994. *Birds Watch 2 - The world List of Threatened Birds*. BirdLife International. Cambridge.

Cramp, S. (eds). 1980. *Handbook of the birds of Europe, the Middle East and North Africa : The birds of the Western Palearctic Vol. 11.* Oxford University Press, Oxford.

de Schauensee, R. M. 1984. *The birds of China.* Smithonian Institute Press, Washington, D.C.

del Hoyo, J., Elliot, A. and J. Sargatal. (eds). 1992. *Handbook of the birds of the world Vol. 1.* Ostrich to Ducks. Lynx Edicions, Barcelona.

del Hoyo, J., Elliot, A. and J. Sargatal. (eds). 1994. *Handbook of the birds of the world Vol. 2.* New World Vultures to Guinoafowl. Lynx Edicions, Barcelona.

del Hoyo, J., Elliot, A. and J. Sargatal. (eds). 1996. *Handbook of the birds of the world Vol. 3. Hoatzin to Auks.* Lynx Edicions, Barcelona.

del Hoyo, J., Elliot, A. and J. Sargatal. (eds). 1997. *Handbook of the birds of the world Vol.4. Sandgrouse to Cuckoos.* Lynx Edicions, Barcelona.

del Hoyo, J., Elliot, A. and J. Sargatal. (eds). 1998. *Handbook of the birds of the world VoL 5. Barn-owls to Hummingbirds.* Lynx Edicions, Barcelona.

Enticott, J., and D. Tipling. 1997. *Seabirds: a photographic handbook of the seabirds of the world.* New Holland, London.

Falla, R. A., R. B. Sibson and E. G. Turbott. 1996. *Birds of New Zealand.* Hong Kong.

Feare, C. & Craig, A. 1998. *Starlings and Mynas.* Christopher Helm, London.

Forsman, D. 1999. *The raptors of the Europe and the Middle East: a handbook of field identification.* T & AD Poyser, London.

Fry, C. H., Fry, K. and Harris, A. 1992. *Kingfishers, bee-eaters and Rollers.* London: Christopher Helm.

Gaston, A.J., I Jones, I., and I.Lewington .1997. *The Auks.* Oxford

University Press, Oxford.

Goodwin, D. 1967. *Pigeons and Doves of the World*. London, British Museum

Grant, P. J. 1989. *Gulls: A guide to the identification (2nd ed.)*. T & AD Poyser, Calton.

Grimmett, R., Inskipp, C. & Inskipp, T. 1998. *Birds ofthe IndianSubcontinent*. Christopher Helm, London.

Hancock, J. & Kushlan, J. 1984.*The Herons Handbook*, Croom Helm, London.

Harrap, S. and D. Quinn. 1995. *Chickadees, Tits, Nuthatchers and Treecreepers*. Princeton University Press.

Harris. A., L.Tucker and K. Vinicombe. 1989. *Bird identification*. The Macmillan Press, London.

Harrison, P.1987.*Seabirds of the World: A Photographic Guide*. Christopher Helm, London.

Harrison, P. 1983. *Seabirds: An identification guide*. Croom Helm, London.

Hayman, P. J. Marchant and T. Prater. 1986. *Shorebirds: An identification guide to the waders of the world*. Houghton Mifflin Company, Boston.

Heinzel, H. R. Fitter and J. Parlsow. 1979. *The Birds of Britain and Europe*. Collins. London.

Howard, R. and A. Moore. 1998. *A complete checklist of the birds of the world (2nd ed.)*. Academic Press, London.

Inskipp, T, Lindsey, N. & Duckworth, W.1996.*An Annotated Checklist of the Birds of the Oriental Region*. Oriental Bird Club, Sandy, U.K.

Johnsgard, P. A. 1988. *The Quails, Partridges andFrancolins of the World*. Oxford University Press, Oxford.

Johnsgard, P. A. 1991. *Bustards, Hemipodes and Sandgrouse, Birds of Dry Places*. Oxford University Press, Oxford.

Johnsgard, P. A. 1993. *Cormorants, Darters and Pelicans of theWorld*.

Smithsonian Institution Press, Washington DC.

Jonsson, L. 1992. *Birds of Europe with North Africa and the Middle East.* Christopher Helm, London.

Kennedy, P. R. 1993. *Photospot: Saker Falcon.* Hong Kong Bird Report 1993:195-199.

King, B. M. Woodcock and E. C. Dickinson. 1975. *A field guide to the birds of South-East Asia.* Collins.

Koenig, C., Weick, E & Becking, J.H. 1999. *Owls: A Guide to the Owls of the World.* Pica Press, Mountfield, U.K.

Lambert, F. &Woodcock, M. 1996. *Pittas, Broadbills and Asities.* Pica Press, Mountfield, U.K.

Leader, P. J. 1994. *Field identification of Dusky, Radde's and Yellow-streaked Warblers.* Hong Kong Bird Report 1994:170-180.

Lefranc, N. & Worfolk, T. 1997. *Shrikes: A Guide to the Shrikes of the World.* Pica Press, Mountfield, U.K.

Lewington, I., P. Alstrom and P. Colston. 1991. *A Field guide to the rare birds of Britain and Eurpe.* Harper Collins, London.

Mackinnon, J. and K. Phillipps. 1993. *A field guide to the birds of Borneo, Sumatra, Java and Bali.* Oxford University Press, Oxford.

Mackinnon, J., and K. Phillipps. 2000. *A field guide to the birds of China.* Oxford University Press, Oxford.

Madge, S. & Burn, H. 1993. *Crows and Jays: A Guide to the Crows, Jays and Magpies of the World.* Helm, Mountfield, U.K.

Madge, S. & Burn, H.1988. *Wildfowl: An identification guide to the ducks, geese and swans of the world.* Christopher Helm, London.

Mever de Schattensee, R. 1984. *The Birds of China.* Smithsonian Institution, Washington DC.

Monroe, B. L. and C. G. Sibley. 1993. *A world checklist of birds.* Yale

University Press. New Haven and London.

National Geographic Society. 1987. *Field guide to the birds of North America (2nd ed).* National Geographic Society.

Olsen, K. M. & Larsson, H. 1995. *Terns of Europe and North America.* Christopher Helm, London.

Pizzey, G. and F. Knight. 1997. *The Field guide to the birds of Australia.* Angus and Robertson, Sidney.

Poole, C. M., J. Y. Park and N. Moores. 1999. *The identification of Chinese Egret and Pacific Reef Heron.* OBC Bulletin 30:35-39.

Porter, R. E, Christensen, S. & Schiermacker-Hansen, P. 1996. *Field Guide to the Birds of the Middle East.* Poyser, London.

Prater, A. J, J. H. Marchant and J. Vuorinen. 1977. *Guide to the identification and aging of Holarctic waders.* BTO Guide 17. British Trust for Ornithology.

Robson, C.R. 2000. *A field guide to the birds of Thailand and South-east Asia.* Asia Books: Bangkok.

Rosair D, Cottridge D., 1995. *Photographic Guide to Waders of the World.* Hamlyn

Svensson, L. 1992. *Identification Guide to European Passerines.* Stockholm.

Svensson, L., Grant, P. J., Mullarney, K., and D. Zetterstrom .1999. *Collins Bird Guide.* Harper Collins, London.

Takano, S. 1982. *A field guide to the bird of Japan.* Wild Bird Society of Japan, Tokyo.

Taylor, B. & van Perlo, B. 1998. *Rails: A Guide to the Rails, Crakes, Gallinules and Coots ofthe World.* Pica Press, Mournfield, U.K.

Taylor, B. & van Perlo, B. 1998. *Rails: A Guide to the Rails, Crakes, Gallinules and Coots of the World.* Pica Press, Mountfield, U.K.

The Australian Museum. 1995. *Birds of Australia.* Australia.

Turner, A. & Rose, C. 1989. *A Handbook to the Swallows and Martins of the World*. Christopher Helm, Bromley, U.K.

Viney, C., K. Phillipps and L. C. Ying. 1994. *Birds of Hong Kong and South China*. Government Printer, Hong Kong.

Walter, M. 1994. *Birds eggs*. London.

Winkler, H., Christie, D. A. & Nurney D. 1995. *Woodpeckers: A Guide to the Woodpeckers, Piculets and wrynecks of the World*. Pica Press, Mountfield, U.K.

Sound guides

Buckingham, R., and L. Jackson. 1983-88. *A field guide to Australian Birdsong*. (Cassettes 1-4) Bird Observers Club, Victoria.

Colver, K.1999. *Stokes Field Guide to Bird Songs* (4 CDs, 60-pg booklet) Time Warner, New York.

Connop, S. 1993. *Birdsongs of Nepal*. Cassette. Turaco, New York.

Connop, S. 1995. *Birdsongs of the Himalayas*. Cassette. Turaco, New York.

Cornell Laboratory of Ornithology .1992. *A field guide to Western Bird Songs* (second edition)(2 CDS). Peterson Field Guide Series. Houghton Mifflin, Boston.

Kabaya, T., and M, Matsuda. 1996. *The songs and Calls of 333 Birds in Japan*. (2 volumes, 6 CDs) Shogakukan Inc. Tokyo.

McPherson, L. 1975-8. *Birds of New Zealand: A Sound Guide* (Cassettes 1-5) McPherson Natural history Unit, Christchurch, New Zealand.

Marshall, J. T. 1978. *Systematics of Smaller Asian Night Birds Based on Voice*. Vinyl record and booklet. American Ornithologists' Union, Tampa.

Mild, K. 1990.*BirdSongs of Israel and the Middle East*. 2 cassettes and a booklet. Bioacoustics, Stockholm.

Mild, K. 1987. *Soviet BirdSongs*. 2 cassettes and a booklet. Bioacoustics,

Stockholm.

Naumov, R.. 1962. *The Voices of Birds in the Nature* (Vinyl record 4 and
    booklet). Melodiya, The USSR Ministry of Culture, USSR.

Roche, C. 1990. *All the BirdSongs of Europe*. 4 CDs and 4 booklets. Sittelle,
    Chateaubois.

Stewart, D. 1999. *Bird Calls of the Broome Region, Australia*. (1 CD) Nature
    Sound, Mullumbimby, New South Wales.

Veprintsev, B., Litvinenko, N., Neufeldt, I., and Y. Shibaev. 1965.

The Voices of Birds in the Nature (Vinyl record 5 and booklet). Melodiya,
    The USSR Ministry of Culture, USSR.

Warakagoda, D. 1997-8. *The Bird Sounds of Sri Lanka*. 2 Cassettes, DHW
    Library of Nature Sounds, Nugegoda, Sri Lanka.

White, T. 1984. *A Field Guide to the BirdSongs of South-East Asia*. 2
    Cassettes. British Library, London.

<Japanese>

Anzai, H. 1998. *Concise Field Guide to Land Birds (New Edition)*. Wild Bird
Society of Japan.

Anzai, H. 1998. *Concise Field Guide to Water Birds (New Edition)*. Wild Bird
Society of Japan.

Iozawa, H., Yamagata, N. and T. Yoshino. 2000. *Nihon no Tori 550: Sanya no
Tori*. Bun-ichi Sogo Shuppan Co. Ltd., Tokyo.

Japanese Society for Preservation of Birds 1988. *A Guide for Bird Lovers*.
Japanese Society for Preservation of Birds.

Kanouchi, T., Abe, N. and Ueda, H. 1998. *Wild Birds of Japan*. Yama-kei
Publishers Co.Ltd., Tokyo.

Kirihara, M., Yamagata, N. and T. Yoshino. 2000. *Nihon no tori 550: mizube no
tori*. Bun-ichi Sogo Shuppan Co. Ltd., Tokyo.

Kiyosu, Y. 1979. *The Birds of Japan Vol.1*. Kodansha, Tokyo.

Kiyosu, Y. 1979. *The Birds of Japan Vol.2*. Kodansha, Tokyo.

Kiyosu, Y. 1979. *The Birds of Japan Vol.3*. Kodansha, Tokyo.

Kobayashi, K. 1994. *Birds of Japan in Natural Colors. Enlarged revised edition*.
Hoikusha Publishing Co. Ltd., Tokyo.

Morioka, T. 1983. *Concise Field Guide to Water Birds*. Wild Bird Society of
Japan.

Morioka, T.,Yamagata, N., Kawada, T., Kanouchi, T. 1995. *The Birds of Prey in
Japan*. Bun-ichi Sôgô Shuppan Co. Ltd., Tokyo.

Saeki, A. 1983. *Concise Field Guide to Land Birds*. Wild Bird Society of Japan.

Takano, S. 1982. *A Field Guide to the Birds of Japan*. Wild Bird Society of
Japan.

Takano, T., Hamaguchi, T., Morioka, T., Kanouchi, T. and T. Kabaya. 1994.
Nihon no yacho (second edition). Yama-kei Publishers Co. Ltd.

Yamashina, Y. 1934. *A Natural History of Japanese Birds Vol.1*. Azusa Shobo,
Tokyo.

Yamashina, Y. 1941. *A Natural History of Japanese Birds Vol.2*. Iwanami
Shoten, Publishers., Tokyo.

Index of Korean Names

Index of Scientific Names

Index of English Names

Authors

Woo-Shin Lee (b. 1955, Yangsan) gained a B.A. in Forestry in Seoul National University and Ph.D. degree in Applied Zoology from Hokkaido University in 1990. He has worked as a research fellow at the Korea Forestry Research Institute of Forestry Administration and has served successively as a governmental representative for CITES, the Ramsar Convention, and the Korea-Japan Conference on Wintering and Migrating Birds. He has been Assistant Professor in the Department of Forest Resources at Seoul National University since 1997, and has taught Wildlife Ecology & Management, Ethology and Conservation Biology. His interests are ecology of bird community in ecosystem and international conservation plan for endangered birds (Cranes and Spoonbills, etc.).

Tae-Hoe Koo (b. 1944, Seoul) is a Professor at the School of Environmental Science and Applied Chemistry at Kyung Hee University, and has taught Animal Ecology and Ecosystem Conservation since 1980. He has a B.A. from Kyung Hee University in Biology, and in 1996, a Ph.D. degree from Kyungnam University in Biology, and he was a visiting researcher at Kyushu University.

In 1978, he studied at the International Crane Foundation (ICF). He has presented academic paper at many international conferences, including the International Ornithological Conferences, the International Waterfowl Research Bureau (IWRB), and the International Crane Workshop. He currently is an executive board of the Ornithological Society of Korea and the Korean Association for Conservation of Nature.

Jin-Young Park (b. 1967) has a B.A. from Kyung Hee University in Biology. After a Ph.D. course at Kyung Hee University, he has served as a researcher in the Wildlife Division of National Institute of Environment Research since 1997. He first became interested in birds when he was 12 years old, and bought his first illustrated field guide of birds at the age of 13. He decided to devote himself to the study of birds soon after, and he has been enjoying birdwatching and studying ornithology since then.
He specializes in the ecology and monitoring of waterbirds and in the bird migration. He is a active bird bander and has been working for Korean Banding Scheme since 1993. He has also been the Korean representative of the Oriental Bird Club since 1994.

Illustrator

Takashi Taniguchi (b. 1947, Tokyo, Japan) has a B.A. from Waseda University in Commerce. He is one of the best bird illustrators in Asia and the first Japanese to have been commisioned by the National Museum of Natural History (Smithsonian Institution) in the United States. He has been in charge of illustrations of many illustrated field guides published by the Wild Bird Society of Japan, including "*Concise Field Guide to Land Birds*", "*Concise Field Guide to Water Birds*", "*A Field Guide to The Birds of Taiwan (Chinese edition)*", "*A Field Guide to the Waterbirds of Asia (English edition)*", "*Concise Field Guide to Land Birds (New edition)*", "*Concise Field Guide to Water Birds (New edition)*" and "*The Birdwatching Series*". He is also an activist in organisations for conservation of the natural environment.

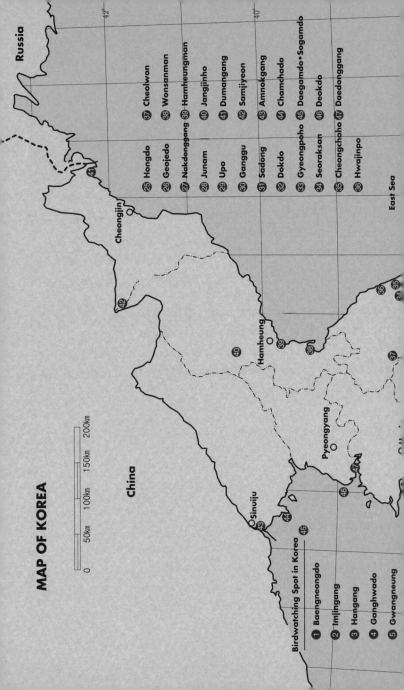